THE THREAT FROM WITHIN

THE

THREAT

FROM

WITHIN

THE INCURSION OF SECULAR HUMANISM INTO CHRISTIAN BELIEF AND PRACTICE

[redacted]

WILLIAM L. MERRIFIELD

TATE PUBLISHING & *Enterprises*

TATE PUBLISHING
& Enterprises

Tate Publishing is committed to excellence in the publishing industry. Our staff of highly trained professionals, including editors, graphic designers, and marketing personnel, work together to produce the very finest books available. The company reflects the philosophy established by the founders, based on Psalms 68:11,

"THE LORD GAVE THE WORD AND GREAT WAS THE COMPANY OF THOSE WHO PUBLISHED IT."

If you would like further information, please contact us:
1.888.361.9473 | www.tatepublishing.com
TATE PUBLISHING *& Enterprises*, LLC | 127 E. Trade Center Terrace
Mustang, Oklahoma 73064 USA

The Threat from Within: The Incursion of Secular Humanism into Christian Belief and Practice

---

This title is also available as a Tate Out Loud product.
Visit www.tatepublishing.com for more information

Cover design by Elizabeth Mason
Interior design by Janae J. Glass
Published in the United States of America

ISBN:978-1-6024725-9-4

07.02.19

// ACKNOWLEDGMENTS

- To God be the glory, great things He has done.
- To my loving wife Jo Ann for forty-two years of love, encouragement, and understanding.
- My sincere appreciation to the brothers and sisters in Christ who supported me in my preparations.
- Among this long list I wish to single out:
- Reverend John Morton for his patience, kindness, and love in helping me see that God really did want me in the ministry.
- Doctor R.J. Gore, Erskine Theological Seminary, for encouraging me to continue my studies to improve myself both in and out of school.
- Reverend and Mrs. Butch Austin for their Christian love and prayers through the years.

CONTENTS

INTRODUCTION

Over my years as an Army Chaplain and a Minister of the Gospel, I have begun, and as a matter of necessity, been required to set aside several studies, which I thought significant. As with many of my contemporaries I have continued to study as God, the Army, and man has allowed, seeking to understand the changing winds of church leadership, the ebb and flow of congregational attendance, and the rise and fall of Christendom. Once again I have taken up the gauntlet and renew the battle to set aside a portion of time in which to express my thoughts and knowledge on paper, as limited as those thoughts and opinions might be, and to express my concerns for the future of the local church.

A Chinese general once said, "to defeat your enemy, you must first know your enemy."[1] To overcome the wiles of the devil we must understand what it is that he is attempting to accomplish, what weapons he has at his disposal, and perhaps most importantly where he is to be found. My battle analysis deals mainly with those threats that are to be found within the modern church. Where did they come from, how did they become threats, and what is their battle plan for the take over of the local church? These are some of the questions that I will attempt to answer.

As with any book dealing with threats and tribulations, the writer must first determine the direction of travel. Does one go from the obvious to the more sinister, or does one jump right into the firestorm? Hopefully by beginning with the more commonplace—those threats that anyone can relate to—I will build a rapport with the reader that will entice him or her to read on to the most menacing threats. As with most such threats, the circumstances of these threats do not come upon an intended victim rapidly, rather it is a combination of events that leads to the final confrontation, each stage building on the other until reaching a climax. I certainly do not consider humanity to have reached the final conflict, nor do I believe that the church will ever achieve total victory over those who would threaten its very existence before Jesus returns to claim His bride.

Books like this often carry modifiers in their reviews such as provocative, challenging, and stimulating if the reviewer likes it and agrees with the premise of the book, and aggressive, incendiary, and even offensive if they don't. I acknowledge very freely, that this book is written somewhat out of emotion. I love the church and my denomination and anything that seeks to undermine their important mission to the world brings me emotional turmoil. Because of the emotional involvement the book does not therefore, I am sorry to say, contain all the words it implies. There are no easy answers to the questions I ask, nor will there be any fast solutions to the problems presented for the reader's consideration. If however, this book brings some emotional turbulence to those who read it, and from the turbulence a proactive response, then I will have done most of what I set out to do.

With twenty-six years as a Southern Baptist Chaplain and having been affiliated with a chapel program in almost every assignment, I preached, counseled, taught varied classes both religious and secular, monitored religious programs, helped establish procedures, fixed responsibility, and provided staff coordination of all religious support programs within the unit's area of responsibility, often supervising as many as twenty-three soldiers and civilians. I had made it my practice to affiliate myself with those Southern Baptist Churches, as well as other denominations near my posting. As a result I have ministered to numerous congregations both military and civilian in whatever position was needed, ranging from interim pastor, Chairman of the Deacon body, to teaching Sunday school, and Bible studies. Having served in various positions and yet having been in reality simply a transient worker; I have had opportunity to observe congregations as both a member in good standing and an outsider simply passing through. The view of a Chaplain and Minister, as this book so easily betrays itself to be, may prove somewhat of a shock to the rank and file of the clergy and lay leadership, or at least to those who hold so staunchly to the belief that the pastor and/or deacons, and only they, have the keys to church and congregational growth and security.

I believe that the majority of people believe foreign missions to be the masculine sport of the age. These spiritual gladiators go forth to the uttermost parts of the world and bravely competing against the wiles of the world for the souls of the lost. It is not my intent to diminish neither the sacrifice nor important of either foreign or home missionaries. However, in comparison to such thoughts, the role of the pastor, deacons, and church lay leaders, and the role of the local church, and the function of the whole; lie in a far different realm of the heroic. In this modern age of rapid communications, I believe that it would be safe to say that the greatest mission field today can be found in the local church and one's own back yard.

If in this book I seem to expect too much of the lay leaders and churches and far too much of the preachers and deacons, my only plea is my inability to read into the Bible a philosophy of ease or of complacent laissez faire. I am a firm believer in the local church—its necessity, its function, and its destiny as given by our Lord and Savior, Jesus Christ. The welfare of that part of the Body of Christ located in the local communities, as I see it, should be of the utmost concern to the congregational parts of the Body.

This is why empty pews, wayward congregants, and dying churches should bring tragedy to pastoral and lay leadership alike. And so, that is what this book sets out to do; take Christians to the church communities with wide-open eyes to see the empty pews, the children without God, the families on the run looking for the beginnings of a church home that would prove acceptable to their God, their denomination, and to themselves, and the threat that has crept into the churches because we were unaware. Hopefully I will draw attention to the fact that we do not need to fear Satan walking about in the world near as much as we need to fear the threat from within the church. Satan and his followers are to be always found in or near the church. The workers of iniquity do not bother those from whom there is no threat, but seek to ensnare those who would call the world to repentance.

Somewhere in this world of Christian debate on the rules and regulations of Christian citizenship we have lost sight of the fact that for the Christian, authority for faith and practice must reside in the Bible and not in the minds of men. All of the truths that are relevant to humanities salvation are to be found in the Bible. How we are to live our lives, how we are to conduct ourselves in the world, and how we are to conduct ourselves with other Christians are to be found within the bindings of Scripture. What the world rebels from is the absolute that states there is no appeal beyond the authority of the Scriptures, and there is no power on earth that can set aside the authority of an omnipotent God.

On the "Letters to the Editor" page of my local paper, a dear soul once asked the question: "Why can't we have religious faith and make social based decisions?" Unfortunately, God has spoken with a finality that frightens a world that more and more wants acceptance without responsibility for any and every lifestyle imaginable. The world desires acceptance so much that they are willing to substitute humanity's traditions, and social principles for God's authority. To answer the dear man's question, It is one thing for the world to unleash untold confusion by setting aside the Word of God for opinions, social principles, and traditions, it is quite another for the church to do so.

Yet in far too many churches and denominations that is exactly what churchgoers are being told today; water down the sermons, lighten up on the requirement for church membership, and stop talking about a literal hell where unrepentant, and unredeemed sinners are going to go. If they don't want to talk about it, they certainly don't want someone writing a book about it. Yet because of my base verse, "*This matter arose, because some false brothers had infiltrated our ranks to spy on the freedom we have in Christ Jesus and to make us slaves*" (Galatians 2:4) I feel even the more strongly that this book needs to be written. I am not trying to anger anyone or turn people off to God, or make the declaration that God does not love everyone of His creations; I just feel that we should with boldness look at the issues that are distressing the church today.

Because of the complexity of some subjects I have chosen to discuss, I need to ensure that the reader understands what it is that I accept as true, and perhaps more importantly, how I arrived at my various conclusions. Unfortunately this requires that I make extra effort to adequately discuss the more academic aspects of some subjects. I will try not to get too bogged down in the finer points of the subject. I would hope that such in-depth discussions would come from the reading of this book. In all cases I will endeavor to keep each chapter simple in language, accurate in statement, practical in purpose, and spiritual in tone.

With the exception of the last chapter I will provide the reader with questions for consideration and discussion. These are provided in the event that some may desire to use the book for a church discussion group. This discussion section of the chapters is more in the nature of an outline or guide than of a discussion. Only a small amount of introductory discussion is given.

In the discussion section, reference will be made to what I considered the more conspicuous dealings of the chapter. These are provided so as to furnish the reader with a brief but comprehensive view of the chapter. Certain instruction or commentary is drawn from each chapter thereby furnishing the reader with a number of topics for study and discussion. For the most part these topics require the searching of the Scripture itself and if properly followed, should give the reader an acceptable knowledge of the contents of the appropriate Scriptures.

The aim is to furnish the reader with a clue to study, not necessarily direct the study. What is said in the discussions that hopefully will follow the reading of each chapter should be in the endeavor to create an enthusiasm for truth, which will in turn lead to a thorough investigation of the subject discussed.

THE LOCAL CHURCH

A Turning Point in History

Some historians have argued that the Twentieth century did not really begin until 1917 at the beginning of the First World War, and came to a screeching halt somewhere around 1989-90 with the beginning of the internal collapse of Communism in the Soviet block countries. In a like manner the Twenty-first century more than likely began well before January 1, 2000. In one sense, January 1st is really just another day in history coming and going like all the other January 1st. In another sense, though, it symbolizes the end of one epoch and the beginning of another. The dates are not so important and neither are the years. What is important is where the church stands in the annals of history? Have we reached a new defining point, a point that will send the world, and therefore the church, careening off the path of righteousness and on to a new track toward the "comfort zone?"

Many such turning points have been recorded in the short history of humanity. For us, the Christians, such turning points were the time of Christ, the fall of the Roman Empire, the Reformation, the Industrial Revolution, and like it or not the Space Age. What do they all have in common? Each point in history forced humanity, and therefore the church, to leave behind the way the culture and society had functioned and for better or worse introduced a new way of living. Regardless of resistance to change, panic, or foreboding, for each of these points in history there would be no turning back to a simpler, safer time.

It is not so much that humanity, or the church, does not embrace change; it's just that the velocity of change has accelerated to an almost unimaginable pace. More changes have occurred in the last century than took place in the ten centuries that preceded it. Changes in the last five years of this first decade of the Twenty-first century may well exceed the changes of the last five decades of the last century. How does the church move into this new century without losing the ageless mandate that Christ gave to the church to make disciples?

Imagine a steam powered locomotive of early Nineteenth century America traveling from east to west across this young nation. At first the going seems to be steady and effortless as it glides through the farm country and across the flat lands of the desert Midwest. Then it reaches the Great Divide, and it is slow going at first, the steep incline requires all the power the steam engine can muster. The mighty locomotive finally reaches the top of the towering mountains, and begins the decent to the desert floor below. The train begins to pick up speed until it has surpassed the recommended safe operating speed. It is an exhilarating ride, but unless the engineer applies the brakes from time to time, slow the forward momentum to a safer speed, the train will soon reach a speed where the brakes cannot be applied without blowing the engine or derailing the train.

In a like manner how does the local Christian church move into the new century without losing the spiritual identity of the church? Denominations are redrawing their Biblical boundaries and reassessing their doctrinal restrictions, struggling to find their place in this new world order. Humanities demand for less intrusion into their chosen lifestyles, less condemnation for the human infirmity that we used to call sin, and more inclusiveness into the life of the church for all individuals regardless of their belief or religion has produced complexity, destabilization, and uncertainties within the local Christian Churches.

Historically Christians have looked to their denominations and their seminaries for the vision and leadership required to lead them ever forward toward the final harvest and that day when Christ will return and claim His own. However, the changes affecting the local church today are far broader than former platitudes, antiquated organizations, and watered down messages that basically offend no one. In order to accomplish this the local church has embarked on a human odyssey without first seeking to understand who or what they really are.

In simple terms there is no one at the brake and the speed of descent into the abyss of non-relevance is increasing. For the most part the Christian churches, most notably those listed under the label "Protestant," have long advocated the priesthood of the believer, and loudly proclaimed the mobilization of the laity for ministry without really putting any of it into practice. And so, before I can begin to discuss those threats within the modern church, I must first seek common ground from which to begin the journey.

The Definition of the Local Church

No one should attempt to set forth an idea without first seeking to define that which they would discuss. The word "church" is used in this book to refer to a Christian congregation—that visible and local group most often referenced in the New Testament.[2] Therefore any definition true to the Christian understanding of the word "church" would have to begin: "A New Testament church…"

A New Testament church of the Lord Jesus Christ is "a local body of baptized believers who are associated by covenant in the faith and fellowship of the gospel…"[3] There are those who would imply that many people today recognize that the term "church" does not invariably refer to a local congregation, but simply brings to mind the image of a building, or even a social group which one joins with no real commitment. Should the social group not meet the needs of the member, the member feels no loyalty to the organization which they have joined, and thereby feel free to simply go off and join another church of like or similar faith. These dear souls tend to view their tithes, if they give such, and offerings as membership fees, and make no connection to the giving of money to the worship experience.

To others there is the understanding that the Church Universal (Capital "C") and the local church (lower case "c") are one and the same. One purpose of this undertaking is to endeavor to make some type of contribution toward correcting errors that have grown out of false concepts of the church. Less I be misunderstood, or taken to task, I do not make the claim to have searched out all of the errors pertaining to an unscriptural interpretation of the church.

One begins with the understanding of what the local church is and what it is not. Jesus Christ established the Church when in his conversation with Peter, Christ stated: "*I tell you that you are Peter, and upon this rock I will build my* Church *(*εκκλεσιαυ)" (Matthew 16:16-18). Here Christ speaks of the Church Universal.[4] In its basic form, "εκκλεσια" (church) simply means an assemblage, a gathering, a meeting, or those who have been called out. It could be better understood as when you come together in an assembly. If one were to accept the Universal Church concept then the autonomy of the separate local church would be destroyed seeing that the individual would hold his or her allegiance to the larger body giving rise to either one person or to an ecclesiastical organization exercising power over the separate churches. Although such a concept is supported by tradition, I can find no such pattern in the New Testament. We need to take care in any discussion of the Church Universal and the local church lest we find ourselves in danger of losing what should be an obvious fact to all of us—the Christian tradition is one great river of thought and not several interconnecting tributaries, "*Your attitude should be the same as that of Christ Jesus*" (Philippians 2:5).

Paul in his letter to the Corinthians writes: "*To the church of God in Corinth...*" (I Corinthians 1:2) and later he wrote: "*To the churches in Galatia...*" (Galatians 1:2). In the first example Paul writes to a specific church, while in the second example he addresses his letter to several local churches. In the first century churches there were no denominations, as we know them today. The New Testament churches were small, self-governing bodies. There were, as in the case with the Galatians, several smaller groups with a somewhat limited association. However, for the most part, these first century churches were both independent and democratic bodies holding sway over only their own assemble. The individual or local church may then be defined as the smaller group of persons, who in any given community unite themselves voluntarily together, in accordance with the guidance given in the New Testament. This uniting of Christians is more than just a gathering; it is better described as a fellowship, a "κοινονια" (koinonia). In Christ Jesus, Christians will find that they may have many variations in their church polity, but no true spiritual differences. A Christian church is a group of people who come together and stay together because they accept Jesus Christ as their Lord and Savior. The glue that binds these people together is Godly love "αγαπε" (agape). "*This is love; not that we loved God, but that He loved us and sent His Son as an atoning sacrifice for our sins. Dear friends, since God so loved us, we also ought to love one another*" (I John 4:10,11). Augustine wrote: "The true Christian will never set himself up over other men… If you would be better than another man, you will grudge to see him as your equal. You ought to wish all men equal to yourself; and if you have gone beyond another man in wisdom, you should want him to show himself wise…."[5] I would conclude my definition of the word "church" by stating that a church is greater than the sum of the people who have thus joined themselves together. In the true Christian church there will always be the presence of the risen Lord in the mist of His followers, calling each member by His grace and power to "*come let us reason together says the Lord. Though your sins are like scarlet, they shall be as white as snow; though they are red as crimson, they shall be like wool*" (Isaiah 1:18).

The Function of the Local Church

Having so boldly given definition to the word "church," we need now to look at the local church's function. A church function should be an essential action without which its basic nature would be altered.

In seeking to clarify the functions of the church, one must always keep in mind the driving force that unites us. The life's blood of the church, in fact its very existence, flows from God. Its vitality however, must be made evident by the coming of the Holy Spirit. Just as it was at Pentecost, so must it be with the local church. Therefore the church finds its function in Christ Jesus and the Holy Spirit. The church hears "*a sound like the blowing of a violent wind coming from heaven and filling the whole house...*" (Acts 2:2).

A great majority of the verses in the New Testament give reference to a local congregation. This then, by the very nature of the word assembly, requires that there be a meeting place. Contrary to many believers in the Christian church today, one cannot rightly be called a member of a church who never attends a church. The membership rolls of a church are intended to contain those souls who are members in good standing, and who attend on a regular basis, those senior members who for health's sake cannot attend are also carried on the rolls and hopefully visited regularly by both deacon and pastor. While I acknowledge the truth that one can worship God anywhere, even on a river bank, I must, in like manner; point to the truth that what the individual will more than likely do is pop a top and bait a hook, and God will not be considered except in an emphatic utterance should a large one be hooked or worse yet get away.

If then Christians believe that we should be obedient to God, then one function of the church would be to gather ourselves together. "*Let us not give up meeting together, as some are in the habit of doing, but let us encourage one another—and all the more as you see the Day approaching*" (Hebrews 10:25). If for no other reason than to find out who is not coming and why, the church membership rolls should be reviewed every year and those who are no longer attending, have gone on to be with the Lord, or have gone to another congregation should be removed from the church's membership and their letter of membership sent on to the receiving church if that be the case (more on this later).

There is a danger in gathering ourselves together. The danger is that some will begin to equate membership with salvation. Just as a minister of the Gospel in the baptismal pool would utter the words: "Upon your public profession of faith in Christ Jesus as your Savior…" even more so should all understand that Salvation precedes church membership. When a Christian comes to join with a church, who has not been baptized by that church, the great majority of ministers will note that the individual comes by promise of a letter from a church of like belief, or by public profession of having been saved and been baptized. There are occasions where local churches require that a prospective member be baptized into the fellowship. This practice has resulted because of the different understandings of the word "Βαπτιζο" (baptizo), which means to dip, plunge, submerge or immerse. One should not confuse baptism into the fellowship of a church with the Scriptural baptism that follows a salvation experience.

I find nowhere in the New Testament where the commandment to be baptized was intended to be applied to the impenitent or unbeliever. "*Peter replied, 'Repent and be baptized every one of you, in the name of Jesus Christ so that your sins may be forgiven…'*" (Acts 2:38). The church is to be comprised of baptized, penitent believers in Jesus Christ. While all are welcome to attend, church membership is reserved for those who have been born again into the Christian faith. One does not attend church for the salvation of their soul, but rather for the good of their soul. The individual who does not know Christ as his or her Savior should always be welcome in the assembly; however, membership should be limited to those who have found faith in our Lord and Savior.

Just as Christ noted, "*the Sabbath was made for man, not man for the Sabbath,*" (Mark 2:27) likewise, the church exists for people. We do not live in a vacuum. I see in humanity today an increasing loneliness in the faces that pass me. There is a longing in the human heart for a place and a people to belong to. The family structure has broken down, there is almost a conspiracy against marriage and true intimacy, true friends are few and far between, and of the friends we have, we can but wonder if pressed how deep the friendship would go. Many in the world cry out that they were born this way, or that way, and in reality have no control over their lives. There is ambivalence to this brokenness; the world is lonely and dying for intimacy but finding that the search for it is too threatening to risk opening themselves to the possibility of finding true happiness. Where can a dying world go and to whom can they turn? Jesus bid them come to Him when He said: "*Come to me, all you who are weary and burdened, and I will give you rest. Take my yoke upon you and learn from me, for I am gentle and humble in heart, and you will find rest for your souls*" (Matthew 11: 28,29).

The church should always be open to all who seek consolation. While membership is restricted, attendance is not. Attendance must be open to all—those who have not accepted Christ as Savior, as well as members of the body. Wherever the church gathers, there will always be the functional responsibility to minister. "*We who are strong ought to bear the failings of the weak, and not to please ourselves*" (Romans 15:1).

In America, church polity tends to presuppose the democratic procedure of voting people into and out of the church. While Christ's discourse in Matthew 18:15-17 does seem to deal with the problem of disciplining church members, the conclusion of the instruction relates more to the impenitent, non-cooperative associate than to the generally accepted concept of disciplinary responsibility toward members. As a Southern Baptist I accept the autonomy of the local church and acknowledge that the New Testament does allow the church to have authority over receiving or rejecting old and new members alike. "*What business is it of mine to judge those outside the church? Are you not to judge those inside? God will judge those outside. 'Expel the wicked man from among you*'" (I Corinthians 5:12,13—see also: Romans 14:1, II Corinthians 2:5-8, and II Thessalonians: 3:6). This does not however, give the church the function of determining the salvation of a soul, which is reserved to God, and Him alone.

But, is that the only purpose for which we gather ourselves together? No, our assembling ourselves together should be for the sake of emphasizing the koinonia. While I believe that Christ intended us to be in the world but not of the world, the internal focus of the assembly should be to bring men and women to Christ, teach them to discern their new identities as believers, and equip them to bring others to a right relationship with God. In simple terms the internal function of the church can be found in the Great Commission. "*Therefore go and make disciples of all nations, baptizing them in the name of the Father and of the Son and of the Holy Spirit, and teaching them to obey everything I have commanded you...*" (Matthews 28:19,20).

All New Testament churches are under the same Great Commission of the Lord Jesus Christ. The problem today is that such a statement carries an authoritative tone, and today's modern individuals do not like to have any absolutes in their lives. Gray is good, and black and white is bad, and the more gray in one's life the better (More on this in Chapter 4). However, for those frail creatures of dust that do recognize and honor the same authoritative commission, surely, they ought to be able to employ mutual motives in spreading a universal Gospel message. If we today can accept and so staunchly proclaim the principle of voluntary cooperation as "*laborers together with God*" (I Corinthians 3:9) with other faith groups, why can't we do it as one faith group believing in the same God? If we can be partners with God, then why not partners with the Children of God?

This adherence to the requirement of the Great Commission brings to the local church two additional functions: 1) that of witnessing to the unbeliever, and 2) educating the assembly. A New Testament church is characterized by its proclamation that Jesus Christ is alive and is the Savior of the world. Any assembly that would be in the Body of Christ must lead its members to witness to those who are not of the body. Any departure from the path, any renunciation of the truth, any retreat, any silence on the Lordship of Christ not only destroys the influence of Christians to the world, it also endangers the life of the church. A church must never be stagnate, it is either growing, or it will die. "*Then the master told his servant, 'Go out to the roads and country lanes and make them come in, so that my house will be full*'" (Luke 14:23). The local church can only accomplish this filling of the house by sharing the Good News that Jesus Christ saves.

But once saved, what then? Are we to simply attend the church, fill the pews, and give our tithe? Far too many people have come to the church, heard the message, and believed, only to hear the same message Sunday after Sunday and year after year, until frustrated in their growth they begin to visit other churches or stop attending all together. Billy Graham is a magnificent preacher, however, I believe that even he would tell you that he was called to be an evangelist and only has one message: "Believe and be Saved." It is a wonderful message! I love to hear it proclaimed; I rejoice in its acceptance, I weep when I hear a pastor preach the same sermon Sunday after Sunday. If that is the message that God has given you to proclaim, be an evangelist.

Paul voiced this same frustration when he proclaimed:

> "We have much to say about this, but it is hard to explain because you are slow to learn. In fact, though by this time you ought to be teachers, you need one to teach you the elementary truths of God's word all over again... Therefore let us leave the elementary teachings about Christ and go on to maturity, not laying again the (1) foundation of repentance from acts that lead to death, and of (2) faith in God, (3) instruction about baptisms, (4) the laying on of hands, (5) the resurrection of the dead, and (6) eternal judgment. And God permitting, we will do so" (Hebrews 5:11-6:3, parentheses mine).

These six things are very important, and I believe that an altar call for decision should be made at every service. However, we should guide our members in their advancement toward Christian maturity from the pulpit as well as from the Sunday school room. It is not enough to just teach the ethical standards of the church in Sunday school; we must also proclaim the beliefs and doctrines from the pulpit.

If queried, most people will readily respond that very little evangelism would be going on anywhere in the world today were it not for the local church. It is in this setting that missionaries, pastors, and church leaders cultivate their Christian Calling. It is here that their talents are nurtured; their zeal for the Word harnessed, and their life's work given direction. Ask most church leaders and they will readily acknowledge that there is a vast difference in the uncultivated and undernourished Christian living either outside of, or on the fringes of church membership and attendance, and those who receive the guidance and nurturing of the local church family.

Lingering a while longer on the subject of teaching, the dynamics of many of the "modern" local churches is discouraging. We have become a congregation of consumers. I plan to discuss what I consider the cause and effects of modern society's encroachment into the local church later, however, there are two items that deserve discussion in this chapter.

First, many congregations have accepted the social values of consumer and leisure now advocated by our society. It is as if they expect to be entertained rather than trained during the worship service and see nothing wrong with being drawn to a more entertaining event that deters them from attendant on Sunday Morning. I would not intentionally offend South Carolina, the state my wife and I have decided to retire in, however South Carolina has two equally good football teams, and debates about which is the greatest is always on going at the church during the playing season. For some unexplained reason regular members see nothing wrong with attending irregularly during many of the away games.

Preach on the big stuff, sex, war, racism, murder, rape, and the congregation will be moved to numerous cries of "Amen" and "Preach On." Preach on such topics as steadfastness, studying the Word, tithing as a form of worship, placing attendance at church over more worldly pleasures, and the assembly grows strangely quiet. Why do preachers do that? Because, it is easier to preach on the big sins than to preach on what Jesus expects us to do because of our relationship with Him. Why do congregations react that way? Because our society says, "If it feels good, do it!" "It isn't harming anyone, and what we do with our off time is nobody's business but our own."

This leads to the second dynamic of teaching the modern local church. The original motto of the United States was secular. "E Pluribus Unum" which is Latin for "One from many" or "One from many parts." It refers to the welding of a single federal state from a group of individual political colonies. On July 30, 1956, the 84th Congress passed a law declaring "*IN GOD WE TRUST*" to be the national motto of the United States.[6] For most of our national existence we have placed emphasis on "Unum," seeking to highlight our oneness, now in this modern age of political correctness we emphasis "Pluribus," stressing our multi-cultural diversity and individuality. From a religious standpoint rather than being one from many, we are in danger of becoming many out of one.

Political correctness is not just an ethnic issue, it can and is encompassing all of the ethnic, economic, academic, and social subgroups that make up the local church. A pastor should always be aware of what he is saying, however, if he must watch his every word or illustration, where is the freedom to share the word? Paul once commented that even the Cretans referred to themselves as "*liars, evil brutes, and lazy gluttons*" (Titus 1:12). One can but wonder how many Cretans left the gathering in a huff? If we are to teach the church, as the Great Commission requires, we must place truth above political correctness. This is not to say that we should not be open to insensitivities that may come from one of our sermons, however, if we must measure, measure, and re-measure yet again our words before we can proclaim them from the pulpit, then let it be done to glorify God, not patronize one group or another.

Returning to the deliberation on function, the internal function of the church is not to remain internal. The church that turns inward and seeks only its own well being is, or is on the way to being dead, seeing that it has lost it first love. "*Yet I hold this against you. You have forsaken your first love. Remember the height from which you have fallen! Repent and do the things you did at first...*" (Revelation 2:4,5).[7] The same purpose must characterize the internal and external function of the church—that of glorifying God.

Externally, the local church is visible, capable of being heard, and tangible. It stands to reason that a congregation of baptized believers in Christ Jesus would be seen, identified, and audible to those who come into contact with its members. Writing on "Evangelism and Missions," Herschel Hobbs wrote

> In simplest terms, evangelism and missions involve sharing what one has received. Persons become Christians by receiving the gospel in the fullest sense of the word. Those receiving it fulfill their roles as Christians by sharing the Good News with others. So it is both a privilege and an obligation.[8]

Just as the Great Commission gave us the internal functions to Baptize and Teach, it also gave us the external function to go and tell. For many years in the Army Chaplaincy I had told young chaplains that ours was a "go and tell" not a "come and listen" ministry.

The Necessity of the Local Church

I do not believe that one can discuss the functions of the local church without also discussing the necessity of the local church. I would not presume to guess at the number of churches in America today. While polls in recent years seems to place the percentage of people in America who believe in a god in the high eighties to low nineties, those same polls show the percentage of Christian churchgoers seems to be in an inverse ratio to the increase in Christian churches.

This reduction in churchgoers comes at a time when religions are becoming a major factor in world events. Islam is playing an increasing role in the social and political changes of Europe, the Middle East, India, Indonesia and most of Africa as well as many parts of America. Many of the ancient faiths are showing re-emergence in numbers and influence. Cults are on the rise in America. From Islam to Wicca, from Hinduism to Christianity, fundamentalism is on the march, and ignoring it or labeling it as fanaticism will not make it go away.

In times of turmoil, in times of world change, humanity as a whole intuitively draws back to the roots of culture and family faith. Many large denominations are shrinking because they have failed to remain true to the doctrinal roots of both their denominational heritage and the Bible. We cannot continue to pretend that no changes have occurred, and as some would so loudly proclaim, there are too many ministers with antiquated methods. However, there is a danger in associating the method with the message. Change for change's sake is not necessarily a good thing. I once heard a general officer say: "New is not better, better is better!" While there are glowing examples of effectiveness and growth, these are offset by depressing examples of ineffectiveness and decline. This is a time of profound change in the local church, but we must not lose the old, old story that has carried us through so many turbulent years.

I have noted in the history of this country that a few hundred years ago, churches were small and rural and virtually the entire country's population attended church. I am sure that there are those who would point to a forced attendant policy, but a closer look at history finds that there was but a short time that such was the case. During the early years of our nation, several additional Christian groups immigrated to America. The Quaker movement began in England in 1647 and was soon to be found in the American colonies.

History shows that they were not welcomed to the new land, and to some extent were persecuted.

However in 1681 William Penn appealed specifically to those groups facing religious persecution. The Mennonites came around 1683, and the Moravians followed by 1735, and the American Methodism took its start about 1766. There were other less numerous groups that settled in America, all seeking the freedom to worship God in their own way.

I chose to believe that the formative factors in American Christianity were the Great Awakenings, or revivals if one prefers that term. The first came around 1726 and fostered such names as: Theodore Frelinghuysen of the Dutch Reformed Church; Gilbert Tennent of the Presbyterians; Jonathan Edwards a Congregationalist; George Whitefield who took up the work of the Wesleys, and others who aided in leading the revival movement to its highest point.

In the early years of the Nineteenth century a second Great Awakening occurred mostly in New England. It was not like the first in either emotional excitement or controversy. But, perhaps more importantly, the second revival aroused all denominations to the significant need to spread the Gospel, both here at home and abroad.

The denominations realized that while the local church could handle the sharing of the Gospel within their communities, the task of sharing the Gospel abroad was a much more formidable task and would require cooperation, giving rise to several organizations to carry on foreign mission work. I know of very few denominations that show any real concern for the welfare of foreign mission work, nor do I raise any hue and cry. I believe, as do others, that our foreign mission work is both productive and on track. Could there be more foreign missionaries? There should and can be if the local churches open their eyes to the responsibility of sending more. However, it is the situation here in America that concerns me most at this moment in time. The decline in rudimentary Biblical literacy and good old fashion Christian ethics that have characterized this nation for most of our history are fast disappearing.

What is the reason then for this precarious situation in the local churches of our nation? Do such polls indicate that our country's population is made up of a less God-fearing populous than in former years? Does it demonstrate that religion is less near to the heart of our countrymen than is true of other nations? Or, perhaps, could these conditions be the outgrowth of a faulty system, the inevitable result of a church distribution spiritually and economically unsound? I give warning that more than one thing must be taken into consideration in any fair-minded attempt to answer such questions.

In seeking the necessity of the local church I believe we can "take a page," as it were, from our foreign missions endeavors. What makes foreign mission work so productive? Having preached Christ and Him crucified for the sins of the world, they teach the indigenous souls, who then go on to teach the local population. Leighton Ford noted: "The growth of any movement is in direct proportion to its ability to mobilize its entire membership for continuous evangelistic action."[9] I intend to come back to this thought later on in the book, space permitting, but for now let us continue with our discussion of the local church.

The Destiny of the Local Church

Christ in his instructions for John to "*Write, therefore, what you have seen, what is now and what will take place later*," (Revelation 1:19)[10] dealt with topics that are relevant to all churches regardless of time and place. It is also a good list of the potential pitfalls that await any church that does not take heed of the true state of present events in today's world and guard itself against secular humanism seeping into the church. Far too many denominations today are seeking to place social principle over Biblical doctrine. To these churches Christ warned that He would "*remove your lamp stand*," or worse yet "*spit you out of my mouth*" (Revelation 2:5 and 3:16). Yet this same Christ also said: "*To him who overcomes, I will give the right to sit with me on my throne, just as I overcame and sat down with my Father on His throne*" (Revelation 3:21). Lest the reader begin to believe that this is just another gloom and doom book, I thought it best to insert the destiny of the local church.

Not long ago someone asked me if I had seen Mel Gibson's movie *The Passion.* I said no, but I have read the book (The Bible) and we win! Some day in the future, perhaps the near future, the saved of all the ages will be gathered together in God's eternal home. The First Church of Jesus Christ of Heaven will be comprised of the same churches on earth, although it will not include any of the unsaved people who are on the church rolls. I tremble in saying that the total membership of the Church Universal will not be equal to the total membership of all the earthly churches, nor will it likely be the same total membership of any one Christian denomination.

Someday the saints will all be gathered into the "εκκλεσια" that I spoke of earlier. Denominations will cease, worldly differences will evaporate, and all Christians will be spiritually merged with all other Christians. The Church will raise triumphant over all her foes, and the infinity of the Church will become reality. The members of the heavenly "εκκλεσια" will have completely sanctified and glorified bodies and souls, as the "*perishable becomes imperishable and the mortal becomes immortal*" (I Corinthians 15:51-53), and earth dissolves away into the heavenly.

But that day has not come yet, and so we must be on guard against the threats that arise within the church both secular and social. "*But there were also false prophets among the people, just as there will be false teachers among you. They will secretly introduce destructive heresies, even denying the sovereign Lord who bought them...*" (II Peter 2:1). Certainly not every church that has one or more of these is to be considered threatened, however, three or more would certainly require that the church take a look at where it is both Scriptural and doctrinal. Although I will cover some of the subjects more completely later in the book, what the readers need to remind themselves of is that the threat is going to come from two sources, the false teachers—which would include the pastor, deacons, Sunday school teacher, and those who would lead Bible Studies—and those congregants that are shallow in their knowledge of the Bible and the doctrine that emanates from the written Word of God. Of all the questions I have asked during this project, the one I have not been able to answer to my satisfaction is, "Why can we not stay on a high level of spiritual devotion and joy?" Perhaps I will research that subject in a later writing.

Questions for Consideration and Discussion

Certainly all Christian churches have high moments when our hearts overflow with praise and assurance and we feel that there is just no way that we will ever drift away from God. However, somehow it happens. Events flood our lives, times and social attitudes change, the world presses upon us to "lighten up," and we awaken to the realization that once again we have fallen away from our treasured state of when we first became born again believers. If we were to chart our emotions, if we were to use a line chart to indicate the spiritual highs and lows, invariably, such lines would show the ups and downs, the highs and the lows of an inconsistent spiritual life.

So then the threat is real, and we must be ever on our guard to protect the sanctity of the church of the living God. Troubles beset us, and we lose for a short time our sense of God's nearness. Allowed to continue, and we become comfortable in the new environment and our witness to the world is removed or at the very least stunted. The one redeeming factor is that, as with King David, so far, we find that life without God goes out of kilter. And so, through the guidance of the Holy Spirit we keep repenting and coming back to God. Amazingly He keeps renewing the relationship and forgiving us. And so as you read on remember "*These things occurred as examples, to keep us from setting our hearts on evil things as they did. Do not be idolaters, as some of them were; as it is written: 'The people sat down to eat and drink and got up to indulge in pagan revelry*'" (I Corinthians 10:6).[11]

1. Have individuals within your church body begun to discuss redrawing the Biblical boundaries based on social changes rather than Biblical doctrine, or re-assessing the doctrinal restrictions of both church and denomination to include the possibility of leaving the denomination or renaming the church? Has there been any discussion on leaving the denominational affiliation off the church sign?
2. Are there those within the body who are very vocal about secular lifestyles being nobody's business but the individual's? Are questions beginning to arise as to what really constitutes a sin or that one sin or another is really just a leftover guilt trip of yesteryear?
3. Has the congregation become more willing to allow anybody to become members, or even church leaders regardless of their former belief or denomination?
4. Does the church ensure that new members attend a new members class to ensure they understand the Biblical requirements of membership
5. Does the church leadership support the principles of the church?
6. Are the church leadership graduates of the denominational seminaries? If not are they Bible college graduates, and of what denominational stance were the places of education? Was the college of attendance accredited, and by whom? Do their beliefs affirm or deny the Lordship of Christ? Do they lead the church through discussion and prayer or do they dictate what the church will and will not do?
7. Do the congregants understand the historical and Biblical basis of the church? Do they understand both the internal and external functions of the church?
8. Is the church visible, capable of being heard, and tangible to the surrounding community? How vibrant are the visitation and mission outreach organizations and programs of the church? Is the church reaching out to the surrounding communities or have the programs offered all turned inward?

9. What is the driving force of the church? If asked the question, "Who runs the church?" does an individual or group come to mind rather then the congregation? Are important issues brought before the congregation for a vote by the church membership, or are issues handled behind closed doors and only the decision announced?
10. Are the congregants erratic in their attendance? Are there members who only show up once a year, or when it is time to vote for a deacon, but have been on the rolls all their lives? Has anybody visited them to ascertain why they don't come more often?
11. Are there members who act more like impenitent sinners or unbelievers than faithful followers of Christ Jesus? Has the person or persons been spoken to by the church leadership, or is it nobody's business what they do for their secular activities?
12. Does the pastor preach on the hard subjects as well as the easy ones? Does he proclaim both Biblical and doctrinal issues from the pulpit? Has he made a stand on denominational doctrine based on an in-depth study of Scripture by himself, the deacons, and the church body?[12]
13. Is there a training program for future potential leaders? Does the church understand the need to support both foreign and home missions through cooperative programs? How energetic are the youth, brotherhood, and sisterhood programs in the church? Do these organizations not only teach but also participate in missions or are their assemblies just another opportunity for food, fun, and fellowship?

COUNTERFEITS AMONG THE ORIGINALS

Religious Evolution

The Greek word "μεταμαπορφουσθε" (metamorphous), contains the concept of a slow and drawn out development, a gradual transformation. Paul summoned the New Testament church to "*Do not be conformed any longer to the pattern of this world, but be transformed* (μεταπορφουσθε) *by the renewing of your mind. Then you will be able to test and approve what God's will is—His good, pleasing and perfect will*" (Romans 12:2). However, as often happens with human endeavors, what begins as a social experiment, sooner-or-later runs off course and threatens to destroy whatever benevolent undertaking was envisioned.

In our search to conform to this world and to bring our religion into a more perfect harmony with other religions we have reached a point where for many professing believers the Bible is no longer their earthly guide into the mind of God. In our search for social standing, political correctness, and religious collegiality, many now declare that they can believe anything they want and still be a Christian. All individuals, because they're Americans, believe that they have the right to reinterpret Scripture in their own image. Even the simplest reading of the New Testament should prove to any honest reader that such concepts violate the very fiber of Christianity.

What is it about humanity that seems to dictate that we must use our minds to reason out each and every situation that confronts us? I don't mean to imply that we should forsake using our minds to reason. However, to be intellectually lazy is to allow others to dictate how we live our lives. The Scriptures tell us to "'*come now let us reason together,' says the Lord. Though your sins are like scarlet, they shall be as white as snow; though they are red as crimson, they shall be like wool*" (Isaiah 1:8). Solomon sought to use reason to discover what was right and pure, and useful for the soul. "*I turned my mind to understand, to investigate and to search out wisdom and the scheme of things and to understand the stupidity of wickedness and the madness of folly*" (Ecclesiastes 7:25). After all of his searching he came to one conclusion—"*This only have I found: God made mankind upright, but men have gone in search of many schemes*" (Ecclesiastes 7:29).

Now, when it comes to the final decision on what authority we are going to base our life's endeavors on, we should reason together, we should determine what the basics are by which we are going to abide, however we need to be ever watchful lest we fall into the trap of rationalism. Simply put rationalism is a state of mind that tells the individual that they cannot believe in anything that the mind cannot explain.

There are, I fear, far too many churchgoers who seem to think that they can come to church and sit in the pews, have no real responsibility to either the church or the Scriptures, answer to no one but themselves, and yet declare themselves justified before God Almighty.

Within this group of nominal Christians, and I am using the word Christian very lightly here, is a growing group that seems to think that the liberty afforded by Scripture gives them the right to believe as they choose while professing to be a follower of Christ. They claim to worship Christ as their savior yet find no contradiction in denouncing the inspiration of the Bible, the need for a personal relationship with God, the miracles of the Old Testament, even the deity of Christ is questioned. What such liberal theology does is deny the fundamental truths of the Christian faith.

As with most words the term liberal has taken on a new description. Taken from the Latin word meaning freedom, its original meaning was "to be generous or bountiful." Its new use however is neither generous nor does it bestow freedom on the user. Just as some words evolve into new meaning, some people are engaged in a form of religious evolution. They seek to bring the Christian faith into alignment with secular concepts rather then the other way around. Rather than praying that God's "*will be done on earth as it is in heaven,*" (Matthew 6:10) they are more prone to pray, "our will be done in heaven as it is done on earth." To put it into simple words, they want to live their lives anyway they choose and still want the assurance that they are good people, that they are morally and at the same time politically correct, and most importantly that they will go to heaven when they die.

Such individuals are not hard to spot. They defer the name of Christ in public lest they offend someone. They are quick to denounce any need to publicly declare their faith. They support the right of every American to believe and worship as they choose yet for some unexplained reason they do not believe that Christians should have that same right.

I am not forgetting that with all of this, spiritual things must be spiritually discerned. Beyond the touch and deepest reach of grammar, dictionary, and commentary, beyond the best use of human device and the most brilliant minds is to be found the illuminating touch of God's Spirit on the eyes of the human soul, and on the intellect of the human mind. However, let no individual rationalize that the anointing of the Holy Spirit is at the service of the lazy, the indifferent, the unwilling, and/or the willfully ignorant. The individual who will not employ the most extreme stretch of his or her own powers, the utmost use of every facility at his or her command to search their Scriptures to discover the will of God, that good, pleasing and perfect will, will not ever discover the "mysteries" of Scripture.

This then is the dispensation of the Spirit. The Old Testament growth, its ceremonies, and the entire arrangement, were but preparatory, prophetic, and characteristic foreshadowings of the New Testament. The Old has cast light on the New, but the New Testament is the God-given crown and clarification of the Old. Far too many Christians today have forgotten, or have never learned, that ideas of church-membership, church ordinances, our ordinations, even the relationship of church and state must be interpreted according to New Testament freedom and spirituality, not what the world wants, or thinks, or even demands.

This is not a call to disregard human law or to overthrow our form of government. The Scriptures call us to submit ourselves to the governments of our own making.

> Submit yourselves for the Lord's sake to every authority instituted among men: whether to the king, as the supreme authority, or to governors, who are sent by him to punish those who do wrong and to commend those who do right. For it is God's will that by doing good you should silence the ignorant talk of foolish men." (I Peter 1:13-15)

Yet this same Bible calls us to submit to God. "*Submit yourselves, then to God. Resist the devil and he will flee from you. Come near to God and he will come near to you. Wash your hands, you sinner, and purify your hearts, you double-minded*" (James 4:7,8). And to the double-minded Scripture says: "*No one can serve two masters. Either he will hate the one and love the other, or he will be devoted to the one and despise the other. You cannot serve both God and money*" (Matthew 6:24). Where governments or humanity demand absolute authority, the Christian must look to Scripture to determine what is to be rendered to Caesar, and what to is to be rendered to God (Matthew 22:21).

More to the point absolute authority, Biblical authority, Godly authority, the type of authority that over rules all other standards of authority is as much an anathema to secular humanism as sin is to the Lord. I have noted elsewhere that humanity, as a whole, does not like words like authority, absolute, and mandatory. Modern mankind does not wish to be told that they must do this thing, or that they must observe any certain type of behavior because law, society, or God has mandated it. Humanity wants to make its own rules. Each person wants to be allowed to seek life, liberty, and the pursuit of happiness, each in their own way. "*In those days Israel had no king; everyone did as he saw fit*" (Judges 17:6).

The modern generations are a jaded group, each believing that their experiences are just as valid as any other person's experiences. They don't want to believe in absolutes—any absolutes. They tend to place experiences over all other forms of understanding. However, for the Christian everything we do is to be judged on the standards that the Bible sets before us. Larry Dixon, a professor of Theology and Church History at the Columbia Biblical Seminary puts it this way, "Our experiences in life, even those that may seem to be supernatural, are to be evaluated by their conformity, or the lack of conformity, to the Bible, the Word of God."[13] Any loss of this authority, any addition to its requirement, any deviation from the truths of Scripture places the individual Christian in harm's way. It opens them to heretical, profane, and sacrilegious teachings.

There are many that do not seem to understand the great truths of Scripture. Although the Bible is intended to be a guide for the believer on how God wants His people to live, its intent is often perverted by sin. It is through this sin, or sins, that God's truth is withheld from the individual. The Gospel of Jesus Christ when rightly received has the power to enlighten the soul, bless the heart, and save the individual. It calls the reader to a higher power of understanding then can be received by mere human reasoning. The mind begins to look to the spiritual resource, rather then human understanding, for that which is good, and righteous, and holy.

However when one allows sin to enter into their life, when they reject or despise Godly teachings, then the source of life and salvation becomes a document for condemnation and destruction. The carnal mind rejects any and all instruction that seems to its reasoning to be unreasonable in its instructions. Paul called it a veiling:

> "...on the contrary, by setting forth the truth plainly, we commend ourselves to every man's conscience in the sight of God. And even if our gospel is veiled, it is veiled to those who are perishing. The god of this age has blinded the minds of unbelievers, so that they cannot see the light of the gospel of the glory of Christ, who is the image of God." (II Corinthians 4:2b, 3)

There are a multitude of reasons for this veiling effect. Human sensuality often incapacitates spiritual sight. The more humanity becomes accustomed to fleshly pleasures the more it blinds the soul and dulls the wit. Worldliness fills the individual with the desires for possessions, and power, and material things that delight the senses. Certainly the list of sins that veil the truth of God from fleshly sight should contain the sin of "Pride"—human pride that fills the individual with fancies of being independent of God, exempt from His judgment and all-powerful in their pursuit of what they need and want and desire.

Watered Down Messages

Francis Schaeffer in the last chapter of his book *How Should We Then Live* began by saying,

> Overwhelming pressures are being brought to bear on people who have no absolutes, but only have the impoverished values of personal peace and prosperity. The pressures are progressively preparing modern people to accept a manipulative, authoritarian government. Unhappily, many of these pressures are upon us now.[14]

His prophetic words fell, for the most part, on deaf ears. The Christian church did not listen; they did not know how to listen. Perhaps having seen the continuous encroachment of government on the freedom of religion they will listen now.

However, if they are to listen then there must be some brave souls who are willing to bring this unpopular message from the pages of the Bible to the pulpit, and from the pulpit to the people, and from the people to the world around them without diluting the message. It would be so much simpler if we could just lay the blame on the preachers and teachers of the Bible, but such is not to be the case. Each of us must bear our own responsibility to carry the Gospel message to the communities that surround us. Each of us is to boldly stand and proudly state that Jesus Christ is the Author of our faith and the Rock of our salvation.

I love our basic doctrine, and I believe that it is, and must always be, the starting place for the new believer. There is no greater message to bring to the world than "Jesus Saves!" However, as we mature there comes a time when we must move on if our faith, and our knowledge, is to grow as God intended it to. And, grow in our knowledge is what we need to do. We need to expand outward and see what the rest of the Bible has to say about a whole host of things.

Somewhere in our individual spiritual walk, the basics, while dear to heart and needful for salvation must be gently and lovingly set aside. Certainly not to be forsaken, but to be returned to from time-to-time, as we progress in our Biblical knowledge and in our endeavor to build upon the solid rock given us by Christ. Perhaps of greater importance, the basics must be saved for further generations of new believers. Where we were once those who needed teaching, we should, in a mature Christian manner, seek to become the teacher. Rather than worrying about what the rest of society is going to say about our claim to salvation through Christ we should be defending the pure unadulterated Gospel, all the Gospel, not just the basics, and not in an abbreviated edition.

In the last part of the fifth and the first part of the sixth chapters of the book of Hebrews, Paul begins a discourse on the dangers of falling away. However, in beginning his discussion, he notes that while there is much to teach the peoples, he finds it hard to because of the slowness in which they have learned. Paul tells the Jewish Christians that by this time they themselves should be teachers, and yet they are still in need of teachers to teach them even the most elementary truths of God's word all over again. Paul is almost patronizing, almost insulting, in his confronting the people with the spiritual condition of those to whom the Epistle is addressed.

This habit of spiritual apathy towards the things of God not only hinders progress but it produces retrogression rather than progression. These peoples had made some profession of faith, but no progress had followed. They had not progressed far beyond the elementary truths of the faith. Upon closer examination of our own spiritual growth, can there be much difference between the Christians of Paul's day and those of the present age? Have we become so contented with where we are spiritually that we don't want to move out of our comfort zone? Are we perhaps concerned that if we mature we will be expected to do something with our faith? "*From everyone who has been given much, much will be demanded; and from the one who has been entrusted with much, much more will be asked*" (Luke 12:48).

I can find in Scripture no stationary position in the Christian faith. Once we pass into God's kingdom, we're expected to move on, progressing as the Spirit of God leads us ever forward. There is no standing still! If we are to believe Paul, it is impossible to bring our Christian growth to a halt. If we're not moving forward, then we are falling away, or backsliding if you prefer a good old Southern Baptist word. If the Christian is not to remain stationary, then, in like manner, certainly there can be found no Biblical approval for watering down the messages that are to be found within its pages. Just because I encourage Christians moving on in their faith, I don't want you to think that I am advocating that we abandon the first principles of Christianity. Paul while encouraging his readers to move on in the faith, listed six first principles of the doctrine of Christianity that his readers are supposed to be acquainted with: (1) *repentance from acts that lead to death*, (2) *and of faith in God*, (3) *instruction about baptisms*, (4) *the laying on of hands*, (5) *the resurrection of the dead*, and (6) *eternal judgment*, but he completes this list by stating "*and God willing we will do so*" (Hebrews 6:1-3). So, let's advance beyond the elementary principles to the higher, deeper, and wider truths of the oracles of God. What does God want us to know? What is it He has been trying to tell us for years now that we just don't seem to get?

Why not pledge ourselves to obtaining a clearer apprehension and a wider comprehension? A clearer fear and reverence for the Kingship of God; a clearer fearfulness for the fate of the millions of lost souls; a clearer anxiety that there was someone we should have told about Jesus and just never found the time, or worse yet did not want to insult their faith in another deity or god other than Christ. Why not develop a wider understanding of what God has in store for those who keep the faith, a wider grasp of the truth of Salvation, and a wider knowledge for the mind of God?

There is a very big "Why Not? The truths that are seized by the mind must be incorporated by the heart and soul; it is not enough to just know something, sooner or later we have to act on it. Mental perceptions should grow into spiritual convictions, and from there into Godly actions. Somewhere along the Christian walk we have to stop reading about the life God wants us to live and start living the life that God wants us to live. Having learned of God the Son, we need to be able to proclaim to the world, "*I know that my redeemer lives*" (Job 19:25). From repentance we must press on to the higher calling and into the enjoyment of the fullness of the blessing of Christ.

> "I pray that you being rooted and established in love, may have power, together with all the saints, to grasp how wide and long and high and deep is the love of Christ, and to know this love that surpasses knowledge—that you may be filled to the measure of all the fullness of God" (Ephesians 3:16-19).

If as we profess we believe in the Bible and all the doctrine that is presented within its pages, then shouldn't we be prepared to live our lives in such a way that we, more or less, become a living Bible to those who see us? Another way of putting this question is: Shouldn't our belief in Scripture result in changed behavior? D.L. Moody said something to the effect of: "Every Bible should be bound by shoe leather." Today's generations would say, "Walk the walk if you're going to talk the talk." "Don't strut your stuff if it ain't enough!"

Young people today are desperately seeking role models that they can emulate. For at least the last three generations the youth of this nation have refused to take the age old advice of "Do as I say, not as I do." This hypocritical concept has been rejected and is often the reason why today's youth has gone off on a search for a better way of life through Eastern Mysticism, Scientology, New Way, and other none Christian lifestyles. They have weighted our words against our lifestyle and found us wanting in the truth department.

Many nonbelievers will at one time or another read our Bible. For other nonbelievers you and I may be the only Bible they ever read. They will listen to our words, they will read our actions, and then they will watch us to find occasion to rebuke or even ridicule us for not living up to the standards we proclaim to have. In a very real way each of us are to be an Epistle of Christ Jesus. A literal literary work, known and well read of all men in every place where we are located whether we be pastor, deacon, or layperson. Our conduct and character should be a living commentary on the Word of God, which we preach to the people. Jesus said of His followers "*...let your light shine before men that they may see your good deeds and praise your father in heaven*" (Matthew 5:16). Poor conduct by professing Christians often results in a poor presentation of the Gospel message. Such behavior leads to what I have so appropriately called "Watered Down Messages."

Minimum Requirements

If I were to ask what are the minimum requirements to "become" a Christian, most people would answer with the "Sinners Prayer," the "Roman Road," the "Four Spiritual Laws," the "ABCs of Salvation," or some other statement on how to become saved. Each of these small but highly effective presentations is intended to lead the individual in accepting Jesus Christ as Savior. However, what if I ask what are the minimum requirements for "being" a Christian? In becoming a Christian there is the single requirement to accept Christ Jesus into one's life as Lord and Savior; there are no other requirements, it is Christ plus nothing! However, being a Christian, living a life that points others to the Lord, well that is a different matter all together. I'm not sure that I could get a consensus on what the minimum requirements are.

There is this marvelous story in Matthew 19:16-22, of one who came to Christ seeking eternal life. "*Now a man came up to Jesus and asked, 'Teacher, what good thing must I do to get eternal life?'*" Jesus told him that if he wanted to enter eternal life then "*obey the commandments,*" to which "*the man inquired, which ones?*" Jesus listed in no particular order Commandments five through eight (Exodus 20:12-16), and ended with a restatement of Leviticus 19:18. Jesus seeing that the rich young man was close to where he should be in his relationship with God rather then give him a list, gave him a choice—a choice of lifestyles. Later the disciples wonder who could be saved, if a rich person couldn't? What the young man, and in a similar manner the disciples, wanted was a list of requirements. However, wouldn't it have been great if Jesus had supplied us with a list of things we could do to gain eternal life?

In some ways there is a wide diversity among Christians. There are of course the normal ones, some are men, and some are women. They come from all races and nationalities. They include in their fellowship young people ranging in all age groups. There are adults of all ages ranging from the young adult to the more senior of our brothers and sisters. Some are members of church staffs, secretaries, deacons, pastors, ministers of education, music, youth development; some are teachers in Sunday Schools, and some teach Bible Studies, others may work with the poor and homeless, or even be missionaries; some because of health or age may sit in the pews, give of their tithe, sing in the choir, or simply be there to lend a listening ear or offer a prayer of concern. They come from all walks of life and are employed in as many vocations.

However, more important than these marks of diversity are the marks of unity that all Christians have. Most importantly in being a Christian is that each individual be a genuine Christian. I don't know if I can do justice to this concept or not. Do you know how it is when you're with a group of fellow believers? Especially when it is a group that is deeply committed to the cause of Christ. There is this sense of oneness that you can feel, a sense of sharing together as brothers and sisters in Christ.

These people do not wear their religion on their sleeves. They do not sound their trumpets in the marketplace, they don't seek to take the finest seat at the table, or the choicest seat on the pew, and they don't demand that others show due reverence to their position and call them by one title or another (Matthew 23:5-7). Their commitment to Christ is much deeper and more genuine than those who do. It comes out in the experiences they share, the prayers they pray, the way they act and talk, the way they relate to other people, not only at church but also in the home and at the workplace. Their backgrounds and experiences may differ, but each is a committed follower of Jesus Christ as Lord and Savior.

Another trait shared by all is a commitment to the group. Denomination notwithstanding, each is a loyal and committed member of a Bible believing, faith sharing, Christian church. This is not just a minimum requirement, it is a Biblical precept, "*Let us not give up meeting together, as some are in the habit of doing, but let us encourage one another—and all the more as you see the Day approaching*" (Hebrews 10:25). This loyalty and love of the church is strikingly present in those who give so much of themselves to the church on a strictly voluntary basis. "*Christ... loved the church and gave himself for it*" (Ephesians 5:25), and so do they.

A third characteristic that is seen in such people is their commitment to the Bible and to the missionary zeal of the saints. Some are preachers of the Word, others are teachers of the Word, still others are hearers of the Word, and one and all are doers of the Word (James 1:2ff). Every one of these people has had personal experiences with the Bible that have strengthened their conviction in its authority and its relevance. Each of these people will take the truths that they have found into their community and share it with those whom they come into contact with. Each and every one of them has a heart for missions and whether God calls them to a mission field or leaves them where they were first planted and harvested, they will boldly proclaim the love of God through Christ Jesus.

Some of the Nicest People

I don't know if you have noticed or not but some of the nicest people you would ever want to meet are to be found in the church. That is until they feel threatened or challenged, then these sugar sweet saints turn into vile venom spraying vipers striking out at any and all that stand in their way. The same diversities that I listed for true Christians will be found among those who profess to be, but in the counting will be found not to be true Christians. I have found that for everything that God has, Satan has a counterfeit; this is equally applied to believers. Oh, they talk the talk, but the walk just isn't there. For the Christian everything we do is to be judged on the standards that the Bible sets before us for Godly living. However, these nice people would rather use experience or even rationalization, to determine who or what their authority in life will be.

Perhaps the most famous illustration of rationalism is Thomas Jefferson. Thomas Jefferson was not a Christian; he did believe that there was a deity, a higher being, however he was also a rationalist. Jefferson in his private pursuit of knowledge took upon himself the task of searching out the "real" Jesus. Taking penknife and pen, Jefferson omitted the paragraphs, versus, and words that he thought were inauthentic and retained only those he believed were fundamentally correct within the realm of human understanding. The resulting work is commonly referred to as the "Jefferson Bible."

Who was this Jesus that Jefferson found? I doubt than any Christian would readily recognize the Jesus of Jefferson's Bible. In his Bible, there is no account of the beginning and the end of the Gospel story. There is no account of the annunciation, the virgin birth or the appearance of the angels to the shepherds. Most miracles are omitted, and the resurrection is nowhere to be found. Jefferson in his intellectual pursuit found a Jesus who was a great Teacher of common sense. His writings on the subject have often been referred to as common sense religion. Jefferson deleted any verses he thought to be unreasonable. His message was the morality of absolute love and service. Its authenticity was not dependent upon the doctrine of the Trinity or even the claim that Jesus was uniquely inspired by God.

Jefferson's intellect, his reasoning, saw Jesus as a man of illegitimate birth but having a benevolent heart. He saw him as a person who set out, without pretentiousness of divinity that others attributed to him, to teach the people about the coming Kingdom of God. Jefferson believed that Jesus ended up losing touch with his intentions and thereby began to believe in himself as the Son of God, and as a result of this loss of focus was punished for sedition by being crucified according to Roman law.

In II Corinthians 4:1-4, Paul wanted his readers to understand that he had not withheld any secrets to eternal life, he had not used any deceptions, and he had not distorted the Word of God. Rather, Paul had sought to bring the truth of what God had done on this earth through Jesus, His Son, to the reader. It is through this truth, plainly given, that Paul appealed to the conscience of every individual.

Our conscience is that part of the mind with which we reason out that which is good, that which is desirable, and that which is needful to our continued existence. Our conscience when functioning properly separates these things into their proper place in the life of the believer. The world often appeals to our interest, our hopes, our fears, and our dreams. Sometimes society appeals to our prejudices, or our superstitions, even our vanity is often brought to bear in determining what we believe and more importantly how we will live out those beliefs. Paul evidently, believed that the mind, the conscience, the intellect, the God given ability to reason should be used to understand the Word of God rather than simply being the final source of our belief.

For the nice people in church they tend to rely on what they can see, and touch, and reason out. There are many that do not seem to understand the great truths of Scripture. Although the Bible is intended to be a guide for the believer on how God wants His people to live, its intent for their lives is often perverted by sin, a sin that they would never admit to having. It is through this sin or sins, that God's truth is withheld from these individuals.

The Gospel of Jesus Christ when rightly received calls the reader to a higher power of understanding then can be received by mere human reasoning. The mind begins to look to the spiritual resource, rather then human understanding, for that which is good and righteous and holy. However when one allows sin to enter into their life, when they reject or despise Godly teachings, then the source of life and salvation becomes a document that the mind cannot integrate with their reasoning. Must like Thomas Jefferson what should have been an intellectual exercise in Godly truth became a source of destruction for the soul. Their carnal minds reject any and all instruction that seems to their reasoning to be unreasonable.

The expression that Paul uses is very powerful in its description of the one who causes the spiritual blindness. Paul attributes this mischievous act, this occasion of greatest evil, this cruel misuse of God-given intellect to one individual—"*the god of this world*" (II Corinthians 4:4). He is known by many names: he is the "*prince of this world*" in John 12:31, he is the "*roaring lion*" of I Peter 5:5, he is the "*dragon*" of Revelations 12:7, he is the "*Satan*" of Matthew 4:10 always seeking to usurp the authority of God, always seeking to bind humanity in sinful bondage.

For Paul there is a personal prince of evil working in both human society and in the human heart. There is one source for this spiritual sightlessness, and one effect in the minds of those so blinded by the rational beliefs of this world. Such individuals are perishing. Perishing in body, perishing in mind, and perishing in spirit. They have become so blinded that they cannot see the light of glory because of the darkness of the human heart.

The church members in Galatians 1: 6-9 were having a similar problem in their church. These nice people, these individuals, these purveyors of provocative perversion, were evidently well-known to the Galatians. They most likely belonged to the group. That they are from within the body makes their culpability that much more heinous. This is not some outside force compelling the Galatians to turn away; they are doing it to themselves. Paul's words give us understanding that this is an ongoing process, and that there may still be time to turn these nice people back to the true gospel message.

These individuals are seen as presenting a different gospel. Paul's use of the Greek word "ηετεροσ" (heteros) shows them presenting their gospel as just another of two alternatives. Paul then forcefully tells the reader that it is "αλλο ηετεροσ" (allo heteros); this is absolutely not another alternative, and that to listen to such heresy causes confusion of the mind and harm to the soul of the believer.

Paul points out two characteristics of these individuals, these nice people. First, they have an unsettling influence. Their words trouble the listeners; they rob the churches of their peace. They lead the members to forsake Christian love and embrace controversial doctrines, wayward teachings, and may even cause a split in the body. To the follower of Scripture there is just something disturbing about a person who not only takes Scripture out of context, but also adds to it or re-interprets it in order to justify their own behavior or belief.

The second characteristic is that they pervert the Gospel. They seek to reverse the Gospel message. They want to mingle belief, or human experience, or even secular law with the atoning death of Christ. Most often they seek to take away this requirement or add that liberty, seeking to make the new gospel "Christ plus something," plus works, plus lifestyle, plus the freedom to sin.

Paul very unquestionably lets us know that he doesn't care who these individuals are. They might be of the body of believers, they might be angels, they might even be found within the association of the Apostles. Whoever they are, and wherever they are to be found, if they preach a different gospel than the one the Apostles, including Paul, preach then they are to be eternally condemned. The problem for us here is that these individuals are so nice, so respected, that we feel uncomfortable in confronting them, but confront them we must. We need to unashamedly say what needs to be said, and do what needs to be done regardless of their standing within the community or the body.

Such heresy, left unchallenged, has the power to damn the soul. As such, such heresy is a sin against God, it is a sin against the believer's soul, it is a sin against the church, and it is a sin against humanity. Such a person worships Satan not God; such a person follows the world, not Christ; such a heresy leads humanity to believe that everyone is right, that no one is wrong, and that only the most evil life will face retribution from an angry God.

Whether the world wishes to acknowledge it or not there is no greater authority on earth than God the Father, God the Son, and God the Holy Spirit. There is no greater gift of God than to receive the Salvation that was purchased with the very blood of the Lamb of God; there is no greater source of truth and authority for the Christian than the Bible, the written Word of God. Not even an Apostle may change the Gospel message that only through Jesus Christ are we saved. No angel in heaven or demon in hell dares oppose the Gospel message that Christ died for the ungodly, that He will come again to claim those who have believed in Him as the Son of God, the Messiah, and the Savior of the world. The grave could not contain Him, the earth cannot explain Him, and Satan certainly cannot restrain Him, nor hold Him back. The Gospel message will go out to the utter most parts of the world and people will believe in Christ and in believing they will be saved.

Paul closes this discourse by restating that any such message and any messenger, who regardless of how nice they seem, or their social standing, or even their church position perverts the Word of God will be eternally condemned. Their fate is assured, their abode in hell reserved, their souls by their own devices will be condemned to eternally be separated from the God who loves them.

But, what can we do, they are such nice people? We don't want to drive them away when they have been so good to our church and they have been so faithful, they are family. We can and must remain firm in our convictions that the gift of God through Jesus Christ the Son is the firm knowledge that God loves us and gave Himself for us. The Bible tells us of that love, and it also tells us how to receive and hold on to the love that binds our wandering hearts to Christ. It is Scriptural precepts not human perception; it is the Word of God, not the experiences of life; it is the Bible, not humanity that gives us the ultimate authority to live our lives both in this world and the next, and it is Christ, not nice people, who is the head of the church.

Self-Serving or Selfless Service

By way of transition to the next subject, there is at least one more characteristic that these nice people have in common—they are not servants, and they certainly are not slaves to anyone. Oh they may be pastor, Chairman of the Deacon Body, or hold any number of church leadership positions, but they do not do anything that does not in one way or another contribute to their self-esteem or self-importance. They may hold a very significant position in the church, but it is not held because of any Biblical authority. They hold it because of tradition or because they feel it belongs to them. They, their father, or grandfather, or even great-grandfather started the church; there has always been one of their own in one or more positions of authority; there are ten or fifteen of their kinfolk buried in the church cemetery; they hold an equally important position in the community; they give the largest tithe in the church; etc.

By example, I have heard of at least two incidents of the person who played the piano at a church using their position to express their displeasure with something that the pastor said or did. In one such incident the individual would play the first part of the service and when the pastor got up to deliver the message she would leave the service, leaving the congregation without someone to play the invitation and closing hymn. In the other instance, the person would remain in the service but again refuse to play the last two hymns even though the pastor would ask forgiveness and beg the individual to play for the congregation. These individuals did not play the piano as a ministry or as a gift to the church; they played for the authority and control it gave them over the congregation, the service, the choir, and the pastor.

A Chairman of the Deacon Body at a small backwater Texas town, not far from the Red River had been the controlling deacon for the past ten years. His wife was the church treasurer; his sons held sway over the nominating, budget, and church grounds committees. His sons were also the Sunday school and Outreach Directors. The church had not been able to hold a pastor for any significant time, nor had they been able to grown even though a new housing area had been build within sight of the church. It seemed that when the pastor preached outreach or growth, the chairman would instruct his wife to cease paying the pastor his salary, and his sons would bully the pastor until he either did as he was told or moved on.

Lastly, I pastored a small church many years ago. The church had split off from one of the larger churches in town, and the person who was the Chairman of the Deacons had footed the cost for most of the building and furniture. I took notice that he would always sit on the back pew during the business meetings. Whenever I would bring up something for vote the entire congregation would literally turn and look back at him. If he had his arms crossed, the measure would be voted down. If he nodded his head up and down, the measure would pass. This was done even though I took everything to him before bringing it to the church. Even so, I never knew if he was for or against the proposal. When I left that church I stopped to drop off the church keys at the chairman's house. I wasn't feeling particularly meek, and I told him I still believed that the church would grow, just as soon as he died!

He remarked that I was probably right, but until then, it was still his church. I said in leaving, "And that's the problem."

In Philippians 1:1, Paul referred to himself and Timothy as "δουλιο Ιησου Χριστου" (slaves of Jesus Christ). This "doulos" was not a hireling; he was not a slave through entrapment or force. The individual, male or female, may have begun as an indentured slave, but when offered their freedom in accordance with Hebrew Scripture they did not desire to be set free. They had come to love their master and his family and willingly chose to remain with them. A doulos then was one who willingly became the slave of another for life. The concept is taken from Deuteronomy 15:16-18.

> "But if your servant says to you, 'I do not want to leave you,' because he loves you and your family and is well off with you, then take an awl and push it through his ear lobe into the door, and he will become your servant for life. Do the same for your maidservant."

We, whether we are leader or layperson, have had the awl of Christ applied to our souls and are forever more called to be a slave to the Lord Jesus Christ, and therefore a servant to His church. This is not forced upon us; we are not coerced into the relationship. We are to enter into the bond freely. But having freely entered, we become subjugated to Christ for life in a ministry of servitude to His children. Jesus told his disciples,

> *You know that th*e rulers of the Gentiles lord it over them, and their high officials exercise authority over them. Not so with you. Instead, whoever wants to become great among you must be your servant, and whoever wants to be first must be your slave—just as the Son of Man did not come to be served, but to serve, and to give his life as a ransom for many. (Matthew 20:25-28)

Lord Acton, a nineteenth-century English academic is credited with saying: "Power tends to corrupt; absolute power corrupts absolutely." He was referring of course to the power of one person or group over another person or group. This is neither unusual nor even unheard of within American society. However, for the Christian to seek to dominate another Christian is to lack respect for the brother or sister. It violates Christ's supreme law of love. We must always oppose wrong and error such as the examples I used above, but in so doing we must "*love each other*" (John 15:12).

Perhaps, as Christians, what we should do is redefine the word "love." The word "love" has many meanings. It means to like, to enjoy, and to admire. It also means tender attachment, sexual attraction, unselfish devotion, benevolent care, Christian concern, and spiritual unity. Most of us understand that in the Greek there are three words that we translate as "love." There is "εροσ" (eros), human love, that sensual desire, that longing for another's body, a love of flesh that if not Biblically approached often explodes into erotic sinfulness. There is "πηιλοσ" (philos), an abstract love, a friendly devotion, a love that is often shared between siblings and life long associates. Third, there is "αγαπε" (agape), God like love, self-giving love, and a self-sacrificing love, a love that a country western song says, "when it comes to love you don't count the cost." It is the kind of love that Jesus spoke of: "*Greater love has no one than this, that a man lay down his life for a friend*" (John 15:13). Each of these definitions of love finds many expressions and each of them has a place in human life. What is needful for Christians is to know what we mean when we use the word "love."

To love with a Christian love is to love as Christ loved us. To love as Christ loved is to express the love of the Father. And to have and to express the love of the Father is to practice the love that never fails, even when human frailties impede the effort (I Corinthians 13). God created humanity to be like Himself, and because He loved His creation He provided for all their needs. And when in sinful disobedience they disobeyed God, He still loved them and their offspring. When they fell from grace, God had a plan to redeem the fallen race. He patiently brought it to fulfillment in His Son Jesus Christ, the "*Lamb of God that takes away the sins of the world*" (John 1:29). Jesus so loved the world that He laid down His life for humanity's salvation.

There are so many examples of Godly love in the Bible that it would make a book in itself to attempt to extract them all and give meaning to their application. Let me just say that this Godly love is Christian love! It is the most precious of all gifts for our welfare and our happiness. We love God because He first loved us. We love Jesus because He became one of us and demonstrated divine love by His service and His sacrifice. We love humanity, not because they are lovable—they may not be love-able—however, we love them because of what they might become if they loved our Lord half as much as He loved them.

There may be some of you who may be saying, "That kind of love is beyond me, I can't reach it." You may be right, probably not, not in your own strength anyway. But if Jesus Christ is not only your Savior but also your Lord and example, and if you trust the Holy Spirit for guidance, the otherwise impossible becomes possible. I have tried to redefine love as I have found it in the Bible, love that is displayed by God the Father, and love that is displayed by Jesus Christ the Son who as the embodiment of Divine love became a human being and lived among us, and who gave Himself a ransom for us.

I don't know, maybe this last part has been an exercise in futility. It is not enough to define the word "love." We have to demonstrate it. We have to put it into practice. We have to live it everyday, and to claim the promise it holds "*for those who love the Lord and are called according to His purpose*" (Romans 8:28).

Questions for Consideration and Discussion

What a church, a congregation, an individual, does is determined to a large measure by what the members believe the Bible teaches. God gave humanity the ability to think and to make choices. Because we could think, we could choose between keeping our fellowship with God, or we could go our own way by following what the world thought. Because we could choose, we were tempted. Would we obey God? Or, would we do what we wanted to do? More to the point, what will you do?

1. Is the congregation, individuals or groups within the church seeking to conform to the world or to the precepts of God? Is your church concerned that in listing a phrase or Bible verse on the marquee they might offend some people within the community?
2. How does your church arrive at a final decision? What is the process by which they determine what they are and are not going to do in and for the community? Is there a Biblical process in place to arrive at such decisions?
3. What does your congregation as well as individuals within your church understand concerning Biblical liberty and individual responsibility? How are such issues addressed from the pulpit?
4. Are there any who consistently denounce the inspiration of the Bible, the need for a personal relationship with God, the miracles of the Old Testament, or even the deity of Christ? How are such notions handled within the church body?
5. While there is no church mandate to pray in the name of Jesus, are there any who consistently defer the name of Christ in prayers as well as mentioning Him in public lest they offend someone? Are there any who feel that the church should downplay their Christianity while advertising their inclusiveness? Once again how are such issues handled?
6. Are there any who loudly denounce any need to publicly declare their faith? What is the church leadership's stance on the right of every American to believe and worship as they choose? How does that agree or disagree with any church sponsored evangelical outreach programs such as visitation?
7. Are there individuals or even groups within the church who are always deferring to what "so-and-so" has to say about Biblical

concepts? Do such individuals defer discussion on issues affecting the church until they can see what other churches are doing?

8. Are there those in the church who consistently place their own life experiences over Biblical principle? Do such individuals argue from a reasonable position based on the changing morals of the general public?
9. What is the church's understanding of a personal Satan? Who do the congregants think he is and how he works within the world, the church, the society, and the individual? Are there those who argue that there is no such person and that it is unreasonable to believe in such a being?
10. Are there any who always seem to have an unsettling influence in the church? Does there always seem to be one controversy or another ongoing in the church? Has the church lost its sense of peace? Has there been such turbulence in the church that some are considering leaving or even a split in the church?
11. Are there those who always seen to be taking Scripture out of context, adding to it or re-interpreting Scripture in order to justify their own behavior or belief systems?
12. Are there those within the congregation that seem to pervert the Gospel? In Bible studies and Sunday school are there any who always want to blend their personal belief, or human experiences with the doctrine of Salvation? Do any seek to remove Biblical requirements or add a new liberty to the gospel message?
13. What is the church's understanding of Salvation? Has an atmosphere of "Christ plus" come into the worship service, the Sunday school, or the Bible studies? How are such topics approached, and how are they discussed?
14. What is the congregation's understanding of servanthood? Are there those who never seem quite ready to serve the church when called upon to do so, such as serving as a deacon or Sunday school teacher, by the congregation?

15. How do the pastor, the deacon body, and the lay leadership feel about being a servant to the congregation? What is their understanding of being a "dolous," a slave to both Christ and the church? Have they made their understanding public?
16. What is the congregation's understanding of selfless service? How is it to be accomplished, and what is the relationship between those serving and those being served?
17. How does the church define Godly love? Have there been any Bible studies on the concept of the three types of love? What is the love relationship of the congregation to one another, to the pastor, to the deacons, and to the lay leadership?
18. How do the church, the leadership, and the congregation show love to the community?

SECULAR AND SPIRITUAL CHURCH ISSUES

Over Churching, The Law of Supply and Demand

Before moving on to what I consider to be the more insidious threats facing the faithful today, I think it best to deal with the more apparent threats first. The first part of this chapter is going to be somewhat disturbing for some readers. There are those of the faith that believe that the Supreme Rule of God means that He "*will*" overturn the laws of economy where the church leadership fails to acknowledge sound financial principles such as the law of supply and demand. To those few I freely acknowledge that God "*can*" overturn any law of nature that He so chooses, however, why then did He allow the laws in the first place if He did not intend that we should follow such laws?

The New Testament church was growing so fast that the Apostles could not handle the daily distribution of food and see after the administrational needs of the congregation and still do justice to the ministry of the Word of God. So they called upon the new church to appoint seven men "*who are known to be full of the Spirit and wisdom. We will turn this responsibility over to them and will give our attention to prayer and the ministry of the word*" (Acts 6:3,4). So came into being the concept of the "διδκοϖοσ" (Deacon). These bodies of men (and women)[15] were then set aside, ordained, to oversee the administrational responsibilities of the church. Over the years the responsibilities have changed and in most cases increased, but the position has remained constant.

I must also acknowledge that few generations think alike. In churches where the leadership is still made up of those generations that lived through the depression years and those following, it is not uncommon to find a "building fund" that is not intended to build anything, but rather is there in case the church falls upon hard times. These dear souls are most likely to think deductively and systemically. The deferment of their personal gratification to the financial well being of the group as a whole directs their moral principles. In contrast, those generations that fall within the cluster of the "Baby Boomers" and beyond can be expected to spend what they have as soon as they have it, with little regard for long-term future endeavors, outside their own retirement funds. They prefer to focus on the short-term. These individuals will tend to think inductively and eclectically and an instant gratification model will guide their principles. I do not debate the pros or cons of either group; I simply acknowledge that they exist.

These facts offer little consolation to those who are struggling with why there are so many empty pews on Sunday morning or that they just don't seem to reach their monetary requirements. These facts also offer a severe shock to church members who have the little white church in the dell along with the little one room red schoolhouse preserved so firmly in their memories. The sad fact is that we have fallen into a rut of taking it for granted that our local churches have not only kept pace with the best of religious life, but have somehow managed to stay one or two paces in front of advancing financial difficulties, if not in theology, at least in interest in Godly things and in piety; all this without the benefit of proper guidance or training.

I do not mean to imply that no individuals are left to whom the church is a sacred trust. In reality there are hundreds of thousands of such individuals all over this nation who will make any sacrifice to keep their church alive and well. However, as with the law of supply and demand, there also comes the law of diminishing returns. It is interesting to note that in many areas it really seems that the fewer churches an area can afford, the more it is apt to have. To quote 60 *Minutes'* Andy Rooney: "Why is that?"

I remember a story about a young pastor at a small church. Like most ministers of the Gospel, he was poorly paid, his suits were somewhat threadbare, but his soul was eager and inspired. He had a message to give to the nations and this small church was where the Lord had placed him to give it. As he stood before his congregation, the inspiration in his young face flickered for a moment as he looked across his small congregation assembled to hear the Word of God. If he had walked outside the little church, he would have seen to his left two other meeting houses, to his right would have been seen a third, and across the street stood yet a fourth church. Four churches of Christian denominations, almost identical doctrine, almost within a stone's throw of each other, and in each not one fair sized congregation.[16]

Lest I be accused of believing in one denomination, a state religion, or of a General Protestant Worship Service much like the Armed Forces provide our service men and women, let me clearly state that I am a Southern Baptist and as such believe in my denomination, and I believe that it includes all the elements of a true Christian faith.

What I refer to here is the problem of the competitive denominations, which affects not only ministers, but the entire Christian population, financially as well as spiritually. The spiritual rivalry set in motion by well meaning yet zealous and jealous denominations, has and is continuing to undermine the present and future welfare of the local church by ignoring the laws of supply and demand. In the military, the senior chaplain must set aside his or her denominational desires, yielding to the greater good of the local Christian (as well as others) population. The senior chaplain does not set aside the denominational requirements of his or her faith, but does place Biblical Doctrine above church polity, meeting as near as possible the needs of the many over the needs of the few.

While attending seminary at Fort Worth one of my fellow students came to class one day very depressed. The professor asked what the problem was and if prayer was called for. The young man relayed how he, like many of us, was ministering to a small Texas Church not far from the seminary. A Baptist and a Methodist congregation were jointly using the building. The Baptist would meet one Sunday morning while the Methodist met that evening and the next week the Methodist would meet in the morning while the Baptist met in the evening. This had been going on for some years.

Because neither could afford a full time pastor he had been providing messages for both services for the past few months. During this time he had been talking to the deacons of both groups about forming one congregation since there was very little Biblical difference in the two groups. This way they could afford a full time pastor and would have sufficient leadership to provide teachers for a proper Sunday school and Bible study groups.

Things had been going well and the young pastor had high hopes that soon there would be an honest effort at ministry and outreach in the community. The deacons of the two groups had been able to agree on everything but a name for the church. Nothing seem to fit, and finally one deacon suggested that the church call itself the "First Christian Church of," to which one of the other deacons announced to the group that he had been with his denomination for the past fifty years and no one was going to make a Christian out of him.

Barring the humor of the story, it is undeniable that the staggering growth and depressing statistics of over-churching and under-attendance confront any honest student of conditions in local churches. In retrospection of my own area, within a fifteen-mile radius of me, there are at least seven churches of my denomination each proclaiming the virtues of the Southern Baptist. Expand the circle to a twenty-mile radius and the number jumps to twelve. What adds to my consternation is the knowledge that I know at least ten people who drive past five denominational churches to reach the one they presently attend. I know one person who drives clear across town to reach a church of like faith and message. I cannot count the number of church hopping people who have left one church for another simply because of a misunderstanding or the strain of being asked for more and more money in order to have a full time pastor and part time staff had become unbearable.

It is most unfortunate that in this age of heralded collegiality same faith denominations cannot bring themselves to sit down at the same table, and having conducted a survey of the existing denominational churches and the ability of the community to support those churches, called a moratorium to building new churches which will only take members away from existing congregations and threaten the very existence of the already active churches.

Yes, someone will say, but churches split! Yes, they do, but this does not necessitate the building of a new church or require that a new congregation take on new or additional financial responsibilities just because they differ on a non-salvation question. In such cases the county or state association should do everything in their power to bring about a Christian reconciliation, and barring that assist the injured congregants in finding a new church home within an existing denominational church.

Mediocre Leadership

Common Place Deacons: Paul in I Timothy said: "*Here is a trustworthy saying: If anyone sets his heart on being an "επισκοπεω" (overseer), he desires a noble task*" (I Timothy 3:1).[17] However, the question begs to be asked: "Why?" Why be a deacon? Setting aside the call of the Holy Spirit and the local church, what earthly reason would a person have for becoming a deacon? Before someone is tempted to ask by what right do I pose such a question, I am not only a licensed and ordained minister, I am also an ordained deacon and have served as a chairman of a deacon body. The Greeks, from whom we draw the language of the New Testament, did not see servant-ship as a worthwhile calling. To them it meant to wait on tables or to provide some other menial service for the benefit of those more affluent and of more noble birth. Plato once asked "How can a man be happy when he has to serve someone?" Dante would later echo this thought by noting that it would be better to rule in hell than serve in Heaven.

Then Jesus comes along and flips that entire concept on its head stating that "*...whoever wants to become great among you must be your servant, and whoever wants to be first must be slave of all.*" (Mark 10:43b, 44). Paul later tells servants:

> Slaves, obey your earthly masters with respect and fear, and with sincerity of heart, just as you would obey Christ. Obey them not only to win their favor when their eye is on you, but

> like slaves of Christ, doing the will of God from your heart. Serve wholeheartedly, as if you were serving the Lord not men, because you know that the Lord will reward everyone for whatever good he does, whether he is slave or free. (Ephesians 6:5-8)

Someone once said that the world measures greatness by the standard of service given, not the service a person gives. Just as great service is measured by the world's standard, even more so is the service of an overseer, be he (or she) pastor or deacon, measured by the standards that Christ set for His church.

To seek to become a deacon should be the desire of every Christian's heart. It should rise from the bowels of the individual and resonate from the heart of Christ. Jesus said: "*Just as the Son of Man did not come to be severed* 'διακονηναι' (be deacon to), *but to serve* "διακονησαῖ" (deacon others) (Matthew 20:28). If Christ had not washed the feet of the apostles, if he had not demonstrated time and again what it meant to serve others, if he had not loved us unto death itself, if he had not done what he did for us, then the world standard would remain unchallenged, and we would be free to take the roll of deacon up without any real Godly commitment to serve others.

I am reasonably sure that there are few out there in church land who have not seen the Wednesday night business meeting come around when it is time to elect those who will fill the roll of deacon. Then much to everyone's dismay, they see friends and faces that have not been in church in months, if not years. Those staunch Christian souls have come for the express purpose of electing those who will oversee the churches business only to disappear into the night until the next time a friend or family member is nominated for the high office of deacon. And if that is not bad enough, not one church leader, not the pastor nor the serving deacons, nor even the members of the nominating committee raises a question as to the right of these people to vote on matters that affect a church that these wayward members do not support with either time, talent, nor tithe.

And so, I am brought full circle to my question: "Why be a deacon?" If one is not willing to learn what it means to be a deacon, if one is not willing to do what is required of a deacon, if one is not prepared to sacrifice time away from work and friends and home and family—why be a deacon? "*...Jesus... turning to them said: 'If any comes to me and does not hate his father and mother, his wife and children, his brothers and sisters—yes, even his own life—he cannot be my disciple. And anyone who does not carry his cross and follow me cannot be my disciple*" (Luke 14:26,27). His discourse on being His disciple was intended to cause those around Him to count the cost. It is not so much that we hate our friends and families, but that we love Christ more. So much more that we are willing to take up our crosses daily and follow Him. Tired, disgruntled with the pressures of the world and finding that there is never enough time to do what we want still "*I press on toward the goal to win the prize for which God has called me heavenward in Christ Jesus*" (Philippians 3:14).

First, I would say to the Christian, that such service, when we are called to it, is not optional. Secondly, I would have to say, as do many other Christians, that God equips those whom He calls to service, be those dear hearts missionaries, pastors, deacons, or teachers. If one were to say that they did not possess the required talent or gift, they should be just as fast to say that God will provide a teacher to show them the way. As Jeremiah said: "*here am I, send me*" (6:8). Third, and perhaps most importantly, the pastor, deacon, and any others called to ministry within the church are, and should always be, held to a higher standard. It is not hypocrisy to demand that those who would hold sway over the Bride of Christ be held to a higher standard. I would that the whole church rise to the higher standards, but to those who take hold of the keys to the kingdom, the Scriptures demand they remain above worldly temptations and free from reproach.

I Timothy, chapter three, disclosed that the elder (pastor) and deacon have much in common, and while the ability to teach is not directly required of the deacon, the deacon should be willing to learn in order to, at a minimum, provide Biblical guidance to those with whom they come into contact. There are also several qualities of a deacon that are to be just as desired in the congregation. The Scripture I'm discussing uses the word "likewise" (verse eight) to connect the requirements of the deacon with those of the elder. The same attributes of the elder: temperate, self-controlled, hospitable, gentle, not quarrelsome, not lovers of money, most certainly not a recent convert also apply to the candidate for deacon. Paul does invoke two additional conditions that would be just as applicable to the elder. "*They must keep hold of the deep truths of the faith with a clear conscience. They must first be tested...*" (3:9,10).

Far too many times the local church holds a business meeting to nominate people for the open positions on the deacon body. These dear souls are then contacted to see if they would be willing to serve the church in this venerated position. Normally the responsibility of determining their qualifications for the position is relegated to the deacon body, rather than a nominating committee, who more often than not does not go far beyond the question of how many times has the candidate been married, and does anyone know of a reason why they would not be qualified to serve. Some brave souls will perchance ask for a testimony from the candidates. But for the most part no real proof of purchase is required.

And here an unsuspected villain enters the story. The villain is a truth, just a reality of life; however, it is a very searing statement. It is an indictment of not only those who nominate but those who accept the nomination. For far too many there is no passion for seeking out the lost souls within the community. There is no passion for visiting the sick or homebound. There is no passion for promoting the Sunday school or the on going Bible study. In far too many churches the deacon will not be found in the Sunday school room, or the Wednesday night prayer service, or often even the Sunday night worship service because they are at home preparing for the up coming workweek. Many churches assign families to each of the deacons for visitation and support, however, there are no real requirements that the deacons visit those families within a definable time limit.

Although often ignored, the office of deacon is not a reward for being well liked or a member of one of the ruling families. It is not a second-class office that holds no real sway over the congregation. It is both a high calling and critical to the life of the local church. If the local church is the custodian of the Gospel, the depository for the Light of the World, then the deacons are the guardians of the gates. They have the responsibility to provide an atmosphere that is conducive for winning the lost to Christ. "*Open for me the gates of righteousness; I will enter and give thanks to the Lord. This is the gate of the Lord through which the righteous may enter. I will give you thanks, for you answered me; you have become my salvation*" (Psalm 118:19-21).

Where there is a standing committee there should be found a deacon present to assist and guide. Where there is an empty teaching slot there should be found a deacon ready to stand in the gap. Where there is a homebound member there should be found a deacon ready and willing to assist the pastor in bringing the Good News and Communion to the sick and homebound. Wherever there is a need we should find a deacon standing in the forefront of the battle to promote, highlight, and expand the work of praying, teaching, preaching, and training the laity to tell others about Christ.

Complacent Church Members: In the military that defends this nation we cannot use, nor should we tolerate, unfit soldiers. The soldier that finds any and every excuse not to properly exercise, both the body and mind, soon becomes fat of body and lethargic in thought. There is no strength of body, no vitality of action, no resistance to unsound military doctrine or orders. There is no growth as a professional. They cannot carry the load, they cannot endure the hardships, and at that moment when most needed, they will fail the mission.

If we place such high value on the defense of the nation, why do we settle for a lower standard in the defense of the faith? Paul said: "*Have nothing to do with godless myth and old wives tales; rather train your-*

self to be godly. For physical training is of some value, but godliness has value for all things, holding promise for both the present life and the life to come" (I Timothy 4:7,8). The church must provide programs that will adequately teach the Word of God as the basic diet for the members, Biblical studies as the norm for exercising the mind and constant encouragement for the inward growth of integrity and moral strength and the outward expression of service.

But, where do we draw the resources to provide such stimulating curriculum? "*Whom shall I send, and who will go for us*" (Isaiah 6:8)? Where are we to find these staunch souls who will teach and lead the next generation? If a civilization cannot build a great nation without knowledge of the history that spawned its birth, how can the church build character without knowledge of the men and women who endeavored to find God and found Him faithful?

I have often noted that akin to the church where no Bible is to be found in the Sunday school classes, is to be found the church where, although there is a Bible, the leaders who teach from it are themselves basically ignorant of its truths. I cannot count the times that some well-meaning soul has quoted *Poor Richard's Almanac* as if it were Scripture.[18]

The Bible is a book of many stories, however, it is also a book of a multitude of human episodes and a depository of innumerable Godly ideas. The teaching and passing on of those ideas is vital to the life blood of the church. To select teachers who take passages from the Bible and pass on their ideas in grave ignorance is to run the risk that all ignorance runs—to repeat the failures of the past and to condemn future members to misunderstandings and false precepts. Luke praised the Bereans for "*they received the message with great eagerness and examined the Scripture every day to see if what Paul said was true*" (17:11). Without proper training ignorance of an inane nature rules and the Bible has no well balanced soul to interpret its wonders and truths.

I have been in a lot of churches where there have been no plans made, no teachers trained, no real programs put together. I blame the church members as well as the leaders. In initial cases usually the church leadership has to take the initiative in making the church feel the need and value of a program. The leadership will not accomplish this by springing the proposition on uninformed church workers and officers two weeks before the planned event. The congregation will not accomplish the program by coming together during a business meeting in late September to nominate the same people who have been doing the job for the past ten years without a break or additional training, just because they do not want to be bothered with the responsibility to do more than just read the Sunday school lesson thirty minutes before leaving for church.

This is neither the place nor moment to settle the blame for this condition on any person or group. It is probably more appropriately the time for a statesman-like move to meet the danger. It is a Herculean endeavor to provide Bible instruction of worth, dignity, and intelligence in every church, but as with the eternal optimist I believe it is an achievable goal. Churches deserve, by God given right, teachers and leaders who will lead the forces of Bible literacy against a creeping godless paganism that the world now chooses to call social principle or secular humanism. This will only happen when complacent church members get out of the pews, get off their knees, get on their feet, and ask what they can do to carry the banner, to defend the faith, to become soldiers of the cross.

Inadequate Preaching

Unprepared: Some of the first things I remember my Drill Sergeant saying over and over again to our platoon of young soldiers were: "Poor preparation, provided for poor performance." And, "If you don't have time to do it right the first time, when will you have time to redo it?" The lessons he was trying to teach us were simple: "Before you do anything, back off and see what has to be done!" In the Biblical sense, count the cost! The calling to be a pastor is a great calling, but a very dear friend and the one who helped me see my calling, John Morton,[19] once told me if you can do anything else, then do it, if not, then heed the call before God gives it to someone else.

I well remember my first sermon at Springdale. I began preaching before I even reached the pulpit and was pretty much through after ten minutes. Brother John said, "Maybe you should get some additional training before entering the full time ministry." He was very kind in the way he put it, and I soon realized that if I were to serve the Lord to the best of my ability, then I would need some really great Christian teachers to instruct me in what I needed to learn, and to do, if I were to become an under-Shepherd. I do not mean to belittle the role of pastor, nor take anything away from the calling, however, a pastor should always keep before him that he is not the shepherd, and the congregation is not his flock. "*I am the good shepherd. The good shepherd lays down his life for the sheep. The hired hand is not the shepherd who owns the sheep. So when he sees the wolf coming, he abandons the sheep and runs away*" (John 10:11-14).

I was not ready, I was not prepared, and I lacked both the adequate training and the ability for the high calling to which I aspired. In hindsight, I now see that there were many at the seminary that also did not have what it would take to endure. For some the cost was too high, and like the rich young ruler, they went away sad (Mark 10:22). For others they were there because their families or their church called them into ministry, and "*the spirit is willing, but the flesh is weak*" (Matthew 26:41). For some the call was valid but the positions they aspired to were not where God wanted them. If there was ever a place where the Parable of the Sower (Matthew 13:3-9) was to be seen in living color it was at the seminary.

I freely acknowledge that there are many lay-preachers who provide well for their congregations. Without taking away from their calling, the real marvel is that so many of these men are of the high sort that they are. More then once I have heard a lay-preacher state from the pulpit "I don't know nothing about theology!" Ignoring the double negative, after the second sermon, I found myself in full agreement with the individual. I believe that these well intentioned individuals would do well to read the Biblical admonition to "*Do your best to present yourself to*

God as one approved, a workman who does not need to be ashamed and who correctly handles the word of truth" (II Timothy 2:15).

So far I have only touched on preaching. Just about anyone who wants to can learn a method. There are several excellent methods of speaking, but that is not to be equated or confused with the message. And that is not the only responsibility of the pastor. I have often told young chaplains that the job of pastor is to be found on the congregational side of the pulpit.

Untrained: There are grave charges being made against many pastors today. It is unfortunate that the church must admit that there are grounds for the charges of incompetence and sexual misconduct[20] among some of the pastors. If one wishes to just preach, then be an evangelist, be a supply preacher, become an interim minister with no real intentional ministry. However, if one wishes to be an under-shepherd, then one must be prepared to learn what it is that will be expected of him or her.

The great English preacher Charles Spurgeon in 1857, out of his own outgrowth and development, founded the Pastor's College. Its aim was simple. It was not a place where one came to find one's calling. He had come to believe that God called men to the ministry and consequently selected them from many different grades of society. It was not in his idea to establish an institution to educate them out of the very position into which God called them, but, rather to supply them with better means for working in their own category and in their own place. He believed that if one were a devout coal miner, a farmer, a mill worker, then he would supply them with better means for working in their own environment.

A student once lamented that the seminary had prepared him to be the pastor of a 10,000-member church, but he couldn't handle a sixty-member church. Not all of that is the seminary's fault. I was amazed at the number of students who took every course they could on individual Bible books, and not one elective on management, counseling, visitation, ministry to the elderly, sick, or abused, ethics, pastoral care, etc.

For those who were called to bi-vocational ministries there were associate degrees, but for far too many the cost of attendance was prohibitive. We have done better with satellite programs and courses, but the cost is still far too high for many lay preachers to afford. Our denominational offices send out countless flyers beseeching the part-time, bi-vocational, and lay ministers to attend a one- or two-week course at one of the major retreat centers for a nominal cost of between one thousand and fifteen hundred dollars. Some will even go so far as to cover part of the cost.

These poor souls struggle just to meet the daily bills. How are they to afford more training for a calling, which will never pay them any returns upon it? Most cannot spare the one or two weeks required, and for those who might be able to find someone to step in, they can't afford the cost. Those who have had the opportunity to complete such courses have demonstrated that such individuals can develop into able pastors. Here is a place where the larger churches in an association could be of significant assistance by offering classroom space and qualified pastors to provide free evening courses in counseling and leadership issues at no cost to the local pastors.

I have presented two illustrations. First, the bi-vocational or non-resident pastor too occupied with the requirements of life to also be a part-time student in search of becoming the best spiritual under-shepherd they can. And second, the seminary-trained student who wasted the opportunity and thus is an incompetent pastor too incapable to be a leader of his people. Lest someone be tempted to separate the two illustrations, I ask that they think about it for a minute or two. It is not so much "isms," "ologies," or even seminary degrees that the local congregations want. Several polls and studies have suggested that the general feeling being manifested in local churches today shows little concern for denominationalism. What people want is someone who will present Bible facts in an acceptable manner and minister to the needs of the people.

Unmotivated: The plain answer, without any apology is simply this: The uneducated unmotivated pastor, as a phase of religious worship in eclipse, has not yet cast an image on the mind of the local church. The local church, the Christian conscience, and I class together all the Christian bodies in this charge, has apparently reversed itself and "*passed by on the other side*" (Luke 30: 30-32) of this distorted situation. I had occasion to speak with a member of a church I had once attended, and asked how things were going. His answer bothered me. He said, "We have a preacher, but we don't have a pastor." I had heard this individual preach before and was bothered by his put down of higher education for pastors. The thought that we would wish to hire an untrained, untested, inexperienced individual, regardless of how long they had been in the church or the community, is not only reckless, it is unforgivable and in fact incomprehensible.

There was an educational commercial a few years back that showed a young boy running along a track gleefully jumping over several very small hurdles. He was just having a ball, and the entire world seemed right to him. Everything was going just great for the young lad until he came to a standard size hurdle. His young face first showed confusion and then bewilderment as he just stood there looking at it as if he were waiting for someone to come and remove it from his path. The message was that when we take it too easy on our children's education, we make it hard for them to overcome the obstacles of life. I believe the same could be said of young pastors.

By example, a young ministerial student, a fair-haired child of his local church community came to the seminary the same year I did. I'm sure you know the type, he had married the fair-haired girl, he had been brought up in the church to know that he was called, he had been brought alone by the church leaders, of whom his father was one, his future was all planned out. He would attend the seminary, receive his degree and return to the community where he would be employed by one of the first available larger churches as their pastor. Yes, he had it made; or did he?

Things did not go well for the young man. The church wasn't as free with the money as first pledged. He and his wife had to each get a job; he working on my maintenance crew and she in one of the seminary offices for less then minimum wage. His ministry downtown to the local drunks and homeless did not go as planned. He could not understand why they were not accepting Christ by the hundreds. I tried to explain that trying to meet the spiritual need without also meeting the physical need was little more than trash to those poor souls. That didn't go over well, and I was accused of calling the Gospel message trash.

He quit the crew, and I heard about him from time to time. His classes were not going well. The professors didn't seem to be interested in what he had to say. The test did not ask the questions to which he had the answers, and no church seemed to call him back after the first sermon. His married life was not fairing much better. Somebody or several somebodies had broken his rose colored glasses. And then one day, I heard that he was getting ready to quit both the ministry and the seminary.

Being the non-confrontational person I am, I took it upon myself to go and seek him out. He was not happy to see me. I asked him a question I have since asked a lot of young chaplains: "Whom are you ministering to?" In other words, what is your motivation? Who called you to the ministry—your church, your father, your God? To my surprise he almost broke into tears. Things were not going as he has been lead to believe they would. I shared something with him that a very wise pastor had once shared with me: "If you can do anything else, go do it, if not…" I told him it was not what his father or church wanted, it was what he wanted, and it was what God wanted for him. I prayed with him, which I have found to be of a great comfort among Christian brothers and sisters in pain. He did not graduate with his class; he graduated two years later. He didn't go home either; he and his wife went where God called them, to the Home Mission field.

I am sure by now that someone wishes to remind me that several of the apostles were unschooled. Yes, but they were called by the Master and were qualified at the feet of Christ.

established on zero[21] based budgeting, and what people thought they might like to do during the year?

2. Does the process incorporate a "needs" assessment, planning, evaluation, and implementation guidance into a total religious support budget? Are individuals required to submit goals and objectives for a planned program at least three months out?
3. Do missions and special offerings often fall short of the goal, or does the church leadership take money out of the general fund to meet the goal? Have the goals remained the same over the years or even decreased in the amount designated?
4. Does the church now, or has it in recent months, failed to meet the minimum offerings required for paying the bills, to include the staff salaries? Does the congregation receive a monthly budget report at the business meeting? Does it accurately reflect the financial security of the church?
5. How many churches of your denomination consistently having less than one hundred in worship are within a five-mile radius? How many churches of like faith and message are unable to hire a full staff or offer even the minimum programs to their congregations?
6. Is your church unable to keep a pastor for more than three years because of budget restraints? Does your church find itself in competition with other small churches in the area for a limited pool of pastors, constantly being forced to up the salary and benefits, often to the detriment of missions and outreach programs?
7. Does your church have a growth plan that looks out at least three years? Has the church ever considered the possibility of joining with another denominational church also struggling to maintain some form of worship that is acceptable and enlightens the members and is inviting to visitors? Why not?
8. Does the church allow the denominational association to assist in the search for new pastoral leadership by offering classes

and Bible studies, or does the church leadership chose to go it alone? Does the church know what kind of pastor they are looking for?

9. How does your church select the individuals who will serve as deacons? Is there a job description?
10. Does the church select a committee that draws nominations from the church body? Does the committee inquire if the individual is not only willing but meets, at the very least, the minimum requirements to serve? Is there a place in the process where the individual being considered is asked to give his or her testimony and how they see the role of deacon?
11. How does the church ensure that only those members in good standing are allowed to vote for the individuals being considered? How is the vote to be taken, by hand, by voice, by ballot? Is the ballot to be secret? Will it be handed out at the business meeting, or will it be mailed to only those on the active rolls? Is an announcement made before the voting that if one does not attend the church at least once a month, they should in all good faith abstain from voting? [22]
12. Is there an active and on-gong training program, not only for new deacons, but also for those who are serving? Who is responsible for the training program? What types of topics are taught, and who teaches them?
13. Does the church have required classes for teachers? Do the teachers attend the classes and are they tested on the desired knowledge? What steps does the church leadership take to ensure that proper doctrine is being discussed and taught in Sunday school? Are there constructive Bible studies being conducted in the church?
14. Is there a time limit on how long teachers, deacons, committee members may serve, and is there a time limit that they must be inactive before serving again? Are there programs available intended to revitalize these faithful workers?

15. Does the pastor have an accredited degree? Does the church have a program to assist the pastor in his theological growth? Do the deacons take time to pray for the pastor and to ensure that his training and library are up to date? Does the church budget for educational courses for the pastor? Is the pastor continuing his Biblical education?
16. Does the church body take an active interest in the pastor's education? Do they budget for periods of time in which the pastor can attend courses without loss of pay? Has the church considered a "love" offering that would send the pastor and his family to a retreat intended to refresh and revitalize his ministry?

THE MODERN CHURCH

What Is the Modern Church

If one is to discuss the modern church, one should first determine what it is and what it is not. What it is not is new. With the exception of twentieth century technology there is nothing really modern about the modern church, except what people imagine it to be. As I dwell on the concept I give way to temptation and quote Solomon, "*What has been will be again, what has been done will be done again; there is nothing new under the sun*" (Ecclesiastes 1:9).

The Book of Revelation, chapters two and three, symbolically gives it readers a representation of all types of churches in every period of history. There are the churches of Ephesus that have emphasized sound doctrine, but in the process have lost the zealous love for Christ, for humanity in general, and for each other, without which all things are but "*clanging cymbals*" (I Corinthians 13:1). They are comfortable in their religion and are quite open about not wanting "those" kinds of people in their worship services.

The churches associated with Smyrna are persecuted churches. They are not outwardly wealthy. In America their persecution could be in the form of secular or even state restrictions. They may well be in countries that require them to go underground in order to meet and worship. As with many of the Christian churches in China today, their leaders may face imprisonment, and they may be denied the legal right to even call themselves a church. Although such churches remain steadfast to the faith, they are in need of encouragement.

Churches in the style of Pergamos are those churches that are in difficult surroundings. Most likely they will be found in a city, a state, or even a country that has given preference to secular humanist belief or one religion over all others. Not much is know of the Nicolaitans in Pergamos other than that they were a group who believed that a little comprising here and there would not hurt the relationship of the church to the spirit of paganism and emperor worship that enveloped the city. Because of this there were those in the church that were teaching false doctrine and thus causing the congregation to stray from the truths of the Christian faith. Such churches today will be found to lean more toward the secular humanistic concept of worship and less toward Godly living. They have not yet forsaken the faith, but they have strayed far a field and need to return to the pure doctrine.

If the church at Pergamos was entraining thoughts on some form of comprise and false teachings, then the church at Thyatira evidently had the corner on the market. Not very much is known of the city other then there were so many guilds that if one wanted to work they had to belong to one guild or another. So caution dictates that we not push the interpretation too far. However, there is to be found in the Lord's condemnation the age-old question of just how far the Christian church can go in accepting secular and contemporary standards and still remain true to doctrine. Thyatira churches are those who have grown so accustomed to compromising that only a massive shift toward pure doctrine will save them.

Sardis was the dead church that was in desperate need of revival. Sardian Christians did not suffer the same level of persecution as Pergamos or Thyatira. In these two cities that portion of the congregation causing problems was minimal, while only "*a few people in Sardis who have not soiled their clothes*" (Revelation 3:4) remained. The churches seemingly sheltered existences may have accounted for its slackness in remaining true to the faith.

As with the church at Smyrna, the church at Philadelphia received no condemnation from the Lord. Philadelphia, from the Greek "Φιλαδελφια" (brotherly love) was a small church however there had been some persecution in which the members had stood firm in the faith and all their adversaries both Jewish and Roman were to be found outside the body and not in the church itself.

Lastly there was Laodicea, the lukewarm church so much in need of repentance. So minimal were its works in sharing or spreading the Gospel message that they are not even worth mentioning. There is to be found in such churches a professed Christianity without any outward show of real faith. Much like the city itself, the church is self-reliant. In worldly matters they may even be wealthy, but in spiritual concerns they are poor and destitute. If one were to seek out such a church, one would only need look at their monthly financial statement. While their giving to missions might be in the hundreds of thousands of dollars, the percentage of their yearly budget will seldom be more than one percent. Because of their wealth they can offer a multitude of programs and services to their congregants.

The Competition for Souls

If there are to be found seven Biblical concepts of the church, then certainly we are to find at least as many variations of the people who will comprise the modern church congregations. So in some ways we do have to accommodate our worship service and therefore our churches to our cultures. There is evidence in the Scriptures that tells us that on occasion Jesus was accommodating in His ministry. The rich young ruler was told to give away all that he had and follow Jesus if he would have eternal life (Matthew 19:16), while the Samaritan woman at the well had no requirements placed on her other than to believe (John 4:6-15). Just as Jesus adapted to the people He was speaking to, so must we. So I am not against adaptation, you have to know where people are coming from if you're going to take them where they need to be.

Jesus understood his listeners' cultural background and adapted his approach accordingly. Jesus ministered in the time of an agrarian society that was for the most part still oral in its tradition. The religious leaders of the day were highly educated; however, the common man was a storyteller. Jesus had His greatest impact when he told parables to the people. When Jesus talked with farmers, he placed His parables in an agricultural setting such as a vineyard. When He talked to shepherds, He used stories that spoke of the good shepherd, being the gate to the sheep pen, and finding the lost sheep. And when he chose to call fisherman to His ministry, He spoke of becoming fishers of men.

In our modern day society we reach out to people who are secularized in their philosophy and their characterizations. When preaching we preach from the Bible, we often use the language of the Bible, our illustrations are Biblically oriented. However, sometimes that terminology is not current, and I'm not talking about the King James Version, I'm talking about the common words we use like grace, redemption, righteousness, holiness, and godliness. Compared to the secular world and the visual stimulants they receive at an ever-accelerating pace, my standing behind the pulpit for twenty to thirty minutes on Sunday morning is not going to be nearly as sophisticated as what they are used to. In simple terms, I can't compete! As hard as I try, as much as I want to, I am never going to be as exciting as those who they see in the entertainment world and on television.

So, how much should we accommodate? How far should we go in creating a church that will compete with the secular world for the souls of those we are trying to reach? If I were playing the devil's advocate to my own question, I might be tempted to ask, "What's the cost of one soul?" When souls are searching, when they are crying out for relief or someone to love them, at that climatic moment in an individual's life it's not going to be a drama, nor group therapy, nor a music video, nor even a tele-evangelist that they respond to. It is going to be the spoken Word, the time-tested Word of God, simply articulated by one individual, whether it's the pastor during the sermon, a church member during visitation, or just a concerned Christian friend at the moment of crisis.

There are many churches today that are seeking to move from a traditional approach to ministry to a more contemporary approach. I'm not against a move to a more contemporary style if it has been planned for, if the leadership of the church understands the audience that they will be reaching not the audience they hope to be reaching, and if the growth plan includes a visitation program to reach the younger generation without leaving the senior generations behind.

In some cases, where the congregation is large enough and diverse enough, there may be two services on Sunday morning, as the church seeks to blend the two traditions in such a way as to reach as many as possible. What normally happens is that somewhere in the future the church leadership finds that what they have rather than two congregations are two churches meeting in the same building. And as is common to all humanity, groups of people get increasingly petulant and pushy in their effort to guard their own worship time and space. Often wanting to grow and unwilling to share what limited resources they have with others, even those of the same place of worship.

Those who attend the traditional worship service are normally auditory learners. They are accustomed to following a textual message given in a reformed style, while the contemporary groups prefer that a variety of preaching styles be used, especially the visual ones. Television and Cyber-space are the great culture-forming components of our society today, and they are powerfully capable of separating people from reality. They entertain the masses in colorful, fast paced, thirty-second imagery. The producers of such entertainment endeavors value style over substance. Society is being programmed to appreciate style over substance.

I have heard preachers who have great style; they really provoke the people into loud amen and even laughter and applause as they move the congregation through the worship hour. Some of the people leave the sanctuary talking about what a great message, and I come away trying to put a handle on what if anything the preacher said of substance. He had an opening text, but it seemed to be a springboard from which to propel him into his message. He had great illustrations to support his opinions, but where were the Biblical truths of the Scripture? Where was the listener to find the principle, the exposition, and the treatise of the text? What was the writer trying to tell us? What are we to do with what we were told?

Is that what we need today to fill the sanctuary? Are we to program new ministers to touch lightly on the serious issues? Do we as ministers really have the option of choosing style over substance? Is this what Paul meant when he said: "*For the time will come when men will not put up with sound doctrine. Instead to suit their own desires they will gather around them a great number of teachers to say what their itching ears want to hear. They will turn their ears away from the truth and turn aside to myths*" (II Timothy 4:3,4)?

I'm not saying that we can't have style and substance. Our preaching can be entertaining, but the people have to leave with the feeling that they have been ministered to and not just entertained. We have a thousand interesting things to say, subjects that will grab the people's attention and hold them fast as they become engrossed in the message and take hold of the truths of God. Effective preaching, and I think that's what I've been talking about, helps the listener to hear the message not the messenger; it helps the seeker to see Christ, not the preacher. In our competition for the souls of humanity, we need to be purveyors of the Word of God bringing eternity and reality together in a moment of truth that changes people's lives and brings them closer to Almighty God Himself.

I know in my own denomination that we were weaned on the concept of baptisms, budgets, and buildings. If we didn't have enough baptisms, if our budgets were not big enough, and if we did not grow the church, then we were not successful as ministers. Somewhere way back in one of my classes someone said that it takes about five years to grow a church and a pastor. The tenure of the average pastor is somewhere around two years, so how much does a church grow in that time, and will the new pastor have to go back to square one? I would be hard pressed to name even one church that does not dream of growing into a large church that will reach millions. But, at what cost, not in terms of money, but in terms of souls? "*What does it profit a man if he gain the whole world, yet forfeit his soul? Or what can a man give in exchange for his soul?*" (Mark 8: 36,37). One of our main objectives is to help people identify sin, and having identified it, then remove it from their lives through accepting Jesus as their Lord and Savior. We need to summon our congregations to move beyond where they are, to respond with repentance where necessary, and to react to the message where called for.

One of my preaching professors said that what most congregations need to hear are more sermons like "Sinners in the Hands of an Angry God," and less self-help messages from the pulpit. We need to take care less in our drive to bring in the people we make them feel good about themselves while they travel merrily on their way to hell. Somehow through all the hype, we need to find a way to offer something that seems to be in short supply. We need to offer hope. Hope that is Biblically based and anchored firmly on the eternal relationship of the individual with God. So, then let's look at the modern church and see if the competition is healthy or harmful and what, if any, consequences it has on our congregations.

The Mega Church: I have heard various definitions of what constitutes a mega church. The general consensus seems to be a church that averages over 3,500 in worship. There are several things that the mega church has both in common and in difference to the smaller church. They have the same functions of other denominational churches, similar worship styles, methods of evangelism, and the training of lay leaders only on a grander scale. Many of the mega churches have their own schools through the high school level and some even leading to theological degrees. They run television and radio programs, they start new congregations and satellite churches, and some even print their own curricular materials.

They have much larger staffs and most of the staff has at least a bachelor level degree. Their pastors have advanced theological degrees, many are published authors, and they tend to stay in the pastorate for longer periods of time than smaller church pastors. The most distinguishing characteristic of mega churches is not their size, nor even the programs they offer. Smaller churches, to a lesser scale, offer the same types of programs and social services such as Day Care Centers to their communities.

During one of my assignments in Germany, I began to help a junior chaplain with his service, seeing that there was no service available for me to pastor. As with any small congregation the chaplain made up the bulletin for each service himself. Likewise there was little or no time for either the piano player or myself to coordinate with the presiding preacher for the upcoming service. Part of my assisting included preaching when the junior chaplain was unavailable. I had covered several services, when I asked the chaplain to come to my office to talk about enhancing the worship service. I asked him if it was his practice or intent to cause the supporting preachers to fail in their responsibilities to the congregation. He seemed honestly surprised at the question. I laid out on the table several bulletins for him to look at. Having given him time to reflect on the bulletins, I said: "Did you notice that when you preach, we sing songs that everyone knows, and when I or another chaplain fills in for you, you list songs that neither the chaplain nor the piano player knows?" By intent or design the practice stopped and both the congregation and the worship experience grew in size. You may be asking what this story has to do with mega churches.

Mega churches are not just larger versions of the smaller church; they differ in their effectiveness and their sophistication. Even as far back as the eighties, the differences between the two types of churches were evident to those who studied church administration. In one of his books, Lyle Schaller said that "mega churches are organized differently, people relate differently, and they minister differently." [23] Mega churches tend to become large because they are effective at what they do, there is a division of labor among the staff, and perhaps most importantly, the staff cooperates and works toward the same goals; proclaiming the Word and providing a meaningful worship experience. This requires that as an effective church grows it also becomes more complex with a larger organizational system and will develop multiple relationships between diverse social groups.

There is of course an adverse relationship to the growth of any church. As a church becomes more effective it usually grows; if a large church ceases to be effective it usually becomes smaller. With both types of churches there are several reasons why growth may cease and the church become diminutive.

The Small Church: Excluding no growth potential, the first and perhaps most common cause of no growth, or decline, in small churches is that the personalities and characteristics of the present staff tend to fight growth.[24] Somebody once called this "squatter's rights." When the present pastor and/or staff have a reluctance to change, regardless of reason, they will do everything possible to undermine restructuring of the staff and redistribution of any responsibilities. There has always been a strange philosophy at work in the minds of small church staffs, especially the unpaid or part time staff. They tend to view the position as belonging to them and their family and not to the church. Any attempt at such reallocation will be viewed by those in the positions as a direct threat to their power base and will be resisted by all means available.

Many a young pastor has seen his tenure come to a screeching halt after having attempted to change the way the songs were selected, or dared to suggest that there was a more efficient way to run the office. The story is told of a new pastor of a small church. As he was putting his things away, he opened the middle draw to find it empty save for three sealed envelopes, one marked "For a Small Problem," one marked "For a Medium Problem," and the last marked "For a Large Problem." Being rather busy, he put them back in the drawer and went about his business.

About a year later he had a problem with the volunteer secretary of the church and remembered the letters. This being what he considered to be a small problem he opened the first letter. It read: "Blame me! I am the last pastor, and if I had done what I should have done you would not be having this problem, so just blame me." This made sense, so he went back to the secretary and said, "This is the last pastor's fault, if he had just done what should have been done, we would not be having this problem." That seemed to defuse the situation.

About a year later he got into it with the music director and the piano player. The first letter had worked so well, he went and got the second letter. It read: "Blame the school! If they had taught you what they should have, you would have been better prepared to handle this problem, so just blame the school." So, the young preacher went to the two individuals and said, "If the school had better prepared me, this problem would not have happened." That seemed to satisfy them.

One year later he had a really big problem with the chairman of the Deacon Body. He ran to his office, pulled the center drawer clean out of the desk and frantically tore the third envelope open. It read: "Prepare three envelopes." The rule to be remembered here is that more responsibility will be equated with more authority, and as such more will always be considered better, while less will not be. Even if the person holding the position is ninety years old and his or her skills have now become a liability rather than an asset, the church will find itself reluctant to redistribute his or her duties.

A second reason has already been discussed to some degree, that of economics. Any reorganization may require that the present salary scales be upgraded. The base question is and has always been can the church afford it. There has always seemed to be a divine mindset with regard to salaries in small churches, especially the pastor's salary—"If the Lord will keep you humble, we will keep you poor." Even when presented with viable evidence to the contrary, most church members believe that their church's salaries have kept pace with those found in other churches of like size. Yet again a word of caution, when dealing with a reluctant staff, one assurance that they will seek is that the position will not decrease in either authority or pay.

A third reason for a lack of growth can be attributed to ineffective supervision. One thing that any officer in the military must learn is that when a Non-commissioned Officer (NCO) says, "That is NCO business, sir!" what is really being said is "It is none of your business." Staff personnel, any staff personnel, will become accustomed to doing their work a certain way. Unhealthy work habits develop, and the staff does not want them changed. Using my NCO analogy, a good supervisor understands that the NCOs do not tell the officer what NCO business is; the officer tells the NCO and the NCO does it. In like manner, a supervisor supervises! To do anything less is to watch work production gradually deteriorate to an unacceptable level. Allowed to continue, and even new workers will lose their professionalism and surrender to the ineffective rather than fight what the supervisor obviously accepts. If you would be a leader in the church take warning: "Silence will always be received as tacit approval by the offending party."

Church Growth: Lest the reader is tempted to declare me much too worldly[25] on the subject of church growth, let me offer the following in my defense. I believe that when we listen, the Holy Spirit guides our ministry to one another. However, at the same time I believe that we should view church growth from the historical, contemporary, and Biblical standpoints.

What are our roots, who were the founding fathers and mothers of the local church, what do we stand for, and how has that changed over the years? How has our community changed, how has the present day realities changed us, and how has the community helped or restricted the method and style of our present day worship service and programs? Lastly, do we, as a church, have a balanced theology of church growth? I'm not sure who coined the term: "holistic" ministries. I know that I have seen that word misused in many a hospital ministry, but what does it mean to the local church? What does it mean to have a balanced theology? Where do we find a theology that meets the needs of the body, mind, and spiritual well being of the individual?

I have in my pilgrim's walk seen far too many churches, and military chapels I'm sad to say, where everyone had a book, and no one had a Bible. There were Sunday schools that never touched on the hard subjects and Bible studies that never opened the Bible. It is not enough to offer every type of social program conceivable, if the programs do not focus on the Lordship of Christ, Christian morals and ethics, the coming kingdom, and the redemptive work that the Lord has entrusted to the church. Regardless of the type of ministry or program, a sound Biblically based church will (and must always) examine their principles of church ministry in the light of Scripture.

The church cannot and must not divorce itself from the programs that God has given us to offer to the lost and dying masses. Christ Jesus has opened heaven's gates to the repentant thief on the cross and to the trusting sinners of all ages. We as His bride are to be His agents to this world. As such we have an explicit, unambiguous privilege and responsibility to serve wherever we have been placed. The local churches are to be "*the light of the world*" (Matthew 5:14). In Revelation 1:20 the church was called lamp stands. I do not think that it can be made any clearer; the local church, whether a mega-church or just a small one, is to be light-bearers to those who are lost in darkness. In some ways we pastors are entertainers, but churches should never be places of entertainment just to draw a crowd.

The Modern Church Membership

So many today, and I include church leadership in this nebulous number, come at the concept of church as if it were just another organization. The reality is that the church is, or should be, more of an organism than an organization. "*The body is a unit, though it is made up of many parts; and though all its parts are many, they form one body*" (I Corinthians 12:12). Although the comparison may escape some, it should not be that hard to envision. An organization should conjure up a vision of structure and programs in which the individuals involved are only vaguely aware of its configuration and the recipients are only loosely related to one another by need or desire.

An organism, on the other hand, should invoke visions of vigorous life and cooperative purpose with all the individual parts functioning together toward the ultimate goal of a vibrant existence. Although a church needs a certain amount of organization, its primary need is to be an organism into which the Holy Spirit has breathed life. All the members perform their diverse functions and exercise their many spiritual gifts in a mutually beneficial and interdependent manner.

I believe a cursory reading of I Corinthians chapter twelve will show that Paul did not equate unity with uniformity. Just as the human body cannot survive unless all its parts are each doing what they were intended to do, even so the Church cannot function as God intended it to unless all the members are free to be all that God projected them to be. In Christ's Church all the members are important and all the members are equally needed. Complete interdependence must exist between the parts with no one individual being a stand-alone leader, or authority unto him or herself. Interestingly enough is that Paul seemed to be teaching that rather then discount the weaker parts of the body, they should be the ones to receive more attention rather than less.

Do you ever get the impression that some of the membership is lost and adrift in a sea of church programs? It should never be allowed to happen of course, but it does. Sometimes, especially in larger churches there are so many programs going on that it becomes easy for an individual to become lost in the self-righteous attitude of some of the more affluent and gifted members who tend to look down on poorer and less gifted members. I don't think I have to belabor this point, such an attitude says you may come and join our program but remember that we don't really need you to accomplish our purpose.

Non-denominationalism: Compounding the problem of unity in the church body there has arisen in the modern church a wave of non-denominationalism. I'm not just talking about churches that meet in store fronts or school gymnasiums. Nor do I simply mean those who once claimed affiliation with one denomination or another but now seek to go it alone, or who will eventually declare their own denomination separate from the founding assemblage once property, resources, and personnel have been securely retained within the grasps of the new denomination leadership. There seems to be a movement afoot in the local churches whereby church members are leaning more toward a non-denominational mindset. They are shying away from denominational ties, and their giving seems to be more inward then outward. Their budgets, while increasing each year, seem to be giving less and less toward missions and outreach programs that don't seem to bring anything of substance to the individual church itself. The focus of this non-denominationalism is the individual, and can be a person, a family, or a group of people and what they perceive to be their needs. What is the implication that this new wave of churchgoers seems to be providing, and what accounts for this rapid growth in church attendance of these types of churches? What is the basis for their beliefs?

The true Christian church is not made up of individuals separated by their individual needs. The totality of all believers constitutes the church. The coveted title of "Church of God" links the local congregation with all the other churches who worship our Lord Jesus Christ. "*To the church of God which is in Corinth, to those sanctified in Christ Jesus and called to be holy, together with all those everywhere who call on the name of our Lord Jesus Christ—their Lord and ours*" (I Corinthians 1:2). Without a denomination, a confederation, an association, call it what you want, many churches lose sight of what the church's true purpose is and become nothing more than a mutual admiration society, serving the good of no one but themselves.

Inactive Members: Coupled with this growth in non-denominationalism there is an equal but opposite group of church members. As near as I can determine there must be several million Southern Baptist Church members who have become inactive. Inactive not in the sense that they are no longer on the church rolls (God forbid), nor that they no longer attend church, but rather inactive in their sharing in the mission and the ministry of the church.

Some of this inactivity can be laid at the foot of the church leaders. Some members are not aware of the objectives of the church to which they belong. Failure of the church to offer, or failure on the part of the new member to avail him or her self of such training can often lead to a lack of interest in the church or its activities. Many churches do not offer, let alone require, new member training. Unfortunately, even older members often have to acknowledge that they do not know Southern Baptist doctrine or are not knowledgeable about what their church stands for. Many years ago there was a saying that no one spoke for the Southern Baptist with regards to doctrine. As a result of such mindsets, we became guilty of not saying anything. "*How, then, can they call on the one they have not believed in? And how can they believe in the one of whom they have not heard? And how can they hear without someone preaching to them*" (Romans 10:14)?

Because of the modern mindset that what a person does is nobody's business, or is between them and their God, some church members have gone back to their old ways of life. Such Christians were called Sunday Service Christians. They live like the devil six days a week but are the epitome of righteousness on Sunday. We used to call this backsliding, and it almost always dictated a visit from the pastor, the deacons, or both. Paul put it this way: "*...for Demas, because he loved this world, has deserted me*" (II Timothy 4:10). At its base it is a retreating from the promises made to God and to the church to live a life that shared the love of God with others.

Some modern Christians have found that the cost is too high to pay. Salvation is a gift, but it carries with it responsibilities. Christ has a claim on those who would be called His disciples. Obedience is one such cost of discipleship. For some reason it is painful for some to meet Christ in obedience. Discipleship is demanding. Sacrifice is necessary. The new birth is the beginning of discipleship. Discipleship is a concept that develops over the years through Bible study, prayer, worship, and ministry to one another in love. Surely there must be an easier way?

In close fellowship with this concept are worldly attitudes. Many church members are affected to some extent by worldly attitudes, however more and more of them are leaving church and Biblical doctrine choosing to be of the world as well as in it. The spirit of this age is secularism. Governments, education, science, technology all report their ability to meet human need without the infusion of Godly requirements into the equation. For these frail creatures false teachings can become attractive alternatives to obedience. The church has always had problems resisting false teachings that would lead believers away from a true understanding of what it means to be followers of Christ. One of the clearest threats to the modern church member is the contention that the need of humanity is not forgiveness of sin, but rather the acquisition of a more perfect understanding of humanity. This type of heresy is nothing more than the old "special" knowledge of Gnosticism. If, somehow sin can be dismissed as being of no spiritual consequence or as something that could be overcome by human thought or action, then sin becomes nothing more than perception.

It's the Message, Not the Messenger: I remember hearing the term: "vocational amnesia" in one of my continuing studies. That is a disease whereby a pastor forgets the two basic responsibilities to his congregants—preaching the word and shepherding the flock. Well there is a disease that often accompanies this disease of ministry, it's called: "devotional amnesia." Here the congregation forgets that it is the message not the messenger that is important.

Perhaps this would be a good place to insert my definition of a pastor. A pastor is an individual who ministers to the congregation in both word and deed. A pastor not only preaches the word, but he visits the sick, cares for the dying, and comforts the living. A pastor understands that it takes time and study to speak a clear, thoughtful sermon. He worries that he does not have near the time he needs for study and his own family because for the pastor the ministry is on the congregational side of the pulpit. Many churches have a preacher, but they don't have a pastor. The problem with a preacher is that he or she never gets to know the people, and worse yet the visitation program seems to suffer if not die outright from his or her lack of leadership.

In previous years the pastor needed to only pronounce the truths of Scripture, and because he had lived those truths among the congregation they readily confirmed them. Today's society calls upon the pastor to persuade the people concerning the gospel and its implications in their lives. We are told that we must somehow preach the truth, yet respect the right and the freedom of an audience to make up its own mind. Okay, so be it. Let the people decide! But keep in mind that Biblical preaching has always cut against the grain of society's rights and freedoms. To affirm this, one need only look to the beginning of the Beatitudes (Matthew 5:3), "*Blessed are the poor in spirit...*" but the world says, "To be a winner, you have to think like a winner." "*Blessed are those who mourn...*" but the world says, "Eat, drink and be merry. "*Blessed are the meek...*" but the world says, "Only the strong survive." "*Blessed are the merciful...*" but the world says, "It's a dog-eat-dog world out there, and it's every man for himself."

"*To what can I compare this generation? They are like children sitting in the marketplace and calling out to others: 'We played the flute for you, and you did not dance; we sang a dirge, and you did not mourn*'" (Matthew 11:16,17). It is like two groups of children calling to one another to "come and join us," and neither of the groups is willing to go. The one group calls out to be entertained. They want to be told that they are good and moral people. They desire to be affirmed as having nothing to fear, and no restrictions being placed on either their worship or their private lives. The other group, the true ministers of the faith continue, as they must, to call out to repent and receive salvation from the Lord, for the day of the Lord is fast approaching.

When I minister to a church I make the assumption that the congregation has enough Biblical knowledge to know where to find the Scriptures. When I was a chaplain I announced the page number in the pew Bible where the Scriptures could be found. I have often challenged my congregation to see where I am coming from in the Bible, and if they couldn't see it to come to me and we would read the Scriptures together. When in the course of moving to another chapel on the same post or in the same area, I would ensure that the people knew I did not desire that they follow me to the new chapel. If they did, then I felt that somehow I had failed them. I had failed to make them understand that it is the message, not the messenger.

A pastor wants to capture a sense of urgency that says that this is not just another interesting alternative, but it is something that is vital to the listener. It is not enough that the pastor knows what he is saying to be true, he has to be righteously enthusiastic about it, and he has to somehow pass that enthusiasm on to the congregation. It is not enough that the pastor has a vision; he has to be able to give that vision to the people in such a way that the people make it their vision, their dream, their mission in life.

It's Not What You Want, It's What You Need: The congregants thinks that they know what they want, and they are certain that they know what they want to hear, but the congregants miss the point when they seek to hear only one type of sermon, or insist that certain topics be off limits to the pastor. Today's congregations are most often found to be a diverse group. In effect, the varied social structures from which they come tend to create moralities of their own, or moralities that are not identical in immediate application with the pure truths of Judaeo-Christian ethics. So many seem to be seeking the easy answer and the quick fix, while loudly proclaiming that the Ten Commandments, the Sermon on the Mount, and the Golden Rule are ineffective, naïve, and of an earlier generation, therefore they have little or no application to the moral problems of today's world.

They want a cure-all gospel message that is in reality little more than a panacea for all the sensual sins that plague humanity. They want to hear that if "others" could just somehow love one another, like we do, then all the woes of the world would be solved. This simple concept allows the individual to leave feeling good about him or herself while placing all the blame collectively on humanity's struggle in obeying the law of love. One could argue whether it is even possible to achieve such a lofty standard given the stubborn self-interest so prevalent in the world today.

They want a philosophy of religion that is characterized by a vain deceit "*which depends on human tradition and the basic principles of this world rather than on Christ*" (Colossians 2:8). There is not, and has never been, anything wrong with a philosophy of religion as long as it is built upon the revelation of God that we have in the Gospel and the Scriptures, and not on the tradition of men. Other religions offer philosophies to be accepted or creeds to be affirmed in the believer's life. Only Christianity invites humanity to make a commitment to a person and to enter into a living relationship with Him. There is to be a continuing companionship between the believer and Christ.

This does not mean that the Christian experience is static and without progress. It does not mean that the type of service, the songs we sing, or even the manner in which we present the Gospel message does not change with the times. But for the messenger of God there must always be certain non-negotiables; among these are that the message has a strong foundation in Scripture, is firmly rooted in Christ, provides a maturing process for the listener, and never leaves the listener susceptible to heretical ideas.

Questions for Consideration and Discussion

When a messenger begins to listen to the congregation on matters of spiritual growth rather than proclaim from the Scriptures those things that the congregation needs to hear, they are in danger of becoming purveyors of error. If these messengers are not brought back into line with Scripture, there is the ever-present danger that their lamp stand will be removed. They will, in the end, become just another group of people living in darkness.

1. Has the church conducted periodic studies on the New Testament Church? How would your church stand up to the Acts 1:8 concept of church? Where would you place your church within the seven churches of Revelation? Perhaps more importantly, where would an outsider place your church?
2. What is the cultural background(s) of your church? Does the cultural background(s) replicate the community's culture that

surrounds the church? How does it differ, and does the church reach out to the surrounding community?

3. Once again, does the church have a growth plan? Do they understand the group(s) they are attempting to reach? Does the plan allow for worship that reaches all ages, social groups, and spiritual maturity? What type of evangelistic outreach programs are planned to support the worship service(s)?
4. Does the worship service often take on the form of entertainment rather than worship? Does the sermon have a viable message? Is there substance to the text? How often do you leave wondering what you are to do with the information you were given?
5. Do the sermons summon the congregations to move beyond where they are? Does the congregation respond with action to the message?
6. What are the goals of the worship service? Does all of the staff work toward the same common goal? Does the music support the message; is there appropriate time for both music and the spoken word, or does the music ministry take most of the time allowed for worship? How does the congregation participate in the worship experience? Is the congregation being ministered to or entertained?
7. Is the staff open to changes in the bulletin, the selection of music, and the worship style? Is the pastor free to exercise his gifts in ministry, or is he locked into the way the last pastor or the church has always done it?
8. With regard to the administrative staff, who supervises? Is there a division of supervision where the pastor supervises the worship staff and either an office supervisor or the chairman of the deacons supervises the administrative staff?
9. What process is in place to handle disagreements between the pastor and a staff member? Does each job have a job description, and is there a period of rating for the individual staff member?

10. Is there a pay scale available for each staff position, or does the deacon body or finance committee determine each year if there is to be advancement in position and pay and who does and does not receive compensation for future accomplishments?
11. Does the church have a balanced theology of church growth? Does the program take into account the changing community that it serves? Is the program reviewed each year and are modifications purposed as needed to meet a changing need of the church, the community, or both?
12. What is the primary focus of each social or spiritual program offered by the church? How does the program(s) offered advance the Gospel message to the community or peoples it reaches?
13. Do the church programs empower or restrict the individual church member's spiritual growth? Do the members feel free to discuss possible new ministries and bring them before the church leaders, or are they met with cold stares and patronizing words that such a program would never work in "our" church?
14. Does the church offer discipleship-training programs? What types and how often are they offered. Are church members activity sought out for such training? Are wayward members encouraged to rejoin the fellowship and to participate in such activities? If an absent member has a problem area or just concerns are there programs available to aid them with their dilemma?
15. Are the sermons Biblically based, and does the congregation seek to follow the teaching of the Bible or follow the preacher? Are the congregants more interested in how the preacher looks then what he says or how he says it?
16. Does the congregation have a vision for the church or do they expect the leadership to just do it and not bother them with any personal requirements to support the ministry?

17. Do the message and the vision of the church have a strong foundation in Scripture? Are they firmly rooted in Christ? Do they provide a maturing process for the congregation? Do they safeguard the listeners from heresies?

THE ASSAULT ON MARRIAGE AND THE FAMILY

Biblical Marriage

Have you ever considered that there is a divine order to marriage? Dietrich Bonfoeffer, while in a Nazi prison, wrote a sermon for a niece who was to be married. In it he said, "Marriage is more than your love for each other. It has a higher dignity and power, for it is God's holy ordinance, through which He wills to perpetuate the human race till the end of time."[26] As simple as it sounds, it was God that performed the first marriage by forming man out of the dust of the earth, and the woman out of man. God had looked at His creation and knew that it was not right that he should be alone and so He created man a helper. I like the word "helpmate" because I think that it conveys both the intent and purpose better than just saying "helper." In our creation God had made us social beings in need of touching and being touched in need of loving and being loved; and in need of belonging to another, and having another belong to you. "*The man said, 'This is now bone of my bones and flesh of my flesh…' For this reason a man will leave his father and mother and be united to his wife, and they will become one flesh*" (Genesis 2:23,24).

However, what does it mean to be united man to woman, and the both of them becoming one flesh? Presumably, that becoming one flesh begins on the wedding night with the consummation of the marriage. There is a majestic mystery in the sexual union that cannot be fully explained. A bonding process begins that will, if unbroken, take a couple through the miseries and wonderments of life. Someone once said, "becoming one flesh was like creating bonding paper." You take two souls put them together under tremendous pressure and the two become one. Once bonded together they cannot be separated without tearing both man and woman, each having spiritually become one part of the whole. This then is why there is a Biblical requirement-linking procreation to marriage, and why sex should not be indulged in outside of the marriage bond; it spiritually as well as physically joins the two. "*Do you not know that he who unites himself with a prostitute is one with her in body? For it is said, 'The two will become one flesh*'" (I Corinthians 6:16).

It is unfortunate that insight into marriage does not come on the wedding night. For many, we start out liking our intended spouses. We like being around them; they have a way of making us feel special. Somewhere around the third to fifth year—give or take according to the compatibility of the couple—an understanding about the relationship suddenly (?) comes to us in a breach of insight in which a flood of new meaning cascades down upon us, and we find ourselves saying: "I love this person, I truly love this person."

However, Old Testament marriage was not all that God intended it to be. The problem as seen by the created is that God also infused into us a free will, the right to interpret His design for us, and to conform, or not, as we chose. As with the original sin humanity by the time of Noah had pretty much muddled things up. We had become wicked and had done every inclination of our thoughts. God saw that our hearts were evil all the time (Genesis 6:5). To paraphrase Paul we had all sinned and come up short of the glory that God had intended for us, all save one. Noah, his wife, his three sons and their wives were all saved because of the righteousness of Noah, and God after promising never again to destroy the earth by water gave Noah a blessing: "*Then God blessed Noah and his sons, saying to them, 'Be fruitful and increase in number and fill the earth*'"(Genesis 9:1).

Moses set down laws concerning marriage and the responsibility of both husband and wives. Because Moses had granted women the right to receive their father's inheritance if there was no surviving son, the women were required to marry within the tribe thereby securing the inheritance within the proper lineage (Numbers 36:8).

This fruitfulness was so important that if a man was to die after marrying and had not produced a child then the next available kinsman was to take the widow to wife, and consummate the marriage, and thereby produce children for the deceased brother ensuring the linage continued. The most notable example of this principle in action is to be found in the Book of Ruth.

> *Then Bo*az announced to the elders and all the people, "Today you are witnesses that I have bought from Naomi all the property of Elimelech, Kilion and Mahlon. I have also acquired Ruth the Moabitess, Mahlon's widow, as my wife, in order to maintain the name of the dead with his property, so that his name will not disappear from among his family or from the town records. Today you are witnesses." (Ruth 4:9,10)

To ensure that proper time had elapsed for both the bonding and procreation recently married men were released from social responsibilities for one full year. "*If a man has recently married, he must not be sent to war or have any other duty laid on him. For one year he is to be free to stay at home and bring happiness to the wife he has married*" (Deuteronomy 24:5).

However, Old Testament men still had hardness of the heart and as such they required that Moses grant them the right to divorce for other than adultery. And so a Hebrew law was written (Deuteronomy 24:1):

> "Why then did Moses command that a man give his wife a certificate of divorce and send her away?" Jesus replied, "Moses permitted you to divorce your wives because your hearts were hard. But it was not this way from the beginning. I tell you that anyone who divorces his wife, except for marital unfaithfulness, and marries another woman commits adultery." (Matthew 19:7-9)

As a sidebar, one should understand that the certificate of divorce was for the benefit of the wife, not the husband. It provided the wife some protection under Deuteronomic law.

By the time of Jesus, divorce was fairly commonplace. Herod the tetrarch[27] had married his own brother Philip's wife Herodias, and by Hebrew law was living in adulterous sin. The Essenes, a rigid religious sect even saw marriage as a fleshly hindrance to their preparation for the coming kingdom of heaven. Neither the ruling Roman government nor the Mosaic laws accorded the women rights that were anywhere near what God had intended. The sacredness of marriage had become but a covenant pawn in the contest of consanguinity to see whose lineage was closest to Abraham.

After the death and resurrection of Jesus, the fledgling Christian faith was to change the face of marriage. Christianity was to achieve sanctity, dignity, and a restoration of the divine order to marriage that God had intended it to have. Christian wives had as much right to claim total fidelity of the mate as did the husbands. "*The wife's body does not belong to her alone but also to her husband. In the same way, the husband's body does not belong to him alone but also to his wife*" (I Corinthians 7:4,5). The wife was still to be the helpmate, but in addition she was now a fellow heir with the man to eternal life. "*Husbands in the same way be considerate as you live with your wives, and treat them with respect as the weaker partner and as heirs with you of the gracious gift of life*" (I Peter 3:7).

The Divine order to marriage was to be achieved by Christ being the Lord of both the marriage and the home. I have long advocated that if both spouses would allow Christ to be the head of the household, then the one role that would not be needed in the marriage would be the role of "boss." The husband and wife were to be a typology of the union of Christ and His church. "*This is a profound mystery—but I am talking about Christ and the church. However, each one of you also must love his wife as he loves himself, and the wife must respect her husband*" (Ephesians 5:32).

There is no Biblical marriage without one man and one woman freely given to each other for life. It is a God given bond that can only end honorably by the death of one or both of the mates. "*A woman is bound to her husband as long as he lives. But if her husband dies, she is free to marry anyone she wishes*" (I Corinthians 7:38).[28] In a very real way it is God's design and purpose; it is God's marriage; it is His joining together with His children to form a more perfect union. For the Christian, marriage is intended to bring glory, and honor, and praise to God the Father, through Jesus the Son.

Modern society has sought to change this Divine arrangement. They seek to remove God from the marriage, and to insert humanist desires in His place. Many couples today want to be married in the church; they want the blessing of the church. However, they want to write their own marriage vows that amount to not much more than "until death do us part, or next Wednesday, whichever comes first." I can tell the reader from experience that next Wednesday will always come first. These young couples want to remove any suggestion of submission by either party. "*Wives, submit to your husbands as to the Lord. For the husband is the head of the of the wife as Christ is the head of the church, his body, of which he is the Savior... Husbands, love your wives, just as Christ loved the church and gave himself up for her*" (Ephesians 5:22-25). The thought that the husband might be accountable to God for his conduct in marriage, or that a wife is to "obey" her husband has become unthinkable. They want a secular contract that can be broken by either spouse without the responsibility of making any real effort at building the marriage, without any condemnation as being the offending partner, and they want the church to endorse and approve of such an arrangement.

Part of the threat in the church today is that there are too many ministers ready and willing to unite the children of long time church members in the bonds of marriage without counseling the couple on what it means to be married in the church. Such counseling seeks to build a bond between the couple and the pastor so that if there are problems in the marriage the couple is not uncertain about whom to turn to for support. Lastly, such counseling ascertains that the two actually understand the grave responsibilities they are about to undertake and are willing to accept the roles that marriage will place upon them.

In the same vein many pastors will agree to do the weddings of a couple that are not members of any church. Out of this there has also arisen a horrible state of affairs whereby the couple is encouraged to join the church in order to be married in the church and thereby receive the blessings of the church. Such requirements often result in the joining couple never darkening the doorstep of the church again. The pastor then either does not seek to understand why the couple has stopped coming, or just writes the wedding off as just another civil service offered by the church. As a responsibility of the church, calling upon the Lord to bless the marriage should be safeguarded as though it were an ordinance of the church and not just an additional duty of the pastor. "*They are to teach my people the difference between the holy and the common and show them how to distinguish between the unclean and the clean*" (Ezekiel 44:23).

There have been times in the military when I have had the unfortunate duty to refuse to marry a couple. Contrary to many churches' understanding of the role of a chaplain in the military, a chaplain cannot be compelled to violate the tenets of one's faith. There have also been times when after having completed the counseling I have elected to perform a civil marriage service in a place other than the chapel because I believed that the marriage had a chance of surviving the military and neither of the individuals were religious.

There was one couple that has always stood out in my mind—she from a staunch Roman Catholic family, and he from a devout Jewish family. Both of these young people were well educated both secularly and in the doctrines of their faiths. Both of them were adamant that their faiths would not interfere with their marriage and that any children born to them would be allowed to choose which faith they wished to observe. Both of them acknowledged that their families had grave concerns about the marriage. I had taken more than eight weeks to counsel the both of them, individually and as a couple, and I was convinced that this marriage would be shipwrecked on the storm tossed shores of divorce.

Neither of them accepted my advice that they were religiously unequally yoked and that trouble would be on the doorstep from the moment they said, "I do."

> Do not be yoked together with unbelievers. For what do righteousness and wickedness have in common? Or what fellowship can light have with darkness? What harmony is there between Christ and Belial? What does a believer have in common with an unbeliever? (II Corinthians 6:14,15)

It was not so much that one was a believer and the other was not, there can also be this unequal yoke between devout followers of diverse faiths.

They did not heed my warnings, or my suggestion that they seek additional counseling before marrying, and would not even accept a parting prayer for their marriage. Another chaplain, who did not see the same dangers that I saw but believed, and rightfully so, that in God all things were possible, married them. I didn't hear much about them until Christmas. We were away on a training exercise, and she had gone out and purchased a Christmas tree and had it decorated by the time we returned. He threw the tree out in the yard and declared that he was not going to allow any Christian symbols in his home, while announcing that a Menorah would be displayed.[29] To further complicate the marriage she was with child, and he let it be known that if a boy, he would be circumcised and consecrated in the Jewish tradition.

She tried to get him to come in for counseling, however, he had no relationship with the chaplain that married them, and I was a "Christian" chaplain and could not possibly understand. Shortly after the New Year we deployed on another training exercise. When he returned home she had packed up, gone to her family and was in the process of seeking both a legal divorce and an annulment by the church.

Just because one or both of the intended are the children of church members does not automatically make them candidates for the church to affix the blessings of the Lord on their marriage either. It is no secret that divorces among Christians now equals, and in some areas surpasses, the secular community. Divorce like a contagious disease, tends to spread and multiply not only in the individual but in the church as well. If not properly treated, divorce will breed divorce. Children of divorced parents seeking to try and understand why the marriage failed, why daddy can't be a deacon or that one or both of the parents don't attend church anymore tend to blame the church rather than the parents. Often seeing such a fine Christian marriage fail, friends of the couple who are also having difficulties in their own marriages abandon their own efforts at reconciliation. Add to this pastors and congregations, that do not offer counseling, prayers, and support to both spouses, become infected just as if it had been an endemic disease. There is a residue that lingers in the church community when a Christian couple divorces, that if not properly acknowledged could disrupt the entire fellowship as family blames family and the members of the church choose sides as to whom is to blame.

Authority in Marriage

There are a multitude of reasons why secular, as well as Christian, marriages are in trouble. One of the more significant reasons for the Christian marriage is the decline of the authority of not only the husband but also the authority and rule of Jesus. I mentioned in the beginning of this chapter a "divine order to marriage." "*Wives, submit to your husbands as to the Lord. For the husband is the head of the wife as Christ is the head of the church, his body, of which he is the savior*" (Ephesians 5:22,23). The main thought here is that Christ, and not man, is the head of the church, also called the "body" of Christ, which means that He is the head of the whole body to include each separate part. "*Make every effort to keep the unity of the Spirit through the bond of peace. There is one body and one Spirit*" (Ephesians 4:3, 4a).

Just as Christ is the head of the husband and Lord of the family, even so the husband is the head of the wife, and the primary one responsible for authority and disciple over the children. "*Wives, submit to your husbands, as is fitting in the Lord. Husbands love your wives and do not be harsh with them. Children, obey your parents in everything for this pleases the Lord. Fathers, do not embitter your children, or they will become discouraged*" (Colossians 3:18-21). With authority of any kind comes responsibility. One of the basic problems in Christian marriages today is that many Christian couples have forgotten that when they were married in the church they invoked the name of Jesus, and as such are called to a higher standard than a secular marriage.

> Therefore, as God's chosen people, holy and dearly loved, clothe yourselves with compassion, kindness, humility, gentleness and patience. Bear with each other and forgive whatever grievances you may have against one another. Forgive as the Lord forgave you. And over all these virtues put on love, which binds them all together in perfect unity. (Colossians 3:12-14)

The bond of holy matrimony is a solemn lifetime undertaking that should not be entered into with carelessness. "*'I hate divorce,' says the Lord God of Israel*" (Malachi 2:16). Any individual who interferes with so solemn a bond as marriage does so at great risk to their spiritual well being. When questioned by the Pharisees on marriage and divorce, Jesus quoted Scripture, and then closed by saying: "*What God has joined together, let no man separate*" (Matthew 19:6b).

While I was at seminary a younger pastor came to me very visibly upset. He and his intended bride had been going to pre-marriage counseling offered by the school. The individual providing the counseling was also a student and about their age and had not been married long himself. During the counseling session the counselor had encouraged them to share past sins. The young lady had confided in them that she had one extramarital affair, they had sex only one time, and she repented of the sin almost immediately after the act. He was devastated by the information and was having problems dealing with her past sin.

He had come to me because although I did not have any more pastoral experience then he, I was about ten years older and had what he considered to be a successful marriage. I asked him if he liked her. Did he like being with her, did he like talking to her, and did he like having her around? He readily affirmed that he did, but he did not understand how she could have done this to him. I enquired if he had known her during the time of the sin. He didn't.

Part of his problem was that the counselor had made known his own emotions upon hearing the news. He had in a separate counseling session questioned whether he could have married his wife if he had known such information. I told the young pastor that God had already forgiven her, and that if he could not forgive her, then by all means don't marry her because she deserved someone better than him. He seemed shocked by my answer. He was not the one who had committed the sin; he was not the one who had not waited for the "perfect" mate.

Yes, I told him, I agree, however I also believed that he was not the one whom she had sinned against unless he was making himself God. I reminded him of another time when one much wiser than we were had said to the crowd, "*...If anyone of you is without sin, let him be the first one to throw a stone at her*" (John 8:7ff). I also told him that this sin had been between her and God, and it really wasn't any of his business. She had shared the information because the counselor had suggested it and because she believed that her intended would not hurt her with the knowledge. I told him that if he could not handle this as Christ would handle it then he should walk away before he hurt her more than he had already done.

He asked what I would do. I thought about it and said I hoped that I would be able to go to my wife and ask her forgiveness for having doubted her love for me. We prayed about it, and he went to her and asked that she forgive him for his sin against her. I have over the years lost track of them, but the last I heard they had three beautiful children and were about to celebrate their sixteenth wedding anniversary. Where God is allowed into the union, there is love.

Unrealistic Expectations

Modern marriage has been defined in a whole host of ways. Well-known scholars, both men and women have written widely read books and developed sophisticated theories on how to have a successful marriage. Most follow a standard counseling path that offers couples a variety of ways to identify and correct misconceptions about their individual marriages. No one secular book has all the answers because humanity is so diversified and complicated, and because secular counselors are reluctant to call sin, "sin." Jesus once asked the question: "*What good is it for a man to gain the whole world, yet forfeit his soul?*" (Mark 8:36). Paraphrasing: what good is it for a person, man or woman to gain the whole world, yet forfeit his or her spouse or family?

But how did Christian marriage go so far a field? Where did the institution of Christian marriage fail to live up to all that God intended it to be? There has been debate at many of the seminaries as to whether Christians have really ever lived up to God's requirements for marriage. In every relationship, even a Christian one, there will inevitably be some taut moments, a harsh word, a misunderstood request, a biting remark that is regretted the moment it was spoken. In the past these were moments for apologies, times when the family went to the Lord in prayer, to the pastor for guidance, or both. Now such instances are moments for reflection as to whether or not to continue the marriage.

With no-fault divorce so easy to obtain, the forbearance, or tolerance if you would rather use a more modern word, has dramatically declined. Couples are not near as forgiving as they once were, and forgiveness is an intricate part of marriage. "*...Forgive us our debts as we have also forgiven our debtors*" (Mathew 6:12). If we can ask God for forgiveness and if we can forgive others, shouldn't we be able to forgive our spouse?

The modern male is not willing to acknowledge his fragile male ego, nor take the time required to build up trust in the marriage so that when he does make a decision, his wife will have no reason to doubt his intentions. The young male of today wants what he wants and as he has been raised to expect, he wants it now. He doesn't mind his wife working; in fact two paychecks are better then one, in the race to see who can accumulate the most play toys. However there has been little change in the male ethos that says, "I work hard all day and when I come home, I want to relax. I shouldn't have to do house work and other things that my mother used to do."

In a like manner the modern female has no reason to work through any disagreement with her husband. Due to changes in society she need not submit herself to any man, be it her father, or brother, or husband. She can at the slightest provocation announce to her husband that if he is not the man she wants him to be then she is free to leave him, and usually our permissive society will allow her to do just that. Much like the male, she cries out for relief by proclaiming, "I work just as hard as you do, and I did not marry you to become your slave."

What both partners want is a stay at home wife, and if that's not possible then they want a 50/50 marriage where each spouse shares equally the up keep of the home. Ah, what a beautiful dream, both spouses giving 100% of themselves to the marriage and the home, each sharing in the burdens of life, and it seems to fit so perfectly with Scripture. "*Two are better than one because they have a good return for their labor, for if either of them falls the one will lift up the other. But woe to the one who falls when there is not another to lift him up*" (Ecclesiastes 4:9,10).

But, what if one of them does fall? As God created us as social beings, He also created us contractual beings. Everything we do is a contract, either with another or with ourselves. In marriage these contracts are most often played out in roles. What if his job keeps him out late and he comes home too exhausted to mow the yard or take out the trash or fix the broken windowpane? What about when she is full with child and can barely reach the sink, let alone bend over to put the dishes in the dishwasher? How about when the child is born and his or her first few months of existence are totally dependent on the mother, and she is too tired at night to hasten to her husband's physical and emotional needs? Given this concept of 100% in a marriage, what happens when one spouse can only give 30% to the marriage? Who makes up the other 70%, and is that fair?

The problem with the dream is that Scripture does not know nor does it recognize a democratic marriage arrangement. If one is so fortunate as to have two spouses who each give 100% to the marriage, you still only have 100% in the marriage. The underling failure in so many marriages is not a new form of conflict; it is an old secular unwillingness to tolerate even the slightest disagreement. In this age of the new modern feminine mystique, the new goal in life is "happiness," and this unrealistic expectation demands that the individual's happiness take precedence over the spouse or even family solidarity.

I remember one of my counseling professors saying something to the effect that "what many couples do not understand is that marriage is not a job that we come home to after leaving work, and divorce is not a two-week notice." It is however a lifetime undertaking that is going to require your full attention if it is to be successful. One does not set their marriage aside and pick it up again at the end of the day. In our modern society men and women can come into contact with more successful, more attractive, more interesting men and women in a workweek, than our grandparents could in a lifetime back on the farm or small town America.

In this age of increased extramarital affairs, there is a fascinating thing about "interested" third parties that one might meet at work—they can almost always pick up on the one thing that the other spouse has been disregarding. Characteristic signs are present when an individual is in a state of crisis. The emotional signs are as apparent to the casual observer as if it were a blaring neon sign hung around the neck of the neglected spouse. For whatever reason, the offending spouse has not seen the signs nor have they heard the complaints. Because both have worked hard and both are tired one spouse may say: "I don't want to talk about it!" Anytime a Christian makes that type of statement to his or her spouse, it is time for prayer and counseling. Silence is one of the harshest insults one spouse can give to another; it says, "What you think and what you need are not important to me."

Marriage Counseling

"We are assembled here in the sight of God and the presence of these witnesses to unite… in the bonds of 'Holy' Marriage. It is our intent as both minister and congregation to invoke 'God's' blessings on this celebration of God's children. If there be anyone who sees just cause why these two should not be joined in the sight of God, let them speak now, or before God and these witnesses forever remain silent." I am sure that you have either uttered these words or heard words much like these used in a marriage ceremony. Have you ever wondered what would happen if someone ever stood up and said, "I know a reason why these two should not be joined together in the sight of God. She doesn't love him, she loves me!"

Well I have been marrying couples for over twenty-five years now, and I have never seen anything like that except in the movies. I have had some rather humorous weddings, but I have never had one interrupted on the basis of one or both being ineligible to be married. However, have you ever considered that there are reasons why a couple should not be married? Thanks to the wise words of John Morton, the pastor who led me into the ministry, I have never married a couple without first ensuring that they received counseling. I do have to admit that the counseling they received has improved over the years, and that due mostly to both experience and education on my part.

I believe counseling to be as imperative to the Christian marriage as the invoking of God into the partnership. I hope that those of you who have received a church wedding were made to understand that by having a Christian wedding you were inviting God to be a part of your family. I came from a dysfunctional family. I was the physically abused child of an alcoholic drug impaired stepfather and the cast off street child of an alcoholic mother. When my wife and I were to be married, the only counseling the pastor gave us was: "Do you know his mother? Can you live with that?"

The glorious truth was that my wife and I had no one to fall back on but God and each other; we had to make it or fail on our own, and no one in the family really cared one way or the other. To our credit, and praise be to God, neither one of us ever considered just giving up. May 28, 2006, we celebrated our forty-second year of marriage. The importance of determination in making a marriage successful should never be underestimated. A robust determination on the part of both spouses must be present or the marriage begins with the likelyhood of failure. Of equal important is that there needs to be someone greater than the couple is to arbitrate for them. "*You know my folly, O God; my guilt is not hidden from you*" (Psalm 69:5).

My dear wife had to work when we were first married, and she had to work off and on for many years after in order to make ends meet. At one point I was working the midnight shift and going to college at night, and she was working in the day time and keeping the home fires burning, so both she and I understand the strains that come to a family who is barely getting by and trying to raise two children, all the while trying to reach an acceptable lifestyle.

When I received my call to the ministry and my wife and I both decided that I would need to attend a seminary for additional training, we learned something about both spouses working. What we learned was that spouses could each have jobs, if possible both could earn retirement from their perspective employers, however, only one of them could have a career. Even in the military, somewhere, at sometime, one of the spouses is going to be asked to give up something for the good of the other, and at that moment one has a career and the other a job even though both might remain employed.

Secular society trying to interject "life, liberty, and the pursuit of happiness" into marriages has caused confusion in the traditional role models found within the Christian marriage. Understanding why this has happened and what effect it has on the marriage becomes so much easier if you can understand one thing: In order to achieve happiness in anything, especially marriage, you must first know what you expect of your spouse and then you must know what your spouse expects of you. It really simplifies the equation if you find this out before the marriage, rather than after the marriage. It also helps if the individual counseling you has your spiritual, as well as your social, well-being at heart.

Individuality can be a beautiful thing. We do not lose our individuality when we marry, however, marriage holds no promise of happiness for an individual who is unwilling to lay aside some of that individuality. The marriage covenant is not unlike the covenant God made with the nation of Israel. "*...I passed by, and when I looked at you and saw that you were old enough for love, I spread the corner of my garment over you and covered your nakedness. I gave you my solemn oath and entered into a covenant with you, declares the Sovereign Lord, and you became mine*" (Ezekiel 16:8). Laying aside this individuality comes easier for some than it does for others. Children brought up in a Christian home, and who have seen this love lived out in the lives of their parents, often pray for God to send such a spouse to them. A truth that many young people do not seem to understand until it is too late is that you will marry whom you date. If you're looking for a Christian spouse, try looking in a church rather than a bar or some other social gathering hole.

I think that I have already stated it, but what amazed me at seminary was the number of students who while working on a Masters of Divinity degree took nothing but Bible study courses for their electives. The Education Department of the seminary offered a Masters of Counseling degree, and so had a multitude of courses students could take to better prepare them for their role as pastor. Yet time after time I would have a spouse come to me because one of my junior chaplains had taken the other spouse's side on the issue. I am not saying that every one of those chaplains was wrong, but if you are to help a couple through their problems, and bring God to the family, you have to stay neutral. And for a Christian counselor to say that there is no hope and that the two should seek divorce surely must almost be an abomination before the Lord.

I am sure that someone will say, "What about the abusive spouse?" You are absolutely right! No person, male or female should have to remain in an abusive relationship. But the great majority of abusive relationships, at least those I have had knowledge of, did not start out that way. More often than not when it is a Christian family involved, one or both of the spouses do not understand the roles that they are each to undertake in the building of a home. The husband tries to force the wife to submit, or the wife dismisses the Biblical notion of a husband's authority as outdated and degrading. Neither of them is willing to give a little in order to reach an equitable solution.

God did not put this authority into force to punish one or both of the sexes. He placed an order to the institution of marriage in order to protect the sanctity of marriage. A wife's willing submissiveness and a husband's earned authority are a protective bubble within which both are free to grow spiritually. When the world comes crashing in on the bubble then Christian counseling is needed to repair the damage. A final word of warning—counseling should never be used as a "last" resort. Far too many times couples have come to me for marriage counseling, and I find out that one or both have already been to the lawyer and are here at the suggestion of their lawyer so they can go to court and claim that "they even tried counseling!" As I stated earlier, "next Wednesday always comes first."

The Biblical Family

Throughout the entire Bible we find that the characteristics of the peoples of God are that they are to have a uniquely different life-style from the societies that surround them. In the Old Testament they were called to be a holy nation. "*Now if you obey me fully and keep my covenant, then out of all nations you will be my treasured possession. Although the whole earth is mine, you will be for me a kingdom of priest and a holy nation*" (Exodus 19:5,6). This meant that they were to separate themselves from those around then and not follow after the way of the prevailing culture. "*From the rocky peaks I see them, from the heights I view them. I see a people who live apart and do not consider themselves one of the nations*" (Numbers 23:9). Just as the people of old, the Christians were admonished: "*Do not conform any longer to the pattern of this world, but be transformed by the renewing of your mind. Then you will be able to test and approve what God's will is—his good, pleasing and perfect will*" (Romans 12:2).

This is not intended to be a chapter on family therapy; however, the reader does need to understand the Christian definition of family in order to have a frame of reference from which to understand the unique features of the family group. God created the family as a social group. It includes adults of both sexes, who maintain an acceptable sexual relationship, normally having one or more children born to or adopted by the couple. The social functions of the family unit are economic, sexual, reproductive and educational. The family was to raise the children to give honor to God, to respect both parents, and to grown up to be good citizens. "*These commandments that I give you today are to be upon your hearts. Impress them on your children. Talk about them when you sit at home and when you walk along the road, when you lie down and when you get up*" (Deuteronomy 6:6). And, "*Be careful to obey all these regulations I am giving you, so that it may always go well with you and your children after you, because you will be doing what is good and right in the eyes of the Lord you God*" (Deuteronomy 12:28). Because of the space allotted there is not time to cover the problem with raising or educating the children born to these unions, however that does not diminish the importance of raising children up in the fear and reverence due the Lord God.

When we, as Christians, read in Scripture about marriage and home and children we should want to live a life that is both acceptable to God and one that will give Him the glory He deserves. In almost every society in every age, the appearance of children into a family has been valued as a blessing. "*Children's children are a crown to the aged, and parents are the pride of their children*" (Proverbs 17:6).

For many years in America it was thought that children enhanced the closeness that couples felt toward one another. If the marriage wasn't progressing satisfactory, well-meaning friends, families, and pastors, all leaning on the old adage that "children will bring the family closer together," advocated pregnancy whether the couple was ready or not. If the husband didn't want children at that time or ever, the wife was told, "Once the baby comes he will love that child, just as if he had wanted it all along." Many young couples still believe that to be the case today, despite several studies showing that children create a family crisis that most parents are unprepared to deal with.

Couples today are waiting longer to have children believing that they will be better able to provide and care for the children later in the marriage. First they want to secure their careers, have fun, and develop their lifestyles, and then when the time is right, they will have one child, two at most, to complete the family. This is what society is telling them is the correct way to raise a family that will be wanted and loved. Where one spouse does not want children and the traditional accident occurs, then rather than risk career and marriage the unwanted child should just be aborted. It's not as though you're killing a living being, and everyone is doing it, and besides what you do with you body is nobody's business but your own.[30]

If the church is going to address the threat of both divorce and failed families then there must be a redefining of the concept of family. Far too many churches today are still trying to deal with family problems from the concept of the nuclear family (one man, one woman, and child[ren]) because that is considered to still be the typical family unit in our society. A family can and is often comprised of only two: a male and a female. There are couples, which for a multitude of medical or social reasons do not want children. There are those who for whatever reason cannot have children and choose not to adopt a child. There are stepfamilies and even extended families where one or both spouses bring children from another marriage into the family, and there may be more than one set of stepparents. There are unfortunately single parent households. There are couples in today's society that do not choose to marry and yet do bring children into the world without the sanction of either the church or the state.

For those dear souls who may be so inclined, there is not just one family structure that is presented in Scripture. The Scriptures disclose several examples of family structures. There were Mary, Martha, and Lazarus—three adult siblings who lived together. The woman at the well had had five husbands, and she was living in a common law relationship with a sixth man. Mary the mother of Jesus evidently chose not to remarry and functioned as a single parent after Joseph's death. Family solidarity and the care of parents were so important to Jesus that from the cross he created a new family group between His mother and John. "... *'Dear woman, here is your son,' and to the disciple, 'Here is your mother.' From that time on, this disciple took her into his home*" (John 19: 26,27).

Questions for Consideration and Discussion

The Christian marriage, and therefore the Christian family, is to be as I stated earlier, a "protective bubble" that allows each individual to grow spiritually as well as physically and socially. It is not, however, a strong citadel in which we can raise the drawbridge at the earliest signs of danger and rest secure behind its walls. Trials, tribulations, ambiguities, conflicts, all await the children of God, and rather than seeking to separate ourselves from them we must learn to live among them without falling victim to them. "*Do not be misled: 'Bad company corrupts good character.' Come back to your senses as you ought, and stop sinning; for there are some who are ignorant of God—I say this to your shame*" (I Corinthians 15:33,34).

1. What is the church's view with regard to marriage? Is marital relations viewed as a lifelong and exclusive commitment or is it more in view with the modern culture and seen as a temporary arrangement? What is the church doing to promote Christ-centered marriages?
2. Does the pastor preach on family issues other than Mother or Father's Day? Is divorce seen as a sin or is it seen as reflecting the mores and views of earlier societies and therefore anachronistic for the modern church couple?
3. To what extent has the church's positions been shaped by the basis of Biblical authority concerning marriage? Does the church affirm the Scriptural understanding of sexual relations only being acceptable within the context of the marital commitment? Are the prohibition of sexual relations outside the context of marital commitment and fornication and adultery openly condemned by the church leadership?
4. Is the church body concerned more about teenagers not having to tell parents when they receive birth control devices, or the fact that teenagers are more and more sexually active and society seems to be unconcerned with the development?
5. Does the leadership affirm the Scriptures' condemnation of premarital sex, trial marriages, live-in arrangements, and divorce? Does the pastor understand the issues concerning marriage and family life and how it fits in the Biblical and social contexts of the congregation?

6. Does the congregation, and more importantly the couples within the congregation, understand the divine order of marriage and that it can only be achieved when Christ is allowed to be the head of the family as well as the church?
7. Does the church have guidelines on the requirements for using the church to be married in? Do those requirements include counseling? Does the pastor counsel? Does the leadership ensure that the pastor becomes proficient, and or maintains proficiency in counseling?
8. Does the counseling include a session on the wedding vows? Is the importance of invoking God in the marriage understood by the couple? Are the blessings of the church in the Lord's name prudently protected?
9. Does the couple understand the Biblical admonition on becoming one flesh and belonging to one's partner? Does the counseling offer, from the Christian perspective, ways to identify, and correct misconceptions about their marriage, to include the traditional role models found within the Christian marriage?
10. Does the couple understand the grave responsibilities they are about to undertake, and are they willing to accept the roles that marriage will place upon them? Does the couple understand the Christian concepts of the wife obeying the husband and the husband loving the wife even as Christ loved the church? Do they acknowledge their responsibilities to one another within the marriage contract or do they seek to rewrite the marriage vows?
11. Does the pastor feel free to not marry a couple even after having counseled them? Does the church allow non-membership marriages in the church? Is the pastor free to decline marrying a non-believing couple? If church membership is required as a prerequisite is the couple encouraged to join and is there a time requirement with membership?

12. Is there a "Newly Married" couples class and are young couples and newlyweds encouraged to attend? Is the class co-taught with an older couple that has a successful and proven Christian marriage? Does the church offer continuing education for those couples willing to teach such classes?
13. When hearing of marital difficulties does the leadership of the church activity encourage the couple to seek counseling from the pastor or some other Christian organization? Do the leadership's own marriages give testament to the Christian commitment that lies at the very heart of marriage?
14. Does the pastor ensure that each session begins and ends in prayer? Does the pastor understand the Christian definition of family as a frame of reference from which to understand the unique features of the family group? Is the pastor familiar with the different types of family structure now seen in modern society, traditional, stepfamilies, extended families, and families with and without children?
15. Has the couple been encouraged to individually seek God's forgiveness for their part of the failure to live up to God's concept of marriage? Does the couple understand that while divorce is permitted because of infidelity, it is not required? Is the couple encouraged to overcome their difficulties and to apply Christian forgiveness to their own situation?
16. Does the pastor understand the need for impartiality and non-condemnation in the counseling process? Does the pastor seek to form a Christian bond with the couple that encourages the couple to seek additional counseling where needed?
17. When divorce does occur within the body of the church does the leadership stress the love of God for the individuals and stress the unity of the body in loving all parties through this crisis? Are both individuals given to understand that the church is there to aid them in reconciling with God and each other?

18. Are divorced congregants encouraged to attend counseling to determine where they have failed before considering another marriage? Are there any classes offered by the church to such individuals with others who may be dealing with the same issues?
19. Are the children of the couple offered counseling to help them understand that this divorce is between their parents and that they are still loved and wanted by both parents and God? Are the questions of the children of the church answered honestly and lovingly?

SECULAR HUMANISM IN THE CHURCH

From Gnosis Beginnings

Having touched on what I hope were the more palatable threats to the church, I now move to the more modern and certainly the more grievous threats confronting the church body. Matthew in his description of the Sermon on the Mound introduces a substantial part of the teachings of Jesus (5:1-12). Although somewhat difficult to correlate, one of the passage's intents is to disassociate Jesus from two opposing groups. He is not a Legalist claiming the supreme value of law over the people, and He is not an Antinomian or Libertine who discounts the value of the law altogether. Jesus does not seek to destroy the law or to even circumvent its true intent. Matthew even goes so far as to quote Jesus in the passage saying, "*Do not think that I have come to abolish the Law or the Prophets; I have not come to abolish them but to fulfill them*" (5:17).

All governments are ordained of God. Those governments that are working as intended have three primary functions. They are to protect law-abiding citizens, punish those who break the law, and promote the general welfare of all the citizens. The institution of government, most especially the United States Government, was never ordained to violate the conscience of humanity in its worship. The Baptist Faith and Message states: "God alone is Lord of the conscience...Church and state should be separate. The state owes to every church protection and full freedom in the pursuit of its spiritual ends...The state has no right to impose penalties for religious opinions of any kind..."[31] Herschel Hobbs goes on to clarify this statement by saying: "Religious liberty is the mother of all true freedom. It is rooted in the very nature of both God and man created in God's likeness (Gen.1: 27). It implies the competency of the soul in religion, and denies to any person, civil government, or religious system the right to come between God and man (I Tim. 2:1-6)."[32]

However, no one should misinterpret this as acknowledging that all religions share the same validation. This is not to be taken to mean that I believe that their way is just as good as mine, or that another's religion is just as valid. Moral tolerance and religious freedom were not intended to mean that all religions are of equal validity. The problem for the modern Christian is determining where tolerance ends and truth begins. It is an age-old dilemma that has resounded through the centuries, and always there have been those who have labeled Christianity as being intolerant because we do not accept them for who they are and what they believe and without any restrictions on their lifestyles.

The Christian faith contains absolute truths, and part of our faith requires an acceptance of those truths, which in turn requires us to turn away from the non-truths that others would substitute in their place. There is a problem with Biblical "truth" and the problem is that it rests upon the assurance that some things are worthy of believing, and some things aren't. The same Jesus who said to the Jews who had believed him, "*If you hold to my teaching, you are really my disciples. Then you will know the truth, and the truth will set you free*" (John 8:31-32), is the same Jesus who said, "*I am the way, the* ***truth****, and the life. No one comes to the Father except through me*" (John 14:6).

Moral codes, whether formal law or informal precepts are necessary to the very survival of social existence. The question has never been "Are there going to be laws?" but rather "Who will make the laws, or in the case of Christians, who dictates the standards by which we live our lives both in the church and the world beyond?" The Baptist Faith and Message encourages us to "be ready to work with all men of good will in any good cause, always being careful to act in the spirit of love without compromising their loyalty to Christ and His truth."[33] Yet Christians are attacked for their belief in Jesus Christ and are told that we should not involve ourselves with politics. Adding insult to the injury, the strongest source of discrimination is from the very government that should be defending our right to speak, vote, and run for office.

In all of this discussion on separation of church and state I can find no evidence that God ever intended for the people of Satan to have any real ability or responsibility in making the world better or in saving the world from utter chaos. Unless I have really misread the Scriptures, the world, as we understand it, will never be saved. And, while that statement is true, it is also true that God is at work in the world saving penitent, trusting souls.

Any correlation between changes in people and conditions pertaining to "*witnessing a great light shining in darkness, sinful people becoming children of God, and making straight the crooked pathways*" (John 1:7-23) has always been related to the responsibility of God's family. In simple terms, God does not place the responsibility to make, teach, or lead His church upon any except his own. In fact God says: "*If my people, who are called by my name, will humble themselves and pray and seek my face and turn from their wicked ways, then will I hear from heaven and will forgive their sin and will heal their land*" (II Chronicles 7:14).

The idea of humanistic intervention in the church is not a new concept. One could trace its existence back through the Old Testament (Genesis 3:5ff), but for this discussion we look to its beginning in the humble foundations of the New Testament Church. While the Christian sees freedom as being strictly limited by God's authority as expressed in Scripture, the so-called Christian humanist seeks to stress maximum freedom under God's law thereby placing a secularized version over the Biblical concept of freedom.

I am sure that there are some who will point to legalism being of equal threat to the church, however, there seems to be a prevailing humanistic wind that blows the church more toward maximum freedom rather than restrictive legalistic codes. It would be so much easier to identify the dangers of both legalism and libertarian ideas if they were not couched in Biblical terms. Both legalism and unrestricted freedom gave occasion for Paul to write the Epistle to the Galatians. One group of leaders, more than likely Judaizers from the Jerusalem church, insisted on all new gentile converts being circumcised and adhering to other Mosaic legalistic codes. Another group was permitting their newly acquired freedom in Christ to degenerate into indulging the sinful nature (5:1-15).

Libertarianism

As with other gnosis off-shoots the libertarians will spend very little time defending their concepts to those of us who are bound to Biblical inerrancy and our knowledge, or lack of knowledge, of Godly things. We are psychologically immature and as such our knowledge is inadequate. Gnosticism has a radical dualism to its precepts. On one hand, there is a God who lives totally separate from the created world. On the other hand, there is humanity who lives in a world of material flesh, a prisoner completely separated from the true God. For the Christian there came Christ into the world, divine yet human, spiritual yet flesh and bone, able to be tempted yet not yielding to temptation, totally God and totally man.

Yet for the Gnostic the only hope for freedom from a repressive sinful world is knowledge—"γνοσισ" (gnosis). Another word that the Gnostics like to use is "Enlightened." To the true Gnostic, anyone who is able to know one's character and foundation becomes a free spirit and superior to those of lesser knowledge or enlightenment. The spiritual person of this type of ideology would normally seek to demonstrate this freedom in one of two ways, either by asceticism[34] or by libertinism. Paul, however, in Philippians (3:1 – 4:1) warned against false teachers and called upon the church to follow the pattern he himself had set for them.

A so called Christian Libertarian said: "Libertarianism manifests certain distinct features of Biblical-reformed religion, and when anchored to Biblical faith and shorn of its sinfully autonomous impulses, points toward a fully legitimate orientation to life: maximum freedom under God's law."[35] Who in their right mind would not long to have total freedom? What libertarians seem to miss is that in order to enjoy the freedoms promised in Scripture there must be a servitude or submission to God. Nowhere in Scripture does God give humanity either the freedom or the permission to sin. God continues to call upon His people to: "*Consecrate yourselves and be holy, because I am the Lord your God. Keep my decrees and follow them. I am the Lord, who makes you holy*" (Leviticus 20:7-8). Once again, in Luke, Jesus even goes so far as to ask the question: "*Why do you call me Lord, Lord and do not do what I say*" (6:46)?

Paul called himself a "δουλοσ" (slave or servant if you prefer the less offensive term) of Christ (Titus 1:1). As with the freed slave of Old Testament times who did not desire to be released from his master, a spiritual ring had been placed in Paul's heart, and he was forevermore the property of Christ (Exodus 21:5-7). Neither his life nor his body were his to do with as he pleased, but rather he was pledged to do the Will of God through Christ Jesus. While "*there is no sin outside of the law*" (Romans 7:7), "*there is no freedom outside of righteousness*" (Romans 6:19). If both of these statements are true then God dictates what freedoms are acceptable to the Christian and not the world. To this argument of maximum freedom, Paul responded: "*What shall we say, then? Shall we go on sinning so that grace may increase? By no means! We died to sin; how can we live in it any longer*" (Romans 6:1-2)?

In his second epistle, Peter first reminds the individuals that there is no private interpretation to Scripture, "*that prophecy never had its origin in the will of man, but men spoke from God as they were carried along by the Holy Spirit*" (II Peter 1:21). He goes on to warn the church that just as there were false prophets in Old Testament time so there would be false teachers found in the church. He then concludes this portion by unleashing an attack on these same heretical practices (II Peter 2:1-22). Lastly, the Epistle of Jude condemned certain offenders who were given to libertine and sensual practices that were contrary to the teachings of the church. As the years passed the world seeking to accommodate as many different interpretations as possible began to look for other less offensive terms to describe various movements. One such term is Secular Humanism.

Secular Humanism

The 2002 Democratic Convention was being televised, and I was watching the protesters debating having been corralled into a centralized area away from the convention site and how they all felt that their First Amendment Rights were being violated. Into this variable warehouse of human understanding of individual rights came one lone protester. No one claimed that he was violent, he threatened no one, he simply carried a religious sign, and one can suppose that like all the other protesters he had an agenda he wanted publicized. By all accounts he was shouted down and run off. One of the protest groups later said something to the effect that "there is no room here for any radicals; we don't need his type here." What was not said but should be of equal interest is the human concept that says, "We believe in freedom of speech, but only for ourselves and our causes."

It seems that today if you do not wish to enter into a sensible civilized debate about an issue where there is widespread disagreement, all that needs be done is label the opposing party. Classify your adversary as a radical or as one having this irrational fear or that phobia or even better yet a fundamentalist,[36] and you negate yourself of the responsibility of even listening to their issues. The secular humanist would have you believe that theirs is the only truly benevolent way of life that offers true freedom to everyone.

Secular Humanism, as defined by the humanist, is a method of thinking and living one's life that aspires to bring out the finest in humanity so that all people can presumably have the best in life. Secular humanists, however, reject supernatural and or authoritarian beliefs such as those found in the Bible. To the humanist constant and un-repented sin, such as a homosexual "lifestyle," is not to be condemned, as Holy Scripture would require. The requirement that Christians live a Godly and righteous life, and abstain from immoral behavior is viewed by the humanist as intolerance shown by "unloving" Christians. "Secular Humanist Christians," if such a dichotomy can exist in Biblical Christianity, see the love of God as accepting all persons without requiring that the sin in their lives is forgiven or that there is a change in the individual's moral behavior.

Their basic affirmation is that each individual must take responsibility for their own lives (within the humanist manifestos). Secular humanism emphasizes reason, scientific inquiry, and individual freedom (as defined by humanism not Scripture), responsibility, human values (as determined by the individual not the society), compassion and inclusion of all lifestyles, and the need for tolerance and cooperation toward those same lifestyles (regardless of their opposition to Biblical teachings). The humanist feels free to set their own standards, to conform or not conform as they choose. The only rules that bind them are those that are self-imposed. By now the Biblical Christian should be having a little trouble with the new concept of Secular Humanist Christianity.

I was once called into the Commandant's office for a review of my yearly Officers Efficiency Report. Although all my other efficiency reports at the Chaplain's Center and School had shown me to be a truly outstanding chaplain and officer, this one showed me to be mediocre in both performance and promote-ability. I questioned the rating and was told by the commandant that I was too "black and white." He went on to say that there was not enough gray area in my life, and he and others had come to believe that I was not capable of becoming more compromising where my faith and ethics were concerned. While he did rewrite the narrative portion of the senior raters section to show that I was an outstanding officer, I had to agree that where the Bible spoke, I could not find myself comprising either my faith or my ethics.

Perhaps never before in modern church history has interest in and talk of humanism been so widespread and so poorly misunderstood by both those who support it and those who oppose it within the Christian Church. The most basic of questions would beg to ask: What kind of philosophy is Secular Humanistic Christianity, and can there really be such a hybrid? At the core of Christian Church history, Secular Humanist Christianity is nothing more than a new form of "Libertarianism," and as such holds the Biblical conviction that God grants all humanity the freedom to sin. God, from the libertarian viewpoint reserves to Himself the earthly and eternal punishment for sin. God does not vest authority in the church or state to punish or condemn sin. Therefore, libertarianism anchored to the often misquoted and taken out of context Biblical admonition to "*not judge, or you too will be judged*" (Matthew 7:1), and supported by its sinfully autonomous impulses, points toward a fully humanist orientation to life—"maximum" freedom under church law! Indeed, one may argue that secularized humanism is a libertarian version of certain critical aspects of the Christian conception which requires that we accept everyone for who and what they are, with the added responsibility to do so without application of certain Biblical condemnations as long as they do not infringe on the same rights for others.

The local churches of America are now engaged in a life (and possibly church) shattering debate to determine the age-old Biblical question: Can the children of light and the children of darkness live together in Scriptural harmony (John 12:35-36, Acts 26:18, I Thessalonians 5:5)? I beg to add the question: Can a person who consistently and un-repentedly refuses to acknowledge the Bible's historical right to declare sin unacceptable to God, rightfully be called or ordained to any position of leadership by any self professing Christian church?

The third article of the Human Manifesto II states: "Ethics is autonomous and situational, needing no theological or ideological sanction." The Secular Humanist Christian would change this to read that the "individual church is autonomous and situational, needing no theological or ideological sanction." By humanist thinking, anyone who wants to should be allowed to become a minister within the Christian Church regardless of lifestyle. I would argue that what the Christian Church at large needs to do is explain Christian philosophy in a more hierarchical manner. We, as Christians, must first set forth our basic Christian principles. By this I mean those ideas that unite all Christians and form the foundations of our belief in Jesus Christ as Lord and Savior.

Once this is done, we can follow with our beliefs about our relationship with the world—beliefs, many of which, by the nature of theological inquiry must (unfortunately) be absolute. Yes! God loves the sinner. He loves all sinners, but He does not love nor will He permit sin to come into His presence, nor will He simply turn His head while those who are called by His name continue to sin without regard for His commandments. Once that groundwork is established, we can recommend appropriate social policies, recognizing the differences of opinion within our ranks without embracing sinful lifestyles (as defined by Scripture) into the ranks of our clergy and lay leadership.

The path to Biblical truth is not easily embraced by the world or by the Secular Humanist who tries to find secular liberty in the church. I stand amazed that so many Secular Humanists have found employment within the teaching professions of Biblical History and as Ordained Ministers in nearly all of the Christian denominations. One would think them incompatible with church doctrine. The reason should be obvious to any clear thinking person. Humanists are committed to the preservation of freedom from belief systems that seek to confine their personal choices. Humanists have so many more freedoms, and so few restrictions upon their lifestyles. As a Humanist, I would be free to set my own standards, to conform or not conform as I choose. The only rules that would apply in my life would be those that I choose to impose upon myself. As a Christian, I seek to preserve the theological belief system that God sets my standards, and that I must seek to conform to His will in my life, or acknowledge that I am not one of His. Lest I be misunderstood, to my understanding of Scripture, a secular humanist is far closer to being a heretic than a Christian.

Sometime ago a tele-evangelist was caught with a lady of the evening. He went on national television and repented before his congregation. His denomination intent on helping him save his ministry called upon him to step down for a period of one year and to undergo watch care by senior leaders of the denomination. He refused noting a higher power and quoting Psalm 51 on his television program, "*For I know my transgressions, and my sin is always before me. Against you, you only, have I sinned and done what is evil in your sight.*" A little while later he was again caught in the same sin, and while he still maintains a small congregation of loyal followers, his ministry is not nearly, nor will it ever be, as great as it once was, and he is no longer affiliated with the denomination.

A secular humanist, while acknowledging that the church leadership has a right to curtail freedom when members act immaturely, would find fault with a denomination that would "excommunicate" the tele-evangelist simply because one does not conform to the "church" program. After all, the offense was not committed in the church or with another church member. This gives rise to the notion that Christians can somehow separate their secular lives from their church lives. If I harm no one in the collective but myself, what harm do I do? Whose business is it that I choose to live my life acknowledging two separate lifestyles? To the question: "Why can't I serve two masters?" Jesus said: "*No servant can serve two masters. Either he will hate the one and love the other, or he will be devoted to the one and despise the other*" (Luke 16:13).

Individual Rights Verses Corporate Responsibility

Many years ago there was a marvelous book entitled *Pastor Behave!* In my travels I seem to have lost it, but the concept that has remained with me was that there were no such things as accidents in ministry. You either went looking for it, or you placed yourself in the position to be tempted by it. Charles Spurgeon is an example: "behind the power of the master preacher was found a character of sterling integrity, high ethical beliefs, and unsullied purity."[37] Purity, that's a word that we Christians don't seem to hear much anymore. Another absent word from far too many church leaders is "accountability." The idea is, or should be, that we are accountable to each other for our behavior and that unacceptable behavior will not be hidden, ignored, or tolerated by other members of the body (Matthew 18:15; I Corinthians 5:1-13).

Corporate responsibility has always been a cornerstone of the laws of God. Although not readily acknowledged by the secular humanist, we are all one in Christ and as such must be held accountable to each other. While many of the requirements of Scripture are spiritual in nature, they also carry equal weight socially, morally and ethically. Their implications and applications influence every area of the Christian's life and relationships one with another and with the world at large.

From the earliest beginnings in Genesis[38] through the conquering of the promised land, the newly formed Hebrew nation found itself in such quandaries at various times in their development. When Moses first returned to Egypt and demanded of Pharaoh to let the people of God leave, Pharaoh required the entire Hebrew populace to make bricks without straw (Exodus, chapter 5). When the people sinned at the foot of the holy mountain, Moses required that the people publicly acknowledge whom they were for and then sent the Levites back and forth through the camp killing "*brother and friend and neighbor*" (Exodus 32:25-27). The Leviticuian laws were binding upon all the people even the outsider within the gates. There was the forty years of wandering while the adults of the nation, less Caleb and Joshua, perished in the desert (Numbers 14:21-30). Achan's sin at Ai caused God's rebuke on the entire nation and led to his entire family, all their livestock and belongs being destroyed (Joshua, chapter 7).

Within the writings of the New Testament there were also accounts of corporate punishment. Herod's proclamation to kill all the boy babies within Bethlehem and the surrounding vicinity in an attempt to kill the Christ (Matthew 2:16), Jesus' denouncement of the cities of Korazin and Bethsaida (11:21), and the parable of the tenants in Matthew 21:33 all give validity to the concept of corporate responsibility. There are numerous examples of corporate responsibility being a good thing for the people of God; however, I wanted to point out that certain restraints are imposed upon those who are blessed with liberty as the children of God.

Truly all of these Biblical events both Old and New Testament were horrendous in their application but were deemed necessary for the good of the entire population. God has the right to punish or reward His creation; both saved and lost, as he chooses. While there is liberty to be found in the law there is an equal but opposite bondage to be found in lawlessness.

The liberty that is to be found in Christ is not to be taken as a justification to the flesh (Galatians 5:16-25). In calling us to be in Christ, God did not promise us the proverbial rose garden. Christian training at times can be relatively rigid leaving very little, or no, room for individual interpretation. Jesus in His calling of His disciples called for uncompromising self-discipline, self-sacrifice and self-denial. He did not promise us exemption from persecution and antagonistic treatment such as He suffered for us. Jesus calls upon each and every one of us to "*pursue righteousness, godliness, faith, love, endurance and gentleness*" (I Timothy 6:11). Being set free from sin means that we have become slaves of righteousness (Romans 6:15-18).

Solipsism: Into the struggle between secular humanism and Christian doctrine for the hearts and minds of America has comes an old, yet new again philosophical theory that most young people have unaware assimilated into their modern understanding of Christianity.[39] The word "Solipsism" comes from the Latin "ipse" meaning self and "solus" meaning alone. The dictionary defines the term as "the theory that the self can be aware of nothing but its own experiences and states."[40] The foundation for this theory is "Cogito ergo sum"—I am thinking, therefore I am, and was re-introduced to the world by Rene Descartes.[41]

It is a strangely persuasive idea, and although not known to many in modern society in its truest form, it has been accepted by people today as meaning that the only thing valid is what the individual has experienced for oneself. It is a surprisingly easy mental process to follow to the "logical" conclusion that every one has had experiences and that those experiences are as valid to them as our experiences are to ourselves. There are several concepts that are similar to solipsism and are to be found mostly in eastern philosophy—Taoism, Buddhism, Zen teachings, all draw a distinction between self and the cosmos.

At its most sinister end the reasoning asserts that this makes the individual like a god, capable of creating a virtual reality in which one can exist apart from any and all orders of conduct established by church or government. At the social level it brings in the secular concept that everyone has a lifestyle and belief system and that those are as valid as any other. It also brings a mindset that Christian faith does not need a literal interpretation seeing that faith like reality is whatever the individual makes of it.

Someone said, "It is unfortunate that some devout Christians can be devoutly wrong." This concept allows the youth of today to discuss a Jesus of faith, without any real commitment to a literal Jesus of history. A "Jesus of Faith," just sounds so Christian. However this allows those who believe this concept to place Jesus in the realm of metaphysical abstract thinking, rather than the historical reality. The diabolical result of such thinking removes the Jesus of the Bible from the realm of verifiability, while professing to hold dear the Christian doctrine of the birth, death, and resurrection. Carried to its "logical" conclusion this type of Christianity completely eliminates the sovereignty of God in the believer's life. "*For although they knew God, they neither glorified him as god nor gave thanks to him, but their thinking became futile and their foolish hearts were darkened. Although they claimed to be wise, they became fools*" (Romans 1:21,22a).

Paul called upon all Christians to live a life that would prove worthy of the calling that we have all received in Christ Jesus. In the fourth chapter of Ephesians Paul acknowledges that contrary to the theory of Solipsism, Christians do not live separated by their own experiences, but rather have one unity of the Spirit. He goes on to state that God called church leaders

> to prepare God's people… so that the body of Christ may be built up until we all reach unity in the faith and in the knowledge of the Son of God and become mature… Then we will no longer be infants, tossed back and forth by the waves, and blown here and there by every wind of teaching and by the cunning and craftiness of men in their deceitful scheming. (Ephesians 4:11-14)

Collegially

Other Faith Groups: Before leaving this chapter there is one other area I feel needs to be addressed. It is the concept of collegially among the differing faith groups. Collegially once meant a sharing of authority among contemporaries. This sharing of authority was intended to be among those of same faith and belief, however as of late it has come to mean a sharing of like ideas and beliefs. More appropriately it has come to mean that one faith should not question or demean another faith. One should be willing to set aside certain precepts of one's belief in order to be sensitive to those in the audience of another faith group.

All across this nation, individual religious leaders of the varying faiths gather together on a weekly basis to discuss how they might better serve the community and bring about a better understanding and tolerance of all religions. They join together to find the common ground, those ideas and beliefs that they share while seeking to minimize their differences. Toward this noble end they form a joint presentation that seems to tell America that all religions are on the same footing, and that there are many ways to reach God.

Men, and women, who preach a totally different message on Sunday, stand staunchly with those of differing beliefs and call for the more faithful of their own faith or denominations to water down the message. Many of the secular humanistic Christian persuasion even go so far as to preach Synagogue sermons from their pulpits. These are Christian sermons that if they were preached in a Jewish Synagogue, or an Islamic Mosque, would offend no one, and certainly would not call those who hear the sermon to any definable action. Yet if one were to attend a service of another religious group, I doubt that they would hear such rhetoric. Certainly it would not be heard in any Islamic Mosque.

While a Muslim Cleric might attend such a gathering the Koran is very specific about being in fellowship with both Jew and Christian. "*O Believers! Take not the Jews or Christians as friends. They are but one another's friends. If any one of you take them for his friends, he surely is one of them*" (Sura 5, verse 56)! And from the same section of the Koran you will find these words about Christians: "*Infidels now are they who say, 'God is the Messiah, Son of Mary;'" and "They surely are Infidels who say, 'God, is the third of three*" (Sura 5, verses 76,77). While the Muslim will acknowledge Jesus, they see him only as a wayward apostle who has turned aside from the truth. "*The Messiah, Son of Mary, is but an Apostle; other Apostles have flourished before him... Those among the children of Israel who believed not were cursed by the tongue of David*" (Sura 2, verses 57-61), and *Jesus Son of Mary*" (Sura 2, verses 79,82).

Before moving on, let it be said of me that I believe that from all I have read, the evidence shows that in all his actions and writings, Muhammad was motivated by a sincere desire to deliver his countrymen from the grotesqueness of its degrading idolatries. It must also be acknowledged that although it justifies blood shedding, persecution, slavery, and polygamy, a charge that could just as easily be said of the Torah, the Koran also deserves the highest praise for its conceptions of the Divine nature. For the serious reader there is to be found in the Koran the power, knowledge, and universal providence and unity of God. The belief and trust in the one God of heaven and earth is deep, fervent, and unshakable. For the believer of Islam there is to be no quarter and no compromise of their faith. Toward this end it can be said that Islam and Christianity are not now, nor unfortunately, will they ever be compatible to one another.

It is interesting that when attending any of a number of ecumenical[42] events today one finds that those of the Islamic faith still pray in the name of Allah, the Hebraic faith still refers to the God of Abraham, only those of the Christian persuasion are asked to forgo the name of Christ in their invocation or benedictions and end with the watered down version of "In thy holy name we pray."

Many years ago I was in Germany at a Fifth Corps Chaplains' gathering. I was asked to give the opening invocation to the group. As was my custom I ended the prayer by saying: "we ask this in your magnificent name, and I, Lord, I ask it in the name of my savior, Jesus." I do not do this to offend others, but rather to be true to my God and my Savior. During the break I was talking with a senior chaplain who was Jewish, when a Protestant chaplain came up and began to take me to task for "not being sensitive to others in the group" of different faiths. There were no others of different faith with the exception of this Jewish Chaplain in the meeting. The Jewish Chaplain looked at me and said: "If I understand your Scriptures, you are supposed to be a stumbling block and an offense to me. I have always thought that if you didn't offend me from time to time you probably were not being true to your faith. I take no offense in you using the name of Jesus." I just wanted to hug him, and the Protestant chaplain very rapidly excused himself. It is an interesting side note that I have never been brought to task for using the name of Jesus in public except by other "Christians."

I do not advocate going out of your way to offend others of differing faiths. In the military we have to work together to ensure the free exercise of faith for all, regardless of our own religious affiliation. We are pledged to uphold the constitutional rights of all who serve our country, and that includes their right to practice their faith in a manner befitting their beliefs. It is because of the freedom of religion clause that we are able to serve the men and women of the Armed Forces anywhere in the world without reservation or restriction. And to those who believe that the Army tells chaplains what to preach I again say "without" restriction!

As a chaplain supervising other chaplains it was my responsibility to ensure that all soldiers received equal opportunity to worship in their own faith. Because we often shared the same facilities we were cautioned, not prohibited, against railing against those of different faiths. This was not a relinquishing of my responsibility to share Christ with others; it was simply exercising my constitutional responsibility in being the chief administrator of the entire chapel staff. When a soldier came to me for advice, counseling, or just to talk, it was always with the understanding that I was a Christian chaplain, and would approach any discussion from that standpoint. If one could not accept that, then it was my duty to provide someone of like faith if possible.

It is the same in the world. If you expect good working relationships, then before you ask someone to live up to your expectations, you must make certain that you live up to theirs. Do not abdicate your faith in an attempt to be a member of the whole. The way I overcame this was by accepting what the Scripture had to say about one's salvation: "*Therefore, my dear friends, as you have always obeyed—not only in my presence, but now much more in my absence—continue to work out your salvation with fear and trembling, for it is God who works in you to will and to act according to His good purpose*" (Philippians 2:12,13). If given the opportunity I will share the Gospel with those around me, if prohibited by the individual, I will let them seek out their own salvation, hopefully with fear and trembling. However, I will not forsake my beliefs just to be one of the group, for that is not collegially it is heresy.

The secular humanist would take issue with this discussion. It violates their concept of the preservation of freedom from belief systems that seek to confine their personal choices. The underlying human principle is the one that states human beings seek approval for their lifestyles without consequences for their actions. In the world of politics it is the belief that we rule by consensus and no one is left out. In the world of crime it is the notion that everyone is a victim and no one is a perpetrator. In the world of religion it is the belief that God loves everyone and no one is going to Hell. However, if the actions of Jesus and the prophets are any indication, then giving an effective Christian witness to the world will unquestionably mean saying and doing things that displease the very people whose approval we covet.

Same Faith Groups: True Christian churches, all have one thing in common, the Lordship of Christ. If Christ is not the Lord of the church, then it is not a Christian church, regardless of what it chooses to call itself. When one Christian denomination takes on another denomination in public it hurts the Lordship of Christ, and it damages the witness of all Christians.

The United Church of Christ has during a past Christmas season (and following) aired a commercial that shows two men in earphones and black shirts acting as bouncers at a Church, deciding who may and may not go in to worship. The United Church of Christ is presenting itself as an all-inclusive church, while the inference is that all other Christian churches are exclusive. All true Christian churches are both exclusive and inclusive. While only Christians may be members of the church, anyone can become a member by accepting Jesus as their Savior. There are Christian denominations that do deny fellowship and communion with those of other churches as well as other individuals of other denominations. However the great majority of Christian churches, to include those with closed communion, do invite and encourage all peoples to come and worship with them.

Such blatant misrepresentation of a Christian denomination by another church of like faith does harm to the whole body of Christ.

> If any of you has a dispute with another, dare he take it before the ungodly for judgment instead of before the saints… Do you not know that we will judge angels? How much more the things of this life! Therefore, if you have disputes about such matters, appoint as judges even men of little account in the church? I say this to your shame. (I Corinthians 6: 1-5)

Paul goes on in this discourse to even say that we should be wronged and even cheated rather than take disagreement outside of the body.

There are some who argue that we Christians embrace separate religious truths. That it is because of this religious separation that we cannot find a moral center for any meaningful discourse with one another. The sinister thing about this type of secular humanistic advertisement by a Christian group is the extent to which it can influence a non-believer that all Christian churches are hypocritical and none have the kind of message that they want to hear. This too is not a new thing.

> "Teacher," said John, "we saw a man driving out demons in your name and we told him to stop, because he was not one of us." "Do not stop him," Jesus said. "No one who does a miracle in my name can in the next moment say anything bad about me, for whoever is not against us is for us." (Mark 9:38-41)

One of the things I enjoyed most about the chaplaincy was that I got to work with so many Christians of different denominations. With few exceptions it was a pure delight to discuss both our differences and our commonalities. When a soldier would come to me to profess his or her faith in Jesus as Lord and Savior, I would seek to determine what denomination he or she was raised in. I have found over the years that if I can contact a home church, and get them to lift up the soldier in prayer, then when the soldier leaves the service he or she will return to their home church. Also, it allows me to insure that both the profession of faith and following baptism is in accordance with the receiving church's doctrine. I lovingly chastise my Christian brothers and sisters of the United Church of Christ and remind them that: "*The body is a unit, though it is made up of many parts; and thought all its parts are many, they form one body. So it is with Christ. For we were all baptized by one Spirit into one body—whether Jews or Greeks, slave or free...*" (I Corinthians 12:12,13). I would add "United Church of Christ or Southern Baptist."

Political Correctness

I am preparing to leave my discussion on Secular Humanist and go on to more pressing and certainly to more controversial matters. However, before going, I think that there needs to be a short discussion on the perceived need for political correctness. Not long ago in the city's newspaper a writer asked in the "Letters to the Editor" section of the paper the intriguing question: "Why can't we have religious morals and at the same time make secular decisions?" His letter like many others asked the same question that some Christians have asked, why can't we leave Christianity in the church and conduct our day-to-day living in a secular manner? Another way of putting these questions would be: "Why can't Christians be politically correct when in the market place?"

For a while I tried to ignore this discordant chorus of voices attempting to communicate this Cultural Revolution. However, political correctness is not just about racial issues anymore. It has become as wide-ranging as all the ethnic, economic, academic, and religious sub-groups that compose our nation. It can be as capricious as a politician who speaks before thinking of the wide ramifications of his or her words or as individual as the one who does not agree with what I have to say.

Some Christians are now beginning to understand that the Christian faith is under attack and many groups feel free to openly persecute Christian beliefs. This past Christmas it seems that many Christians and even some Jewish leaders were beginning to speak out against the so-call separation of church and state, believing that political correctness had gone too far. In the newspapers, as well as the major news programs, there have been several shameful well-publicized instances of absurd and relentless attempts to prohibit Nativity scenes while allowing Hanukkah Menorahs and even some Islamic symbols in public buildings. One town in Florida was even threatened with a lawsuit for having a "giving" tree in their city hall. For those unaware, a giving tree is a tree that has the first name of children who are in need of clothing and toys if they are to share in the Christmas spirit. To their shame they removed it. Some schools are forbidding Christmas Carols, and encouraging the politically correct but non-specific "Happy Holidays" rather than the traditional "Merry Christmas."

While a chaplain, whenever I would dare to preach on a controversial topic, regardless of how mildly I would word my sermon, I could almost always count on somebody getting very upset with me and walking out of the service, calling the Commanding General to complain, or both. If I preached my pro-life convictions that before God formed us He knew us and called us, and to end a life before it begins is arrogant and sinful, at least one pro-choice person would stand up, give me an angry look and leave the service. If per chance I preached against sin and mentioned the homosexual "lifestyle," someone who had a homosexual in their family would walk out, and I could more often than not expect a heated letter, phone call, or e-mail having me to know that it is not a lifestyle but that those poor souls were born that way. (I plan to address this concept of being born Homosexual in a later chapter.) If I mentioned the need for Christian parents to become more involved in public school systems, a teacher would leave declaring that I had insulted the profession, or worse yet was inciting the people to violate the separation of church and state.

Dear brothers and sisters, the Constitution defends the freedom *"of"* religion, not the freedom *"from"* religion. Any dear soul who declares that religious people have no place in secular, political, or economical discussion or office is, more than likely, a secular humanist in their beliefs and does not want to hear an ethical or moral debate based on Christian precepts that require we take the high ground rather than the road of least resistance.

While every Christian should seek to relate the Scripture and God to all people, I do recognize that we do live in a multicultural country where every subgroup wants to be seen as significant, and every person wants the freedom to worship, or not, in their own way while wanting to limit the influence of others of differing faiths both in and on their lifestyle. This would all be well and good if they did not want to enter into a one-sided faith relationship with Jesus, while seeking to force their secular beliefs on the Church Universal. By one-sided relationship I mean that they want to be a Christian, but they want to keep one or more sins to themselves without having to repent and acknowledge that they, like the rest of us, "*have sinned and come short of the glory of God*" (Romans 3:23).

As both a chaplain and a minister, I don't believe that we are called to be psychologists, however I do use such methods in my counseling. I know somewhat of the life lived in the Spirit, and I use that also. I have a little more than a modest knowledge about Christian morality, and I am both unashamed and unafraid to confront others with the truth. Yet for all of my knowledge I have learned this much: in pastoral ministry, anywhere, under any circumstance, the Bible is a powerful force to be reckoned with. When I read the Bible, God enters into the conversation. I shall endeavor in these next hypersensitive chapters to be as sensitive to the subject as I can, while remaining as true to the Bible as possible.

Questions for Consideration and Discussion

When I am honest with myself I don't feel very smart about the subjects I discuss. I try to prepare myself as best I can with limited resources. When I prepare a sermon I try to do textual criticism. When I take on a new program, I try to determine if it has been successful at other churches. When discussing secular concepts and ideas, I try to see from where the other person is coming, and I try not to inject more of the Scripture than the individual can bear lest I bring the discussion to a sharp close.

1. What is the church's understanding of the separation of church and state? How does the church see the role of religion and politics? How does the congregation see their role within this understanding? How are political differences between congregants handled within the church's boundaries? Are the congregants free to discuss such differences while affirming their Christian love for one another?
2. How does the church as a whole, and the congregants as individuals, see other religions? Do the church members understand the tenets of their faith well enough to discuss it with others of differing faiths? What is their understanding of cooperation with other faith groups? Does the congregation understand that tolerance of another's faith is not the same as acceptance of that faith's validity?
3. Do the church leaders research a group before giving validity to the group and affiliating the church with the group's benevolent causes? Does the church understand the requirement to remain true to the cause of Christ even over and above the secular cause that may well be worthwhile in its endeavor?

4. What is the church's understanding of "freedom in Christ"? Where do the congregants place the limitation on such freedom, and what is their justification for those limitations? Does the church have any discernable limitations?
5. Are there individuals in the church who place secular knowledge above Biblical precepts? Are such individuals in leadership positions? Has the congregation been trained in how to determine Biblical doctrine from false doctrine?
6. Are there individuals who maintain that no one has the right to tell anyone else how to live their secular lives? Do such individuals advocate separating one's public life from church life? Are there those within the church who espouse the belief that most Biblical precepts are antiquated and no longer valid for the modern Christian?
7. Where there is widespread disagreement does the church undertake a study to properly understand all sides of the issue? Do all members seek, if not to understand, at least to listen to the other side of the argument?
8. Do the church leaders ensure that such studies orient themselves around the Scriptures and what the Bible has to say about the issue? Is the leadership willing to call the issue by what it really is, or do they seek to find a less offensive name for the movement?
9. Is there one group that is unwilling to believe what anyone else may see as a better way? Can they justify their beliefs with Scripture, or do they seek to bring in an outside spokesperson as their source of knowledge?
10. Do they seek to belittle or shout down any dissenting voice? Do they reject or support supernatural intervention and/or authoritarian beliefs such as those that are found in the Bible?
11. Is there a group or individual in the church body that decries any mention of church discipline, while affirming the individual's personal responsibility and their right to live as they see fit without church interference?

12. Is there any group or individual who holds sternly to the belief that the church must show tolerance for and inclusion of all lifestyles, to include the cooperation toward those same lifestyles regardless of their opposition to Biblical teachings?
13. Has the church been schooled on the Human Manifestos, and do they understand where they differ from Biblical teachings? Is the congregation given to understand that not comprising where faith and ethics are concerned will be viewed as intolerants and unloving by the world at large but are in fact Scriptural precepts?
14. Do the congregants understand that God has never given humanity the freedom to sin? Does the congregation understand the admonition to "not judge, or you too will be judged?" Are the members prepared to both judge and be judged by the same Biblical standards? Are all the members, including the leadership, held to high Biblical standards?
15. Are there appropriate policies that while recognizing the differences of opinion within our congregations, and affiliated churches, do not allow for embracing sinful lifestyles, as defined by Scripture, into the ranks of our clergy and lay leadership? Do the church search committee members understand those policies, and do they research the applicant's resume to include speaking with the last church's lay leadership?
16. Does the church have standards for their leadership, and is the leadership held to those standards? Are the job descriptions and ethical and moral requirements spelled out for those who would be leaders?
17. Is the church willing to undertake watch care for a leader whose sins have become known to the church? Is there a process or procedure in place to deal with wayward leaders or are they just passed along to the next unsuspecting church?
18. Does the church membership live up to the idea that we are accountable to each other for our behavior, and that unacceptable behavior will not be hidden, ignored, or tolerated?

19. Does the church, or do members of the church, place individuality above corporate responsibility to the body as a whole? Is the individual's understanding of Scriptural prohibitions or freedoms seen to be as valid as anyone else's even when it flies in the face of Scripture?
20. Do the youth or members of the church often center their discussions around a Jesus of faith, without attempting to understand the Jesus of history? Does the church membership recognize that Jesus the man is also Jesus the Christ?
21. Does the church understand the difference between the free exercise of faith and the Biblical restrictions place on the believer to be true to the Christian faith?
22. Do the church members understand that their leadership will not require, nor will they support, abdicating one's faith in Christ in an attempt to be a member of the civil community as a whole?
23. Does the pastor feel free to preach on any and all sins without fear of offending someone in the congregation?
24. What is the church's understanding of sin and repentance? What do the congregants understand concerning this topic, and where do their differences conflict with Scripture?

FEMINISM[43] IN THE CHURCH

Clarification of Intent

My base subject as the title of the book implies is the threat from within (the church). Lest I be misunderstood from the beginning of this chapter and thereby be discounted by at least a part of the group I hope to reach, I find myself in need of opening remarks. I do not believe that either the original establishment of the feminism movement or the changing role of women in the church poses any threat to the church. However, as with other benevolent endeavors excesses arise that in their zealous pursuit of truth, as they understand the concept of truth, violates the intended purpose. These excesses lead to a shift in the original goal, and more often then not the leadership, and what started as an admirable pursuit can and most often does cause great damage.

It is therefore with trepidation that I undertake to approach such a volatile subject. My interest in the subject, combined with my lack of total knowledge of it, dictates that this section of the book stretch, almost to the breaking point, the prescribed boundaries of the chapter's title. My research, because of time and limited resources, is not exhaustive, and I do not claim to have the final answer. I leave final answers to those with more scholarly aims and abilities. However I believe that it is important to see where we came from in order that we might better understand where we are going.

I do not believe one can get to the desired subject of this chapter without, at least, a cursory look at feminism in Scripture, in tradition, in early American movements, and of course the modern feminist movement. Then, and only then, will we be ready to look at the "radical" feminist movement and the threat it poses to the church. I will to the best of my ability attempt to keep each area of discussion as short as possible while covering the intended material at a level that will be academically acceptable to the majority of readers.

Because of the title of the chapter there are those who will instantaneously presuppose that I am 1) anti-feministic or 2) chauvinistic and/or 3) against women ministries in the church. Let me state for the record and to be honest with the reader that I personally have not been convinced of the correctness of the interpretation that supports women as pastors. However, I will just as emphatically state that if only men are called of God to be pastors, and they fail to heed the call in sufficient numbers to fill their denominations pulpits, then it is man's fault. If such is the case then it is only natural that if a man cannot, or more probably will not, do it a woman will, and the men of the denomination should have nothing to say about it, seeing that they failed to heed God's calling. Allow me to consign one more thought for your consideration; the ordination of women to the pastorate is *"not"* a Salvation question and therefore should never be the cause for a break in fellowship among Christians.

To support such a position, I need only go to the Book of Judges (4:4-22). Here we find the prophetess and judge Deborah. Deborah has a mission for Barak the son of Abinoam. His mission is to take ten thousand men and destroy Sisera, the commander of Jabin's army.

Barak obeyed the summons but lacked the faith to go it alone. He wanted someone else near and visible whom he could lean on. To such a feeble faith certainly the arm of a woman would give more confidence than the Arm of God. The Scriptures state, "*So Deborah went with Barak*" (Judges 4:9) but not before telling him that God would give the victory not to him but to a woman. The battle went well for the Israelite Army, but Sisera fled the battlefield, and while he was resting a woman killed him. There were two hearts that did not tremble before Sisera and his chariots of iron. These belonged to Deborah and Jael, the woman who killed Sisera. I doubt that anyone could argue the fact that these women were raised up and energized by God for their respective ministries.

Biblical Concepts

Old Testament: Genesis, chapters two and three record the creation of humanity. I believe that I would be safe in saying that very few dispute the acknowledgement that humanity (man and woman) was created in God's image. I believe that I can also safely state that Eve was created by God to be Adam's equal, friend, and helpmate. Eve was the first to sin, however to her credit she blamed the serpent while Adam blamed God. "*The man said, 'The woman you put here with me – she gave me some fruit from the tree, and I ate it'*" (Genesis 3:12). As a consequence of the sin, God placed Adam in authority over Eve. "*...your desire will be for your husband, and he will rule over you*" (3:16). This part of the consequence of the fall was that the woman was to have a deep desire for the man. However,

> the supremacy of the man was not in tended to become a despotic rule, crushing the woman into a slave... a rule which was softened by the sin-destroying grace of the Gospel, and changed into a form more in harmony with the original relation... a rule on the one hand, and subordination on the other, which have their roots in mutual esteem and love.[44]

If we place a Christian understanding on this authority of Adam over Eve, it was to be a willing submission on Eve's part, and an earned privilege on Adam's part, and nowhere do I find that it was to be enforced by man or law. Again for the Christian, "*Now as the church submits to Christ, so also wives should submit to their husbands in everything. Husbands, love your wives, just as Christ loved the church and gave himself up for her*" (Ephesians 5:22,23).[45] What we often miss is the verse that precedes this discussion: "***Submit to one another** out of reverence for Christ.*"

At this point according to one feminist interpretation[46] it was during the events following the fall, that Adam usurped the equality of Eve, establishing a characteristic of Man's fallen-ness (i.e. the effort by men to subjugate women). What is strangely absent in this interpretation is where God was during this subjugating. He was, at least according to Scripture, still providing guidance and He was still communicating with humanity. "*Then the Lord said to Cain, 'Why are you angry? Why is you face downcast? If you do what is right, will you not be accepted? But if you do not do what is right, sin is crouching at your door, it desires to have you, but you must master it*'" (Genesis 4:6). In addition to this, if a person (male or female) accepts Scripture, then would it not be seen as disobedience on the part of the female to attempt to overthrow the leadership of the man? And, wasn't it disobedience against God's instructions that lead to the original sin?

From Genesis 11 on we read of women as matriarchs, two of which were Sarah (chapters 11-23) who gave birth to Isaac in her old age, and Rebecca (chapters 24-27) who showed both spirit and courage choosing to travel a long journey to marry a stranger, and then later aiding her favorite son, Jacob, to steal Esau's blessing thereby becoming the Patriarch of the Hebrew Nation. In Exodus 2 there is Jochebed who defied the Pharaoh's order to kill all Hebrew male infants thus preserving Moses, the deliverer of the Hebrews. Later in Exodus (chapters two and fifteen) and Numbers (chapter twelve) we read of Miriam, Moses' sister, who was a prophetess and national leader. In Joshua 2-6 there was Rahab, a humble woman who believed in God and helped the Hebrews win their first major military victory at Jericho. In Judges 4-5 there was Deborah, whom I spoke of earlier who was for many the Biblical "Joan of Arc."

One cannot mention women of the Old Testament without giving homage to the Book of Ruth. Ruth the widowed Moabite daughter-in-law of Naomi returned to Bethlehem with Naomi against the strongest urging of Naomi. In reply to Naomi's insistence that Ruth return to her own people, Ruth gives an endearing vow of courage, love and commitment:

> Entreat me not, to leave you, or to return, from following you, for where you go, I will go, and where you lodge, I will lodge; your people, shall be my people, and your God, shall be my God. Where you die, I will die and there I will be buried. May the Lord deal with me ever so severely if anything but death separates you from me. (1:16,17)

She left her family and her country; she adopted the Hebrew faith; uncomplainingly, she worked in the field to support both herself and Naomi; and most importantly, among her descendants was Jesus the founder of our faith.

There was Hannah in I Samuel 1-2, Abigail in I and II Samuel, and Esther in the book of the same name, who became the wife of the Persian King Ahasuerus and through her courage saved her people. I have not time to mention all of the women in the Old Testament who took an active part in the building and defense of the Hebrew Nation. These women were not limited to just being the matriarchs of the nation, they were wives and mothers, businesswomen and educators, merchants and farmers, a teacher to the young and a compassionate benefactor to the needy (Proverbs 31:13-31).

New Testament: With the coming of Jesus, the incarnation of God in flesh, the role of woman takes a somewhat radical alteration. Rather than being someone to be subjected or behave toward as chattel, Jesus treats women with a new kind of respectability.[47] He accepts their ministry to Him (Matthew 26:6-13; 27: 55-56; Mark 15:40-41; Luke 8:1-3). One of the last words spoken by Jesus from the cross was to assign the care of his mother to John (John 19:25-27). Great significance is often placed on the fact that Jesus appeared to a woman first after his resurrection (John 20:11-18). Of equal significance are the facts that no record was made of Jesus 1) calling a woman to be an Apostle, 2) a woman being in the inner circle, nor 3) appointing a woman to rule over the disciples. These three reasons being the base for many men and women believing that all ministries save one (the role of pastor) are open to women.

The Book of Acts records the apparent participation of women in the proclamation of the Gospel at Pentecost (Acts 1:14; 2:1-4). Peter in his quote of the Prophet Joel in his Pentecost Address gives specific inclusion of women in the ministry that was to result from the out-pouring of the Holy Spirit. "*...your sons and your daughters shall prophesy... even upon bond slaves, both men and women"* (2:17a-18). The man of Macedonia in Paul's vision led him to Macedonia where one of the first converts was a merchant woman named Lydia (16:14). Priscilla and her husband were tentmakers and fellow worker in the faith with Paul. It was Priscilla and her husband Aquila that taught Apollos the full Gospel when he came to Ephesus (18:24-26). The prominence of women converts is evident throughout the Book of Acts.

However, women were not merely converts to Christianity in its earliest phase but were also workers in the spread of Christianity. Paul refers to many such co-workers throughout his letters. Phoebe is thought to be the bearer of Paul's epistle to the Romans, and is commended to their hospitality by Paul.

> I commend to you our sister Phoebe, a servant'διακονον'(dea coness) of the church in Cenchrea. I ask you to receive her in the Lord in a way worthy of the saints and to give her any help she may need from you, for she has been a great help to many people, including me." (Romans 16:1,2)

At the end of Romans Paul sent greetings to twenty-eight people, ten of them women. Paul even goes so far at to note that Junia is not only a relative but is considered in high esteem among the apostles (16:7). Priscilla and Claudia are named in II Timothy 4:19-21. For the sake of brevity I chose this point to move on with my discussion.
As most are familiar with the qualifications for deacons in I Timothy 3:8-11, I wish to simply take note of the word "women" in verse eleven. The Greek work here is "γυναικασ" (gynaikas). Accord-

ing to Leonard Swidler, among others, most of the Greek Fathers of the church agreed that in this context the necessary characteristics were "for bishops, deacons, and women deacons." He went on to note that: "those who argue that it refers to the wives of deacons overlook the lack of a parallel with bishops wives…."[48]

I would be less than honest if I did not note that there are general inferences in Scripture that point to the possibility of women fulfilling any role in the church. The Great Commission (Matthew 28:19,20) is understood by most to give the responsibility of proclamation and nurturing to all believers. Acts 1:8 gives a similar injunction to all believers to be witnesses. I Corinthians 12:6,7 says that God, through His Spirit bestows "*the manifestation of the Spirit*," (i.e. spiritual gifts) "*on every believer.*" These gifts are to be used to build up the body of Christ, which is the church. Certainly the women of the church will point to Galatians 3:28, where Paul states that there is no such thing as male or female, bond or free, Jew or Gentile. However, to take this verse, as commentary on anything other than the fundamental concept of the priesthood of the believer is to run the risk of taking it out of what I believe is its intended context.

Ordination of Women

One cannot leave this section of the discussion without addressing the question of the ordination of women. I am personally hard pressed to relate Paul's restriction to the role of deacon for three reasons: 1) Paul spoke so highly of Phoebe and referred to her as a deaconess, 2) deacons by tradition work together in a deacon "body" with each having a singular vote on any issue, and 3) no one deacon is supposed to exercise authority, outside of the total deacon body, over the church. I believe that I am safe in saying that for many in opposition to women being ordained the issue is a Biblical one. Although there are several texts that are relevant to the discussion the one most crucial to the issue is found in I Timothy 2:12 where Paul writes: "*But I do not allow a woman to teach or exercise authority over a man…*"

Remember part of my reluctance in accepting women in the pastoral role is based as much on what the Scripture does not say as what it does proclaim. What Paul did not say was that he does not allow a woman to be ordained. For that reason alone, perhaps this passage should not be viewed as a blanket prohibition of women's ordination. I believe that I am already on record as advocating the ordination of women to offices of ministry with the exception of pastor. So, then, what is the issue for the majority of those concerned? A textual look at the Scripture noted would show that what is being prohibited is "*teaching*" and "*authority*," specifically over the men. Since the context of the prohibition is clearly one of consideration for church leadership, I do not believe that one should attempt to force a wider application of the text.

Okay, then the most logical question to follow would be: what "*teaching*" and what "*authority*" are prohibited? The verb Paul used is "διδασκειν" (didaskein). In a general sense, it means to teach, to impart information. In an ecclesiastical sense it means to be a "doctor of the church" or a formal theologian, in simple terms a pastor. I draw this conclusion from the use of the corresponding word for Rabbi, which is "διδασκολοσ" (Didaskolos). The discussion becomes a little more Byzantine when we attempt to understand the prohibition on "*authority*." There are different types of authority. The two most common are those of expertise and juridical authority. Having already discounted any attempt to force our application on the academic and political world, it seems the least restrictive exegesis is to limit the prohibition to juridical authority. Most evangelical denominations regard the ordination of a pastor as carrying with it juridical authority. Within the same concept those same denominations rarely give such authority to their deacon bodies.

I am sure that there are scholarly people who will not agree with my explanation of Paul's prohibition. I equally believe that exegetically my view will be seen to be in line with the majority of serious students of Scripture. If then God gifts a woman with gifts best utilized in traditionally male dominated roles, there appears to be no Biblical injunction, save Paul's disallowing women to have authority over men. It should also be noted that the only "singular" role in the church that could possible exercise such "*authority*" is the role of pastor.

Traditional Feminism

I believe that I have shown by both Old and New Testament evidence, that women played a vital role in the advancement of religion throughout its development to include the first century of Christianity. The history of the church under the "Fathers," however, indicates a return to past egalitarian attitudes that excluded women in the concept of equality. Somewhere between the last decade of the first century and the mid-second century of Christianity, the church fathers began to restrict the status of Christian women that bordered on misogynist,[49] a trend that would continue through the Middle Ages to the modern era.

The role of women as defined by the early Roman Catholic Church was either as child-bearer or a life of celibacy dedicated to serving humanity and God. By the time of Constantine, women were working in the church under the supervision of men. Following 374 A.D. there appears a Monastic life usually attributed to Marcella. Double monasteries for male and female were established following the fall of the Roman Empire and were in existence up through the tenth century.

In the later centuries unmarried women with no family were always in danger from false testimony. Many found livelihood by being midwives and medical purveyors of herbal placebos for both real and imagined ailments. Sometimes this would include potions that were intended to charm a suitor, fend off evil, punish a wrongdoer, or ensure that good luck and prosperity would follow the holder.

The problem with this form of endeavor was that if the woman became too prosperous, or the buyer was not happy with the results she could find herself charged with witchcraft. If a child was born deformed, an individual died, or worse yet the intended victim did indeed fall prey to misfortune, the town fathers took a dim view of such enterprises, and more often than not, the woman found herself at the end of a dunking chair until she drowned or confessed.

Assuming that she survived this ordeal she was tied and thrown into a river to see if she would sink or float. The problem with such a test was that if she drowned then she was innocent, and the town fathers saw that she got a decent burial and the accusers got what few belongings she might have had. If she floated then this was seen as cursory evidence to support the charge, and she was burned as a witch, and the accusers got what few belongings she might have had. For better or worse women found themselves subjugated to men—be it husband, father, or even brother—and their only real hope lay in the family finding a good man that would be both provider and loving husband.

Because woman's economic role was tied to the family as procreator, her sexuality became of primary importance. Laws to protect the legitimacy of the heirs, which she would produce, left her in an auxiliary role, and it followed that she became a secondary type of person. Even when a woman would by birth right become queen, the average woman still found little protection in the laws of the land. Husbands had the right to beat, disfigure, and with little fear kill their wives on the slightest provocation. There were in the latter part of the eighteenth century some movements toward, if not equality, certainly protective laws that provided the more affluent ladies with some forms of judiciary relief.

In more recent centuries, the role of women in society had as a rule continually been restricted to that of home-based functions—caregiver to the young, sick, aged, and dying; teacher; nurse; maid; house servant; laundress; and some subordinate positions in institutions of education, business, and economics. For the average woman who lost her husband, as a rule, she was left destitute, and unless there were family members or another man willing to redeem her (and any children she might have) from the brink of poverty, the woman had little to look forward to but debtor's prison, sweatshops and workhouses, or as a last resort, assuming she was still young enough, plying her wares as a lady of the evening, prostituting herself to the very society that offered little or no welfare assistance.

Given these dire happenings there had to be reform! There had to be great awakenings that would call Christian men and women to re-evaluate the traditional roles of women both in society and in the church. It is to the detriment of both state and church that the reevaluation was so long in coming. It is also disheartening to see the feminist reforms now leaning toward a distorted "Liberation Theology," where the oppressed must become the oppressor at any cost.

Early American Feminism[50]

Janet Wilson James[51] summarized significant historical events and persons in the American women's religious movement. In 1630 Anne Hutchinson defied the minister of the church at Boston, daring to hold Bible studies in her home. Another significant woman religious leader was Mary Dyer. Both of these women gave birth to deformed children. The ministers of the day judged this to be God's punishment for the women's heretical leadership thereby releasing the church leadership from any requirement for intelligent, serious study of the changing role of women.

The Quakers were the first Protestant group in America to demonstrate religious status for women. They rejected theological and social distinctions that the Puritans had considered essential to an orderly society. Women and men were both free to avail themselves of revelation and salvation. Priesthood and the traditional role of pastors were cast off, with the sacraments, and the remnants of ritual. A sort of spiritual cleansing of religion in which the baby was thrown out with the bathwater, or in their case the baptismal water. Women could be called to lay ministry as well as men, and they exercised government over their own meetings; of course there was still no ordination and no financial compensation offered to the women.

During the Great Awakening in New England women's activity quickened. In some churches they voted in business meetings, and many undertook religious teaching and Bible studies in their homes. As early as 1806 women, awakened to a sense of their duty to aid and to save local unfortunates, formed a charitable mission society. The role for women in Baptist churches had as a rule been restricted to that of Sunday School teacher, fellowship dinners, piano and organ playing, and involvement in women's missionary organizations.

The modern missions movement in America looked to women as their source of existence. Women always led the way through their missionary societies, and fund raising activities. The highest role recognized for women had been that of missionary. By 1824 the women's organization was a regional body with seventy auxiliaries supporting eleven missionary evangelists.

Revivalism opened the way for greater involvement of women in religious work. Charles Finney encouraged women to speak in mixed prayer meetings and presided over the radical experiment in co-education at Oberlin College that produced Antoinette Brown, the first ordained woman in America. Response to women was mixed. Ministers applauded Dorothea Dix in her crusade for human treatment of the insane. But in 1837 clerical wrath fell on the Grimki sisters for their advocacy of antislavery causes through the revolutionary means of speaking to mixed audiences in churches and public halls. In the 1840s Phoebe Palmer, a Methodist, began holding weekly parlor meetings for prayer, a movement that continued to grow into the 1850s.

As early as 1855, female assistant missionaries outnumbered the ordained males. The overall picture for missions by all Christian denominations indicate that throughout history, women have comprised from one-third to two-thirds of the missionary force. Women served as missionary partners with their husbands, but women such as Lottie Moon and others opened new frontiers for single women in missionary service.

Because of the mixed reception, women began to abandon the traditional churches in favor of experimental religious societies that promised equality. Among these were to be found the Shakers, the Oneida Community, Mormons, Seventh-day Adventist, and the Universal Friends. Such organizations as these became a refuge for the nomadic and for women trapped in intolerable marriages.

Following the Civil War, America experienced revival from about 1870 to 1917. This revival spirit continued to loosen institutional structures and thereby to create opportunities for women. Mainline churches expanded their missionary agencies and women found new frontiers in non-denominational enterprises like the Woman's Christian Temperance Union and the Young Women's Christian Association. Among the varying sects and schematics, religious initiatives by women were encouraged. Women preached freely. Some charismatics, like Alma White, Mary Baker Eddy, and Aimee Semple McPherson, became founders of new denominations. Interestingly, the social gospel movements of this time did not take up the cause of women's liberation.

Tension was created by women's aspirations for leadership. Congregationalists approved an autonomous women's board of foreign missions in 1868, and the Northern Methodists and Northern Baptist followed suit in 1869 and 1871. The Methodist General Conference of 1880 confirmed women's entitlement to positions as Sunday school superintendents and class leaders, but discontinued licensing women as local preachers and turned down Anna Howard Shaw's appeal for ordination. The General Conference of 1888 approved deaconesses but refused to seat Frances Willard and three other locally accredited female delegates.

At the Southern Baptist Convention in 1885, lest some think I hold my own denomination less accountable, two of the seven Arkansas messengers turned out to be women. Delegates changed the constitution to make it clear that only men could be messengers.

> Not until 1888 were women able to centralize in a Women's Missionary Union. When the union's president gained the privilege of reporting directly to the Convention in 1929, a number of male delegates walked out, necessitating a compromise whereby the session was held in the Sunday School rooms of the host church rather than the sanctuary.[52]

Modern Feminism

In the waning days of 1941 this country found itself in a struggle like none other it had ever faced before. A struggle of global proportion with freedom and our very way of life hanging in the balance; the call went out for young men to defend this great country and indeed the world itself against totalitarianism. In the months that followed another call went out to the American people—a call for more guns, more tanks, more ships, more planes, more food, more everything. With the cream of our manhood engaged in mortal combat, who would answer this call? The call was answered. They came by the thousands and by the millions. They plowed the fields and planted the crops. They stood shoulder to shoulder with their fellow workers. They build tanks and ships and planes. Some faced hardships and death in the Armed Forces to support our soldiers, airmen, and sailors. No one can doubt the contribution and sacrifice that the American woman gave to the war effort. The question begs to be asked: "If they had not come, could we have won?"

The men of war came home and picked up where they had left off. This caused a lot of women to suddenly find they were being told to give up their jobs and go back to being the weaker of the sexes, a role many were not willing to accept. Perhaps as a result of the need for leadership in the churches following World War II and in reward for their leadership during that critical time, women began to be afforded more teaching and leadership roles. Russell Prohl, writing in the mid 1950s noted that the Protestant Episcopal

Church, meeting in 1955, refused the women's section of the assembly voting privileges. However, also in 1955, the General Assembly of the Presbyterian Church in the U.S.A. resolved henceforth to approve the ordination of women to the ministry. And in 1955 the Methodist Church granted equal legal status to all the clergy regardless of sex, a right that had earlier been granted to women of the clergy in the Disciples of Christ.[53] Virginia Brereton and Christa Klein in a joint article noted that in 1970 the Lutheran Church in American and the American Lutheran Church voted to ordain women. In 1976 the Episcopalians followed. They concluded "the ministry has become a possible life's work for women in all of the 'mainline' Protestant churches."[54]

Essential to the development of the women's role in the church is the feminist hermeneutical movement. Phyllis Trible used her skills as a scholar to apply one of the tools of higher criticism to develop a feminist approach to God. Aided by modern historical methods, this effort to discover Scripture anew is generated by women's need to find models and themes with which they can identify. Prohl suggested that there are two extremes to be avoided in the female hermeneutic debate: 1) the Traditional interpretation that has been schizophrenic, emphasizing Paul's "anti-woman" passages while ignoring the pro-woman philosophy of Jesus and the unisex statements of Paul, and 2) Absolutism literalists, shunning tradition as they either deny or reinterpret Paul's problem passages to support their own presuppositions. [55]

Georgia Harkness focused on the central issue of the present time, the ordination of women to the ministry by noting "the ordination, far from being the culmination of women's expanding participation, is another beginning point in a history of beginning points."[56] Perhaps a statement from the Southern Baptist Convention acknowledging the Scriptural validity of, and allowing, deaconesses in the church and a return of women to the chaplaincy as Home Missionaries will be our next critical step?

I acknowledge the complexity of the problem. There are an enormous number of women today with theological training and more than a few with ordination who are still being disbarred by their sex from appointment as ministers of congregations within their own denominations. While acknowledging each denomination's right to follow their understanding of Scripture, I also acknowledge that we must never be afraid to re-evaluate our reasons for opposing the ordination of women to the role of pastor, and for limiting them to all other roles in the church save this one. Scripture and Scripture only, unaccompanied by the radical feminist movement's view of the world, must be our measuring stick. We cannot yield the body of Jesus to the prevailing and oft changing wind of social relationships and role expectations between men and women in the world, just to please the world.

I sincerely hope that I have shown that "feminist," as with "fundamentalist," is not a dirty word. There was need for reform, and there was need for us to move back to the relationship with one another that God intends man and woman to have in Him. The rise of the feminist movement, based on its early goals, was both justifiable and needed.

To the determent of the National Organization of Women (NOW) the more rational ladies were shouted down and replaced by the more radical elements: the homosexuals, the abortion groups, those who wanted any and all moral laws concerning behavior overturned, marriage as society understands it reversed, and children, through adoption by homosexual couples, legally subjected to these abominations. The battle cries of this group became: "no one can legislate morality" and "what a woman does with her own body is her business." The American Civil Liberties Union (ACLU)[57] very quickly joined them in their pursuit of eliminating any sense of morality and moral outcry from schools, judicial proceedings, and government, by attempting to shout down and discredit any Christian voice from social and political endeavors.

One would have thought that "Christian" men and women,

groups and denominations would have only to read the various passages on homosexual behavior and the proper relationship in marriage to condemn such immoral stances.[58] It was to their credit that many women and groups did distance themselves from such declarations. There were however several Christian denominations whose leadership having already been infiltrated by secular humanists, not only gave credence to the movements, but against their own books of disciple, even began the heretical action of ordaining as pastors and bishops practicing homosexuals on their word (which of late has proven false) that they were, and would remain, celebrate, if such an action is possible by an unrepentant and sinful group of people. Against God's Word these denominations slander other more fundamental denominations and activity, seeking to not only deny the Word of God but to change it to fit the changing morals of the secular world.

Radical Opposition

Tradition Base: Many individual, to include some Christian, denominations repudiate women's ordination on the grounds that it runs contrary to church tradition. These bodies that see tradition as a second source of divine revelation, equal in authority to the infallibility of Scripture, will also see ordination of women as going against such tradition and therefore an act of disobedience against God. Fortunately most of us do not have such a problem. We should and do give due respect to tradition, yet at the same time we continue to seek improvement on, and correction of, fallible traditions.

Chauvinistic Base: Any chauvinistic position, should to the Christian male, be as repugnant as it is offensive and demeaning to the women. It is in its most inane form, an assault on the Biblical equality of dignity given both sexes. The concept on which such positions are based is the concept that subordination equals inferiority. If this concept were anywhere near truth, the Christian faith would perish seeing that on the one hand we understand the Trinity to be build upon the co-equality of the Father, the Son, and the Holy

Spirit, while also acknowledging that Jesus subordinated himself to the Father to the point of death on the cross. Jesus was not inferior to the Father, nor is the Holy Spirit inferior to Jesus, thus any Christian opposing women's ordination must disassociate themselves from the chauvinist methodology.

Most often, those who deny chauvinism and at the same time hold no real affiliation with the traditional view find themselves leaning toward personal experience. Their "experience" tells them that "women cannot be trusted in positions of authority," which is, on its own merit, a chauvinist statement. This and statements like it tend to be based on emotions rather than reason, it is instinctive rather than logical, and it is perhaps the most slanderous of statements that only underscores the folly of such concepts.

Feministic Base: If I have not done so, perhaps I should pause and give my understanding of the definition of "feminism." Feminism, in its purest form, is the theory that men and women should be equal politically, economically and socially. I do not include in my definition theologically, because for me, God has already ordained that such equality already exist whether society recognizes it or not. Within my understanding of the definition of feminism I do not find any differences or similarities between men and women, neither is there to be found any excluding of men or furthering of only women's causes. The more radical forms of feminism do place such distinctions on the definition.

First Wave: In my research I found at least eleven definitions of various groups of feminist ranging from "cultural" feminist who advocate fundamental personality differences between men and women, to the more radical "separatists" feminist who advocate the separation of women from men. As if there were not a sufficient number of groups, I even found a "Feminazi." This is a feminist who is trying to produce as many abortions as possible. I was unable to determine if it was only male fetuses to be aborted or genocide of a group or race of people. For the most part varying assemblages of feminists are grouped into three overarching categories; "First" wave, "Second" wave, and "Modern" feminism.

The National Organization for Women was founded in 1966 and had its beginning as an outgrowth of the turbulence of the changing times. In its commencement it crossed social and racial lines and numbered its membership neared the million-mark in followers. The late Cleric Pauli Murray, the first African American women to be ordained as an Episcopal minister was one of the founders of NOW.[59] Among the twenty-eight founders was Betty Friedan, author of the *Feminine Mystique*,[60] the book that many herald as launching the Women's Liberation Movement. She became its first president. By 1970 the radical movements of NOW had reduced its membership to a little over 3,000, with an operating budget of less then $40,000.[61] NOW was on the verge of becoming just another obscure radical movement.

Second Wave: Somewhere in the mid-70s, there began a shift in assessment and strategy within the NOW organization and the second wave of feminism began. Social feminists began to move to the forefront, challenging capitalism as well as male supremacy or "patriarchy." They more closely associated themselves with the Black feminist movement, even though the Black feminists generally opposed assumptions of a common sisterhood. There was also a reinvigoration of the Liberal feminism movements of the '50s and '60s in which the stated goal continued to be equality between the sexes in all spheres of public life. It was during the '70s that some socialist feminists tried to develop sophisticated theories that would integrate Marxist and feminist aspirations. This group was quick to endorse Liberation Theology, as it gave religious validity to the concept that the oppressed could only find true liberation by becoming the oppressors.

Lesbian rights have been on NOW's priorities since 1975. By the latter half of the '80s many of the NOW leaders were, for the most part, both lesbian and radical feminist. Rosemary Dempsey the plaintiff in Belmont versus Belmont, a landmark case that defined lesbian partners as a nurturing family, became Action Vice President for NOW from 1989 to 1997. It was also during this time that they began to move away from the investigation for overarching explanations for the inequality and subordination of women and began an organized movement toward specific issues and the election of women, and men, who championed their cause.

NOW presently quotes a membership of around one-half million with over 500 groups in every state. I have not to my satisfaction been able to ascertain whether the Lesbian feminist movement is an integrated part of NOW or not. If it were not imbedded into the organization then I would assume that the membership of NOW would denounce it as both harmful to women's causes and not relevant to modern feminist activists. There has to my knowledge been no such outcry. Just the contrary is to be found in their active involvement in challenging anti-lesbian and gay laws, same-sex marriage, and homosexuality as an acceptable lifestyle.[62]

Modern Feminist: The modern feminist is a late twentieth-century product of both the feminist and secular movements. They do not seem to view themselves as feminist. They do not necessarily align themselves with NOW, and they tend to shy away from homosexual movements while accepting homosexuals as a natural part of society. They were raised to believe that homosexuals were born that way. I have no way of gauging how they are accepting the new methodology of choice rather than genetic engineering. They believe in the equality of the sexes and equal pay, advancement based on achievement rather than gender, and denounce any authority that would seek to limit their own personal growth or agenda.

From what resources are available the modern feminist is having trouble relating in marriage, even though they profess to believe in the traditional family model, with shared chores and parental responsibilities. They seem to be religious in their beliefs, but see social and religious life as being separate. Both of these belief systems are interesting seeing that their secular education has tended to minimize the importance of both parental and theological supervision and involvement in their young lives. Without seeing themselves as such, the modern feminist is a type of cultural feminist and see nothing wrong with male bashing in commercials, movies and television, yet is quick to denounce and take offense at any social endeavor that is seen as less then nurturing to the female persona.

I undertook the project of intentionally watching commercials this past Christmas season. I removed any commercial that did not involve both genders in them, or in which the sales pitch was aimed at only one gender. In total I found nearly seventy commercials, of which sixty-four of them showed the male character, boy or man, to be inordinately dumb, or socially absurd. By example, a Toys-R-Us commercial showing two boys trying to get out of the same door to get the sales advertisement, beaten to the ads by a girl who triumphantly walks into her room. The closing shot shows a sign that reads: "Boys drool, Girls rule." A commercial showing a man who says that he had the carpenter gene standing in front of a shelf tiled so badly that a cup slides off while a young girl walks away totally disgusted by the man, who presumably is the girl's father. A girl replacing cookies her brother had placed for Santa with a "blooming onion" from Outback. I could go on but the point to this is that commercials, as well as television programs increasing show the male youth that they are stupid, incompetent, objects to be laughed at, and are not good role models even for themselves. So, where is the equality that feminist are in search of?

As with the Human Manifestos of Chapter 6 the goals and designs of the individuals, on the surface, appear to be honest, forthright, and benevolent in their aspirations. Yet when viewed in the growing academic theorizing on sexuality, identity and politics find themselves in direct opposition to the Bible and the moral teachings of the Christian Church. These women both radical and modern are now finding themselves in the vanguard of church leadership and as such pose a direct threat to Biblical authority, and the reverence that all Christian's should have for God.

Questions for Consideration and Discussion

One of the churches all-time favorite hymns is entitled "Amazing Grace." The writer of the hymn understood the heart of the gospel—the good news of God's grace in saving and preserving sinners. Grace points the reader to those qualities of God that cause Him to deal with us in kindness, mercy, acceptance, and salvation. I would hope that any discussion on the subjects I have written about would employ these same qualities.

1. What is the church's understanding of women in Christian ministries? Has the church, both laity and leaders, undertaken an in-depth Bible study on women in the Scriptures? What is the general consensus of the church concerning the women's role in the church?
2. What is the church's understanding of the role, responsibility, and authority of the pastor, the deacons? Does church tradition allow for women deacons? How did the church arrive at this understanding? What do the women leaders of the church have to say on this issue?
3. If God gifts a woman with gifts best utilized in traditionally male dominated roles, which roles does the denomination allow ordination for, which roles does the individual church allow? Is the individual church allowed to determine such roles?
4. How do the women of the church see their roles in the church, in the home, and in the context of the traditional Christian male, female relationship?
5. Are the concerns of the women of the church taken seriously by the leadership? How does the church, both laity and leadership, approach such topics? Is there a division of thought and how are the differences handled?

6. If the denomination limits the role of pastor to men, are there sufficient male candidates for the number of pastorates in need of pastors? How do the women of the church interpret both the church's understanding and the Biblical passages used to limit the pastoral role to men only?
7. To what extent do men support the ministries of the church, both male and female? How active are the women's and men's groups in the church ministries?
8. Does the church encourage women to seek out and support ministries within the church to include missionary endeavors? Are these ladies included in meetings that affect such ministries?
9. Is there any tension in the church created by women's aspirations for leadership within the church? How are such situations handled and how are the solutions presented to the church body?
10. How does the church approach such subjects? Does the pastor preach on women's and men's roles in the church, in the home, in the family? How do the young women of the church view these roles? How is the church affected by the secular cultural understanding of these roles?
11. Are the lives of the leaders, both men and women, testimonies to the truth of what they proclaim, or is there a double standard being applied concerning leadership roles?
12. Has there been a loss of respect for Biblical authority in the church body? Does the church body affirm or deny the Biblical views with regards to marriage, family, and home? How does the church handle the contrast between what the society and the church believes?
13. Are there those in the church who seek to change the understanding of female restrictive passages, or who disavow many of Paul's writings as either being written to a specific

church for a specific reason and therefore not relevant to our age, or as not having been written by Paul at all?

14. Are there any who seek to develop a feminist approach to God, by either disavowing the Scriptures that give descriptions of God's masculine nature, i.e. Father, He, His, Him? Are there any who state that those who view God as masculine total misunderstand the nature of God? Are there those in the church who are seeking to interject into the worship service neutered verses that give no gender references to God, or to those who follow Him?
15. Are there any who continually attempt to redefine the genders, i.e. emotional animals rather than male and female created in the image of God, consumers or even customers rather than members or congregants, or various human personifications operating out of the dictates of the society apart from a relationship with God?
16. Are there any in the church who openly proclaim that no one, not even the church can legislate morality to its members? Are there women in the church who hold to the belief that their body is their own, and that their husbands, and even Scriptures, should have no say with regard to the abortion of an unwanted child?
17. Are there those in the church who keep their maiden name or require that hyphenated last names be used? Are there those who decry Christian marriage as an outdated and sexist holdover of male dominated societies?
18. Are there people in the church who slander the more fundamental denominations for their stances on male, female relationships, abortion, and immoral lifestyles, seeking to not only deny the Word of God, but to change it to fit the changing morals of the secular world?
19. Are there any in the church who are actively involved in movements challenging anti-lesbian, gay laws, same-sex marriage, and homosexuality as an acceptable lifestyle? Do

they advocate the homosexual lifestyle as being genetic rather than chosen? What Biblical justification do they offer for such beliefs and actions?

20. Are there young women in the church who see nothing wrong with male bashing in commercials, movies and television, yet are quick to denounce and take offense at any social or religious endeavor that is seen as less then nurturing to the female persona?
21. Are there any teachers who advocate a more liberal position with regard to women's issues over and above those of both men and women?

SEXUAL IMMORALITY

Heterosexual

I have struggled with the title for this chapter. I thought to call it "The Homosexual Debate." This is I believe to be one of the greatest in-house threats facing the church today. I also believe that this threat came into the church by way of both the secular humanist and radical feminist debates. However, it is not a threat just because it is a sin, it is a threat because it is insidiously attacking both the church's mission on earth and the relevance and inerrancy of the Bible, a subject which I will take up in Chapter 11.

No matter how I approached the outline for this chapter, I could not see how I could discuss the homosexual incursion into the very life of the church without first discussing sexual immorality among the heterosexuals. The problem is that heterosexual sins are no more acceptable, nor are they any more palatable to God than those of the homosexual. Sin is sin, and even though we try to abstain from sin, Paul's discussion of his own struggle with sin comes back to haunt each of us in our daily struggle to remain true to God's requirements.

> I do not understand what I do. For what I want to do I do not do, but what I hate I do. And if I do what I do not want to do, I agree that the law is good. As it is, it is no longer I myself who does it, but it is sin living in me... So I find this law at work: when I want to do good, evil is right there with me. (Romans 7:15-21)

There is also a problem with calling this chapter "Sexual Immorality." The problem is that the secular humanist, the radical feminist, as well as the homosexual communities are fast to call into dispute either the term used, or the agreed upon definition of the term used. They seem to find no reservation in almost proudly proclaiming that heterosexuals have as many problems if not more than the homosexual community, and most of the homosexual problems are caused by homophonic heterosexuals. So in Christian fairness to any opposition, I begin this discussion with the definition of external and internal sins.

The concept of sins of the flesh, or external sins as opposed to internal sins, or sins of the intellect or soul, has its basis in the individual's primary purpose in taking sexual pleasure. By example the person who physically completes the act of adultery, commits external sin, and the individual who just thinks about it, commits internal sin. Jesus called it a sin of the heart and said: "*You have heard that it was said, 'Do not commit adultery.' But I tell you that anyone who looks at a woman lustfully has already committed adultery with her in his heart*" (Matthew 5:27).

Fornication: Fornication is the sin of willing intercourse between two unmarried persons. Prostitution is a form of fornication.

> Do you not know that your bodies are members of Christ himself? Shall I unite them with a prostitute? Never! Do you not know that he who unites himself with a prostitute is one with her in body? For it is said, "The two will become one flesh." But he who unites himself with the Lord is one with him in spirit. Flee from sexual immorality. All other sins a man commits are outside his body, but he who sins sexually sins against his own body. (I Corinthians 6:15-18)

With fornication it is not necessary that both parties should experience pleasure or that one or the other should achieve orgasm. Since the intention is not procreation, but pleasure, one or both of the parties could even be sterile. Like all other external sins there is always the cruelty of scandal, ruination of family, and loss of standing within the religious community. All of which requires the duty of repairing the spiritual harm done.

Neither the church nor the Bible forbids gratification in the sex act. With the coming of age of the secular educational system, the old wife's tales of blindness and hair on the hand no longer scare children facing puberty. Children today are being taught every conceivable birth control with the exception of abstinence and that sex is pleasurable and something to be desired outside of marriage. I have even heard on the news that the ACLU was threatening to sue the government for a government run web site because it stated that abstinence is the only proven safe method for prevention of becoming pregnant and/or contracting a Sexually Transmitted Disease (STD). It seems that the ACLU was concerned that the site was advancing a moral value.

However gratification is of secondary purpose. The primary purpose of sex was, and remains, to benefit the people. The "right" to sex and the pleasure it produces is not an inalienable right. You will not find it in the Constitution, nor should it be there. The "privilege" of sex implies the moral responsibility to propagate humanity in an orderly fashion. This should only be done in the bond of marriage. I'm not sure I can do justice to the concept of "orderly propagation," however, as I understand it orderly propagation includes not only the bearing of children, but it includes the duties to care for body, mind and soul. "*Don't you know that you yourselves are God's temple and that God's Spirit lives in you? If anyone destroys God's temple, God will destroy him, for God's temple is sacred, and you are that temple*" (I Corinthians 3: 16,17). As a rule, these duties can only be performed in a stable union of one man and one woman. Homosexuals do propagate, but it is an artificial propagation by means of recruitment of others to their lifestyle. This recruitment is normally done at as early an age as possible.[63] For the church, and it follows for the Christian, marriage is the only state where sexual pleasure should be permitted.

As out-of-date, old-fashioned, antiquated, archaic, choose your own adjective, as this sounds, sexual pleasure of any amount has a legitimate place only in the state of marriage. No amount, no type, no preference has meaning outside of marriage. Outside of Christian and secular marriage[64] the individuals are free to engage with others or to break off the relationship on a whim. To use a Biblical term, there is no "becoming one flesh;" in modern terms there is no real commitment. More to the point the individual who chooses to take of forbidden sexual pleasure, heterosexual or homosexual, completely disrupts the natural law and is guilty of external sin. (The concept of "natural law" is discussed in the next chapter.) Lest I be called to answer by senior citizens, let me state for record that pleasure in sex does not end with the end of the reproduction cycle. Pleasurable sex does indeed continue on well into the later years. My discourse was on the sin of sexual pleasure outside of marriage.

In the majority of cases all attempts at teaching abstinence as a viable alternative to sex outside of marriage has been widely discouraged. The concept of the secular humanist is that we are all creatures of emotion and therefore cannot contain our animalist desires. They have even gone so far as to advocate laws that limit parental control over sexually active teenagers. The Christian parent who thinks that they do well by teaching their children to use contraceptives "if" they are going to have sex not only does the child harm but sins against God seeing that they have not trained their children up in the way they ought to go (Proverbs 22:6). The teenager today is almost made to feel as if they are an outsider or some kind of freak if they don't want to engage in sex. It is time that we loudly proclaimed that it is "OK" not to have sex before marriage!

Certainly for the secular humanist the use of contraceptives, given the incursion of AIDS into the heterosexual community via needle sharing, prostitution, extramarital affairs, and contaminated blood supplies has become a must.[65] For the uneducated, one is normally susceptible to AIDS only if they are engaged in a "high-risk" sexual activity. Unless the medical community and our government are lying to us, then if you are in a one-on-one relationship for life, you don't do drugs, you do not need a transfusion, and your mate has remained faithful to you, barring some other accident you are not at risk for AIDS, as the secular community understands risk.

By example, I read somewhere that a group of parents had been invited to a school to discuss sexual activity with teens. During the discussion one of the parents mentioned the concept of abstaining from sex until marriage and was all but laughed down by both the teacher and the other parents. During the course of the evening the group took a break to have refreshments and to get acquainted. The parent who had mentioned abstaining, still stinging from the rejection, hung back and did not participate in the intermission activities.

When the group came back the teacher told the group to assume that the intermission activities was a sexual encounter, that one of the individuals had AIDS, and based on the number of people you had shaken hands with, and the number of people they had shaken hands with, all of the group had contracted AIDS. The teacher than began stressing the reasons teenagers needed to be taught about the use of condoms and safe sex. The parent who had mentioned abstaining held up his hand to ask a question. His question was: "If someone had not shaken hands with anyone else, was that person to assume they had AIDS?" The teacher answered that if someone had not shaken hands with a single person in the group, then they could consider themselves safe. The parent then announced to the group that he had "abstained" from shaking anyone's hand and therefore did not have AIDS.

Adultery: The Good Lord knows that there are more than a few instances in which adultery has done irreparable damage to one part of the body or another. I doubt that there is anyone who has not seen, or heard of, a minister losing his family, his church, and his ministry because of an illicit affair with either someone in the church or someone they met during a convention, a visitation, or in a second job. I myself have known several chaplains who have had adulterous affairs, and at least one who was a closet[66] homosexual, and have heard of others that have committed such sins. Some of these chaplains have managed to remain on activity duty, either by changing denominations, by submitting himself or herself to counseling, their denominational endorsing agency did not choose to use disciplinary measures, or some got away with it because they knew someone high up that covered their sin. However, for most: "... *you will be sinning against the Lord; and you may be sure that your sin will find you out*" (Numbers 32:23).

If, as an example, I were to discuss the Sixth and the Ninth Commandments, "*you shall not commit adultery*" and "*you shall not covet your neighbor's... wife*" (Exodus 20:14,17). There are homosexuals that will very quickly tell you that they are in a "monogamous" relationship and that only the state bars them from calling it a marriage. The term itself has changed in meaning. Monogamous now means having only one partner at a time, and anyone who has had less than three partners in the past five years is viewed by many in the medical community to have been monogamous.

There was a time when everyone understood that the Sixth Commandment was in reference to 1) heterosexual relations, 2) at least one of the participants was married to someone else, and 3) required a physical and an emotional element in order to consummate the sin. Ah, but along comes the Internet and suddenly our understanding of adultery is turned on its head.

Electronic Affairs: A married person who is engaged in chatroom flirtation is really involved in an electronic affair. They are playing an emotional game of cheating on their spouses by "safe" dating. They have no real intention of taking it any farther than an online mutual admiration society. Their intent is to stay anonymous in the relationship and move on if it becomes too involved. They tend to make it up as they go, saying exactly what they think the other person wants to hear. They want to keep the relationship light and stay away from serious issues. In the beginning, they are more apt to manipulate than be manipulated.

The problem is that many people are very serious about meeting others on the Internet for the purpose of establishing a meaningful relationship. They don't know that the person they are communicating with is married and unhappy or just plain bored with married life. The married person does not realize that they have personal tastes and cultural expectations that they bring with them to the electronic site. These cannot be hidden for long and the responding person, believing that there is a romantic attachment forming, builds on the perceived need of the intended partner. The individual, normally a man, becomes flattering and complimentary.[67] This feeds the married person's ego and the expectations of the affair leaves reality and enters the intra-psychic zone of cyber-space.

The cheating spouse then begins to be pre-occupied with the Internet and begins to spend more and more time online to achieve the same level of satisfaction. They may have more than one "Handle" with which to carry on several affairs at the same time. They may even begin to entertain telephone calls when their spouses are at work, home, or deployed. They tend to become deceptive about their online use. They may even change their personal patterns to coincide with Internet usage. They begin to neglect the spouse, and, at this point, the spouse becomes suspicious.

When confronted with the affair(s), the offending spouse will normally refuse to be drawn into an argument. They will downplay the importance of the online relationship. The Internet partner is just a good old boy or girl. It is, after all, only a platonic relationship. Avoidance, passive aggression, and pretending will only delay the inevitable moment of reckoning. The trust level is broken just as cleanly as if the offending spouse had gone out to a club or bar and met a "real" person.

Emotional Adultery: Emotional Adultery is the next level of involvement and is far more complicated. It can evolve from the Electronic Affair, or the individual can be looking from the start. Men will often begin by seeking out cyber-sex. Their intent is one of self-gratification. As with emotional affairs, they will go to great lengths to hide online meetings from their partner. They normally enter a "Matching" chat-room unintentionally and accidentally become aroused and then later actively seek emotional gratification at the next session. Women feel unappreciated, unloved, and ineffective in their marriage. They are trying to avoid loneliness through increased activity on the Internet. They want desperately to be kept constantly busy and surrounded by caring people. Design or accident has damaged their self-esteem and emotional integrity. Either way the road leads to the same junction.

Electronic affairs become adultery when the person or persons become emotionally involved.[68] By this time, the emotional baggage comes into play. It is also at this point that the person becomes vulnerable to "predators." A predator on the Internet is someone who seeks a certain type of prey. They can be looking for financial gain, sexual relationship, physical bondage and harm, or simply a need to manipulate a weaker individual. They can come across as "the greatest person I have ever 'met' in my life." In most cases both male and female, the individual has not physically met the person they have fallen in love with.[69] And that is only a cursory discussion of the modern term "adultery."

By the example of the Internet one may think that I digress, however, the point was the changing definition of adultery. The type of sin must be determined by how the pleasure is taken, as well as the circumstances that accompany it, the internal sin being as grave as the external sin. Within the contexts of Scripture all sin is a forbidden choice. When Jesus was in the desert and being tempted by Satan (Matthew 4:1-11), Satan could not compel Jesus to sin, he could only tempt Him. In the same manner Satan cannot compel a Christian to sin, it is a willful choice. "*No temptation has seized you except what is common to man*" (I Corinthians 10:13,14). When an individual first chooses to arouse an illicit pleasure, they are guilty the moment they make the choice, even if unsuccessful in their attempt to consummate the sin. "Oh," one may say, "but what if the sin comes upon one unaware?" Ah, yes, the young lady who passes by in a very stimulating dress. I used to tell my young soldiers that it was not the first look that gets you in trouble it is the second look. I told one young soldier to visualize his grandmother in that dress. He looked at me for a moment and then said: "Well you certainly ruined that thought." Temptation is just that, temptation, and is not a sin until the person accepts it and internally or externally acts upon it. If you find any common ground in the discussion to this point then you are left with the understanding that sin is a choice.

Before moving on there are some additional factors that need to be taken into account. The sin of Adultery can be single or double, depending on whether one or both of the co-conspirators are married to other persons. In Christian marriage the parties have contracted before God to give to one another the exclusive rights to those acts that result in the orderly propagation of the race. "*The husband should fulfill his marital duty to his wife, and likewise the wife to her husband. The wife's body does not belong to her alone but also to her husband. In the same way, the husband's body does not belong to him alone but also to his wife*" (I Corinthians 7:3,4). Adultery is such a serious violation of that solemn contract, that it is referred to as a "tearing of the flesh," and the injured party is permitted to divorce the adulterous spouse if they so choose. Divorce is not mandatory; many couples have chosen to seek counseling and have gone on to rebuild trust and reclaimed the sanctity of the marriage bed, however, it is an acceptable option.

Abortion: At this point the secular humanist and the radical feminist will have trouble with the thought that their bodies belong to anyone but themselves. This in natural order brings me to the sin of abortion. Abortion is the intended expulsion of a fetus, which cannot live independently of its mother. The sin of abortion comes under the Fifth Commandment, "*Thou shall not murder*" (Exodus 20:13). God set forth this commandment to remind us to properly preside over not only our bodies, but also the bodies of others. The human body is God's property; it is He who created us, and as such we belong to Him. As such we cannot dispose of human bodies as we see fit. What is confusing to me is that most people, who believe in abortion, do not believe in the death penalty. They see nothing wrong with the taking of an unborn life that has harmed no one, but are appalled at the thought that a violent hardened criminal would be put to death for his or her crimes against humanity.

If Old Testament Scripture is to be believed, then a human being must be regarded as having a body and soul upon conception (Judges 13:2-7; Job 31:15; Psalm 51:5, 6; 139:13; Isaiah 44:2, 49:1; Jeremiah 1:4,5). There has in the last few years arisen a debate within the Christian Church by pro-abortion advocates putting forth a theory of "Ensoulment." This is the theory that the unborn does not become a living being until its first breath of life. I believe this to be erroneous because it assumes that God gives the breath of life to each individual directly: "*And the Lord God formed man from the dust of the ground and breathed into his nostrils the breath of life, and man became a living being*" (Genesis 2:7).

First, if we assume this to be correct, then when does the female fetus become a living being seeing that God gave His breath to the man, and created the woman out of man? "*So the Lord God caused the man to fall into a deep sleep; and while he was sleeping, he took one of the man's ribs and closed up the place with flesh. The Lord God made a woman from the rib he had taken out of the man*" (Genesis 2:21). Second, Scripture states that God gave His breath to Adam and the inference is that Adam and Eve passed it on via conception. "*Adam lay with his wife Eve, and she conceived and gave birth to Cain. She said, 'with the help of the Lord I have brought forth a man'*" (4:1). A search of Scriptures would show that God created humanity in His own image, and thereafter humanity created humanity in its own image and likeness. "*When Adam had lived* 130 *years, he had a son in his own likeness, in his own image*" (5:3). Third, there is scientific evidence that the unborn can respond to the human voice, can feel pain and discomfort, and if Luke 1:44 is to be believed is capable of feeling emotion. Not to belabor (no pun intended) the point, the word "βρεπηοσ" (brephos) is used in the New Testament to describe a child whether it is unborn, new-born, or infant (Luke 1:41; 2:12,16; Acts 7:19; II Timothy 3:15; I Peter 2:2).

Sinful abortion is intrinsically wrong, and no external circumstance can justify it, even when the state permits it. To abort a fetus because no contraception was used or it failed, because it is not a convenient time, or because the circumstances are unpleasant or even criminal, should be unacceptable to the Christian. I know that this discussion must sound hard and unloving, especially coming from a man, however the Christian is called to do the harder right, never the easier wrong. I know that there are hard areas; incest, rape, and diseased conditions of the fetus, conditions or events that test the soul and break even the hardest heart. However to take the life of the unborn in the case of a rape where the mother's life is not in danger is to punish the child in lieu of, or in addition to, punishing the father.

I have over the course of my twenty-six years in the military chaplaincy counseled many young female soldiers who were having problems because they, believing that there was no other alterative, aborted their child. Some cases were for rape, one was for incest, and the majority were teenagers whose families or the father of the child offered little or no help outside of paying for an abortion. Aside from believing that there were no other alternatives, they had one other thing in common, they all felt that they had killed their own child.[70] In many cases society had not only forgiven them, but also told them that everybody was doing it and it was okay and that they would be just fine. For most of them their families had forgiven them, and in a few cases they had gone before the church confessed their sin, and the church had forgiven them and even assured them that God forgave them. What no one had taken the time to do was help the young ladies forgive themselves.[71]

I have to always come back to the Christian thought: for the Christian, unless there is a case of double effect, alterative courses of action must always be sought. I do not believe, nor can I find in Scripture where God either intended or requires that a woman die in childbirth. When there are ectopic pregnancies, cancerous wombs, the state of the fetus or the condition of the woman dictate that one must die or both will die then there is a justifiable case before God for double effect. However, in all other cases Christians should advocate other alternatives to abortion.

Religious Vows of Celibacy: Paul said that it was good for a man not to marry, however, "*since there was so much immorality each man should have his own wife and each wife her own husband*" (I Corinthians 7:1,2). Vows are considered to be religious in nature when they are taken publicly and in accordance with the manner prescribed by the denomination, and are administered by an ecclesiastical official. This is true whether it is a marriage vow or a vow of celibacy. Even if it were not Scriptural, for the Christian the very virtue of religion would compel us to keep the vows we make before God. "*When a man makes a vow to the Lord or takes an oath to obligate himself by a pledge, he must not break his word but must do everything he said*" (Numbers 32:2).

First, whether internal or external, all sexual sins committed by a person under a religious vow of celibacy whether in the privacy of their own home or in a sacred place is sacrilege, regardless of whether the sin was committed with a willing accomplice or a victim, such as a child or a person who has come for counseling. Secondly, when such sins are committed in a place that the denomination has dedicated to the worship of God such as a parish house, a church, or a chapel, the congregation has the right to not only question the conversion experience of the individual, but they have the responsibility to demand that the license and ordination be surrendered.[72]

If the sin is also listed as a crime against society, the congregants have the additional legal obligation to turn the individual over to the civil authorities for prosecution. I cannot find in Scripture, nor do I understand as a person, how any denomination or ecclesiastical order could just send such an individual on to another unsuspecting parish or church.

Pedophilia: Before moving on to the discussion on homosexuality, there is one more area that needs to be addressed here in the heterosexual section of this chapter. Pedophilia is from the Greek "παιδοπηιλια" (paidophilia), "παισ" (pais) meaning boy or child, and "πηιλια" (philia) meaning friendship. It is also understood as pederasty from the Greek "παιδεραστια" (lover of boys). It is the condition of a person whose primary sexual attraction is toward prepubescent children.

The Diagnostic and Statistical Manual of Mental Disorders 4th edition, American Psychiatric Association, includes a diagnostic criteria for 302.2 "Pedophilia." There was a time when homosexuality was considered a mental illness. The North American Man-Boy Love Association (NAMBLA) and "The Human Face of Pedophilia" both advocate legalization of consensual sexual relationships between boys and men. As with the first iteration of the genetic vs. environmental factors debate, many pedophiles are claiming that they were born this way and should not be penalized because like the homosexual the orientation is immutable.

However, even the dictionary defines pedophilia as the "abnormal" sexual desire in an adult to engage in sex with children. It is a human atrocity that is found in heterosexuals and homosexuals alike. Until the past few years female pedophilia was almost unheard of. There have been four cases in the newspapers within the past year of female teachers having sexual relations with male students, one of them twice, even after having given birth to a child while serving a term in prison.

Pedophiles will often refer to themselves using their preference i.e. boy-lover or girl-lover, sometimes choosing to be known as child-lovers, although we are told that most are not sexually drawn to both sexes. For the most part pedophilia is confined to the male of the species in more than 99.9% of the cases involving the church, and the great majority of those involve men and boys. Although there can be one, I do not know of any case of pedophilia in a church involving a woman.[73]

The Catholic Church in America is riddled with homosexuals, the majority of which are proving to be pedophiles. This is not to negate the Protestant church and its problem with pedophilia. What is unconscionable and an assault on the mind of society is how so many of these individuals, Protestant and Catholic alike have been moved to other churches where they were free to continue their sexual assault on children and this horrendous sin goes on unabated. Forwarding a church letter on a member who is not a member in good standing or who has committed a sexual crime against humanity violates the very concept of God and His people being holy. It is a sin of the church and requires that the entire congregation repent and make restitution to the victims.

Homosexual

This is not intended to be a comprehensive discussion of homosexuality. I need to acknowledge that in the space I have allotted myself, that there is no way I can do exhaustive work on the passages or the hermeneutics in applying those passages to homosexuality. The word homosexual was not in general use when the Bible was written, and therefore the Bible speaks about the specific term in only two places. The word itself, I believe, was first used in 1869 in a German article. The word homosexual translates literally as "of the same sex." My problem with giving the Greek rendering of the word is that the word is a hybrid of the Greek prefix homo meaning "same" (not to be confused with the Latin root which means "human") and the Latin root sex meaning just that "sex." Homosexuality was removed from the Psychiatric Association's list of mental disorders in 1973. While still used to describe sexual behavior, when referring to individuals the term is now considered to be archaic and derogatory. The preferred terms are "gay" for men and "lesbian" for women.

However if not mentioned by the modern term, certainly the Bible does have a number of passages that talk about same-sex sexual relations. I will not deviate too far into the scientific evidence for the hypothetical "causes" of homosexuality. The assessment of that evidence, as near as I can ascertain ends in an impasse over the issue of genetic versus environmental impact.

What I will do is attempt to focus on the use of the Bible and the texts that are important for discerning a Christian position on the topic of homosexuality as sexual immorality. Certainly one cannot attempt to discuss such a volatile subject without considering at least some of the views. The problem is which ones. There are a plethora of explanations that have been applied to Scriptural discussions of homosexual activities in an attempt to, if not eradicate any relevance then certainly to, ease any Biblical restriction on such sexual activities.

General Abuse: Perhaps the most prevalent argument is that the Scriptures do not give general prohibitions against homosexual activities per se but rather against abuses "in" homosexual activities. The more modern version of this perception is that homosexual behavior can be perverted and sinful, in the same manner that heterosexual activities can be perverted and sinful. By the careful linking of the two sexual activities, one can then logically (rather than exegetically) presuppose that neither sexual orientation nor specific acts in and of themselves would then be sinful outside of perversion. If one follows the logic of general abuse, then expressions of homosexual passions exist that would not be harmful to one's fellow citizens.

However, there are no positive discussions of "moral" homosexuality to be found in the Scriptures, just as there are no positive discussions on adultery, greed, theft, or coveting that would not be harmful to one's neighbor.[74] In fact, this entire discussion has lead to a division between what is a sin and what is a crime. By example, adultery has always been a sin, but with the exception of the military where it is linked to good order and discipline the majority of society does not see it as a crime.[75] The majority of societies on the other hand have always considered rape a sin and a crime. This has lead to confusion, and by way of confusion, to a secular question: "Should something that is not a crime be considered by society as a sin?"

Should the reader be tempted to say such a thing would never happen in the Christian Church, let me very clearly say that it is happening now. Permit me to drop just a few examples: 1) the ordination of three openly gay Lutheran clergymen in California, 2) the appointment of homosexual priests and Gene Robinson, a non-celibate homosexual man as Bishop of the Episcopal Church USA of New Hampshire. Their denomination in their 74th General Convention of the Episcopal Church USA took to them the task of considering two issues related to homosexuality—the blessing of same-sex unions and to decide whether to confirm a practicing homosexual as bishop, which they did, 3) When California was providing social marriages to gay couples a United Methodist Lesbian minister married her live-in-lover. While to the denomination's credit they found the lesbian minister guilty of violating the Book of Disciple, which bars "self-avowed" practicing homosexuals from ministry by a vote of 12 to 1. To the denominations detriment the vote to defrock was 7 to 6, the minimum required to act; and the Philadelphia congregation declared that the offending minister could continue to perform most of her duties, 4) as noted in Chapter 3, the United Church of Christ has come out with a commercial that blatantly accuses all other denominations of excluding homosexuals, among others, from attending the local church, and offering membership into their inclusive church.[76] I believe that if these churches will search their Scriptures they will find that they have much in common with the church at Thyatira, in that they are a compromising church and in need of doctrinal purity (Revelation 2:18,19).

Fetal Development: In all fairness to others there is the "Fetal Development" hypothesis. In general this basically states that individuals may be genetically predisposed to homosexual desires, via fetal hormone exposure such as testosterone or luteinizing. Within the genetic discussion there are also theories involving maternal stress, consumption of certain drugs, increasing levels of antibodies that somehow trigger differential brain development, and deficiencies within the mother's immune system. There has been some discussion that being born late in life well after the birth of other siblings could have some impact on the sexual predisposition. However I beg to remind the reader that these are theories and not proven fact.

Fixation: To add to the discussion we need to look at the "Fixation" hypothesis. This view states that sexual orientation is fixed early in human development. The questions to be answered by this view is exactly when does this happen and how. For the most part this type of theory holds that gender identity happens in the early stages of childhood. In the non-scientific world this is considered to be something that the child sees in the gender roles of adults, the way adults treat young children, passive fathers, aggressive mothers, enjoyable homosexual encounters as an infant. It is also possible that a random event in the development of the child influences a child's eventual sexual orientation.

Choice: Lastly, this hypothesis presupposes that where society widely accepts homosexuality as "normal," more individuals will be prone to experiment with and as a result of the experimentation adopt such a lifestyle. Most sins are not ugly. They are not unpleasant to either the eye or the senses. If they were either of these things then the normal person would not be tempted to engage in such repulsive activities. Is one born that way, or does environment draw one into the lifestyle? I think that by now everyone reading this book has come to the conclusion that I believe homosexuality as with all other sins to be a choice.

Granting homosexuals the legal right to social positions such as teaching and boy and girl organizational leadership positions, has given grave concern to those who accept this concept. It is here that we find the idea of homosexual recruitment of individuals into the lifestyle as early on in adolescence as possible. Since tracking of homosexual lifestyles has only really begun in the past decade or so, there is no real way to prove this yet. The apprehension is that by the time it is proven, the damage to American youth will have already been done and society will have been desensitized to the danger. Depending on which groups estimate you chose to use, the most common estimates range from three to ten percent of the population being homosexual, with one percent being female and three percent being male. For this theory, sexual orientation is a conscious choice. There is wide discussion as to whether this choice is made casually or if it can be changed easily once accepted. Secular humanistic understanding leads to the conclusion that such individuals should be treated with respect and/or compassion and that they should not necessarily be discouraged from acting on their impulsive erotic desires.

What If: From time-to-time, I like to play the "what if" game—What if you're right and I'm wrong, and what if I'm right and you're wrong? I have found that it is a game that most secular humanists, liberals, radical feminists and homosexuals do not like to play. Oh, they don't mind the "what if I'm right and you're wrong" portion of the game, but they quickly lose interest when it is time to reverse the roles. These groups of people when they cannot get their way by ballot are super quick to resort to lawsuits and liberal judges to force their concepts and ideas of liberty and justice for all, even when the majority, by the public vote has defeated the question.

So, what if you're right? If a person is born homosexual, how can a just and loving God condemn them for being and doing what they were born to be and do? If God created a group of people to be a certain way, then certainly He cannot condemn them to perdition for being what He created them to be and still be a just and loving God. God's righteousness and His omnipotence give Him the right to do with His creation as He sees fit. However, to condemn a group from birth, to remove any and all hope of redemption, would be to give to God the very attributes that we will not tolerate in society and detest in ourselves.

There is only one person in the Bible that I find that was born to be, if in fact he was born to be, the "Son of Perdition," and that was Judas whom betrayed Christ to the religious leaders. "*While I was with them, I protected them and kept them safe by that name you gave me. None have been lost except the one doomed to destruction so that Scripture would be fulfilled*" (John 7:12). So, if God created you homosexual then He cannot condemn that which He Himself declared good, "*God saw all that he had made, and it was very good*" (Genesis 1:31). If you were born homosexual, then the Bible is not to be believed in its dictation and its precepts on salvation and righteousness, and society should not place any restrictions upon where you work, whom you marry, nor what lifestyle you choose, "if" you were born that way.

My turn! What if I am right? What if you were not born that way? What if your lifestyle is not acceptable to God and the Bible is correct in its condemnation of homosexual behavior and the lifestyle does harm society as a whole? Well, first of all according to the Bible God did not create nor intend same gender sexual relationships. "*So God created man in his own image, in the image of God he created him, male and female he created them*" (Genesis 1:27). Proof of God's intent can also be seen in God's instructions to Noah that only male and female pairings were to be brought into the Ark (6:19; 7:2). Secondly, God does condemn homosexual behavior (Genesis 19:4-13; Leviticus 5:3, 18:22, 20:13). I have deliberately restricted my use of Scripture on creation and God's intent to those books found in the Pentateuch because the New Testament is built upon the Old Testament. "*In the past God spoke to our forefathers through the prophets at many times and in various ways, but in these last days he has spoken to us by his Son, whom he appointed heir of all things, and through whom he made the universe*" (Hebrews 1:1,2). There are other texts in Old Testament Scriptures that all deal with homosexuality and or those who practice it (Judges 19:22-24; I Kings 14:22-24; 22:43,46; II Kings 23:4-7; Ezekiel 16: 49,50; and Daniel 11:37).

But, what about the New Testament, what if anything does it say about homosexuality as a lifestyle? When questioned about marriage, Jesus gave an all-encompassing condemnation of all sexual relationships outside of the male-female model as established in Genesis 1:27. Marriage was to be one man and one woman bonded together for life. It was only through the hardness of humanities heart that divorce was granted for other than adultery.

Paul in the book of Romans noted that God's nature and His intent was made clear to sinful man through nature itself so that humanity was without excuse. "*...For since the creation of the world God's invisible qualities—his eternal power and divine nature—have been clearly seen being understood from what has been made so that men are without excuse*" (Romans 1:18-20). His reference to the unsaved exchanging the glory of the incorruptible God "for an image" refers to the creation account of Genesis (1:23). He then goes on to speak about the depraved condition brought on by a sinful nature (1:26). C.E.B. Cranfield noted that "φνσικην" (natural) means "in accordance with the intention of the Creator," and "παρα φνσιν" (against nature) means "contrary to the intention of the Creator."[77] I think that what needs to be understood here is that Paul approaches this discussion from the movement of humanity, historically speaking, and while each individual's experience may differ, the result, that is homosexuality, is still to be considered a sinful perversion of nature.

Paul uses a term, "αρσενοκοιτηδ"[78] (homosexuals), that is only found in two places in the New Testament, I Corinthians 6:9,10, and I Timothy 1:9,10, both of which comprise a sort of sin-list of which those who persist in these sins will not inherit the kingdom of God. Later on Paul will note that when someone becomes corrupted and doesn't believe the Christian way of life or lives the natural integrity and morality of an unbeliever who attempts to live a good if not righteous life, the consequences of such actions are a hardening of both the mind and conscience resulting in mental, and soon to follow physical, perversion.

> To the pure, all things are pure, but to those who are corrupted and do not believe, nothing is pure. In fact, both their minds and consciences are corrupted. They claim to know God, but by their actions they deny him. They are detestable, disobedient and unfit for doing anything good. (Titus 1:15,16)

Jude the half-brother of Jesus gave warning to the church about allowing such individuals to misinterpret the word and allowing for immoral behavior within the church. Jude's use of the combination of two words, "υπεχουσαι" (heteros and sarx meaning flesh) and "ετεροδ" (other) to point to the homosexuality, not to the inhospitality of the Sodomites. *"In a similar way Sodom and Gomorrah and the surrounding towns gave themselves up to sexual immorality and perversion. They serve as an example of those who suffer the punishment of eternal fire"* (Jude 7). Lastly, Revelation 21:27 gives grave warning that nothing impure will ever enter the city of God.

I am sure, that there are those who will find fault with my simplistic approach to the homosexual side of the "what if" game. Certainly there are more arguments to be made on the part of the homosexual. There is the argument that Paul was imposing Jewish laws and customs; there was the cultural setting he was operating in; there is certainly homosexual activity by heterosexuals to be considered. However, for all the arguments, as logical as they may seem, homosexuality as viewed through the eyes of Scripture is a spiritual and physical abnormality. It is the result of the fallen-ness of humanity, it is a disease of the soul, it is in opposition of the nature of humanity to which God has called us, and it is a sin that must be repented of, if salvation is to be achieved.

Questions for Consideration and Discussion

In the parables of Jesus, He often presents God as the gracious and seeking Father who longs to have His children safe in His love and care. We are all created in His image, and He loves us, all of us, regardless of the lifestyle we have chosen. It is not the individual that God hates, it is the sin. Even so, as God cannot allow sin to come before His holy presence, the sinner, any sinner, can be excluded from His Kingdom if they chose the sin over the Savior. What is often forgotten in discussions is that if you're saved through Jesus the Son, you are a child of God. If you are not saved then you are but a creation of God. Sometimes people disappoint and hurt us. Word may come that a sibling, a grandchild or other relative has come out in the open as a homosexual. If such has happened then remember that as a Christian you are to pray for such an individual, and you are to love such a person. Hate should have no place in the Christian heart.

1. How are we as Christians to relate to those people who cast aside moral and religious standards? Should church members be treated any differently than non-church goers? If so, how?
2. Can the church accept such persons (as Jesus did) without judging them and yet without excusing their misconduct or sin?
3. Do the church and congregations seek to bring the individual back into fellowship with the church, or do they simply remove them from the membership? In other words are the church leadership and congregation more like the Pharisees or like Jesus?
4. What is the congregation's understanding of sexual sins? Does it include both heterosexual as well as homosexual? Where does the church stand on such sins?
5. What is the congregation's understanding of external and internal sins? Have there been any efforts to include classes for the youth on sins of the flesh? Who conducts such classes?

6. What, if any, sexual related subjects are taboo or off limits for discussion, and why?
7. How does the church handle a member, leader or laity, who is caught in the sin of external or internal fornication?
8. What if any sexual topics are being discussed with the youth of the church? Who is conducting these discussions? What are the youth's thoughts on abstention as both a deterrent to pregnancy and STDS?
9. What are the youth's understandings of sex outside of marriage? Have the youth been guided through a Bible study and are they encouraged to take a pledge to remain a virgin (both male and female) until marriage?
10. Have there been such sins within the body of the church? What has been the reaction of the leadership and the laity? What does the church do with the unrepentant offender?
11. Does the church as a whole condemn sexual immorality as unacceptable not only for society but especially for the members of the church?
12. If a member is found to be engaging in sexual immorality how does the church handle it?
13. If the offence is not a criminal offense, what Biblical support does the church use in admonishing the offending member? Does the church make every effort to bring the offending member back into fellowship?
14. How does the church handle sexual immorality such as fornication, adultery, and pedophilia? Are the offenders reported to the civil authorities or simply passed on to the next unsuspecting congregation?
15. If the member refuses the offer of counseling and prayer, how does the church exclude the individual from participating in church functions until the member repents?

16. If an offending member seeks to move their letter, how does the leadership of the church handle the request? How does the church leadership handle the situation if the offending person is a leader or staff member of the church?

THE MORAL AND ETHICAL DILEMMA[79]

Moral Education

95% of Americans believe in God, 87% of Americans claim to be Christians, and less than 50% of those claiming to be Christians also described themselves as "absolutely committed to the Christian faith."[80] These individuals are known as either "Sunshine" or "Sunday Morning" Christians. They attend church on an irregular basis and have no qualm in missing church for other "more important" social functions. They proudly proclaim their faith, when there are social or political advantages, and disavow themselves from their faith when it may prove detrimental to their secular endeavors.

Their knowledge of Scriptures are limited to what they've gleamed from the last pastor they heard speak, and they have passed on to their children nothing of the religious education they might have received from their parents. Their morality is based on secular humanism and what may or may not assault their individual sense of moral outrage. More than likely they have grown up with two working parents or in a single parent home; they have abdicated their responsibility for teaching morality to their children to the secular education system. Now the children of America are killing themselves, and the parents don't have a clue as how this has happened and they blame the education system for having failed to instill in the students a high regard for human life.

In this age of rapid telecommunications, instant gratification, thirty second bits of information, and the constant cry of non-Christians for believers to keep their faith out of the public and political domains, many believers have compartmentalized their Christianity; they have kept their spiritual lives separated from their secular lives and with this shift in behavior has failed to live up to, and/or pass on the moral and ethical behavior that God requires of His creation.

> Those who live according to the sinful nature have their minds set on what that nature desires; but those who live in accordance with the Spirit have their minds set on what the Spirit desires. The mind of sinful man is death, but the mind controlled by the Spirit is life and peace, because the sinful mind is hostile to God. It does not submit to God's law, nor can it do so. Those controlled by the sinful nature cannot please God. (Romans 8:5-8)

An important part of Christian Theology is moral theology. Moral theology places before the individual, and the assemblage, the basic ideals of righteous living according to the Scriptural principles of reason and faith. Anyone who is interested in helping young people during their formative years to develop appreciation, acceptance, and to live by the moral code of Christianity recognizes that moral theological education is not only the answer, but it is the authoritative dictate of God (Proverbs 22:6). Father Anthony Alexander, a Catholic educator and theologian once noted that, "One of the great failings of modern education is that while it teaches students how to make a living, it does not teach them how to live." [81]

There was a time when universities and colleges encouraged students to consider moral education. There was even a short period in elementary education when teachers were involved in moral and ethical education. Conversely, as America moved into the second half of the twentieth century traditional moral-filled education in the home, in the school, and especially in higher education was clearly on the decline.

For the most part this highly important component of education was, and, in most cases, is still being left to the parents. Unfortunately there are large portions of American youth who are not receiving instructions on morals or ethics from anyone. Recognizing this fact, the Army as well as the rest of the Armed Forces began devoting a greater amount of time attempting to teach values to their incoming service men and women. Commanders who have never before taught the subject began introducing it into their training schedules. At the same time, the Army is attempting to do so while avoiding the subtleties of drawing a moral distinction between right and wrong.

One need only listen to the evening news concerning war crimes, desertions, and misconduct on the part of our service men and women to see how well that is working. "*The Lord says: 'These people come near to me with their mouth and honor me with their lips, but their hearts are far from me. Their worship of me is made up only of rules taught by men'*" (Isaiah 20:13).

Increasingly young people are entering adulthood without benefit of family upbringing in the social graces of good behavior. I believe that it is not, as some declare, a generation of immoral individuals, but rather a generation of "amoral" individuals. One would surmise that the concept of "right" versus "wrong" would be the simplest moral, and social, principle to grasp. A basic assumption has been that every society, every group, and with few exceptions every individual has a basic working knowledge of right and wrong behavior.

> Indeed, when Gentiles, who do not have the law, do by nature things required by the law, they are a law for themselves, even though they do not have the law, since they show that the requirements of the law are written on their hearts, their consciences also bearing witness, and their thoughts now accusing, now even defending them. (Romans 2:14,15)

According to humanism, the intellect leads the will. By means of the will, the intellect practices good deeds. However, what happens when the intellect does not receive sound, clear, and inspiring instruction in moral truths? What basis of knowledge does the individual draw upon to determine if something is right or wrong? "*The heart is deceitful above all things and beyond cure. Who can understand it?*" (Jeremiah 17:9). An important part of moral education sets before us the basic ideals of right living according to principles of reason and, like it or not, of faith. All of us who are interested in helping people, young and old, live moral and ethical lives recognize that moral education now constitutes one of the more important duties of society. "*Finally, brothers, whatever is true, whatever is noble, whatever is right, whatever is pure, whatever is lovely, whatever is admirable—if anything is excellent or praiseworthy—think about such thing*" (Philippians 4:8).

As the Bible presents it, the history of Israel began with the migration of the Hebrew patriarchs from Mesopotamia to their new homeland that would become Israel. The moral and religious training of the people from their childhood up was regarded by the Hebrew people from the very beginning of their national history as one of the principal objects of life. Speaking of Abraham the Lord said: "*For I have chosen him, so that he will direct his children and his household after him to keep the way of the Lord by doing what is right and just*" (Genesis 18:19).

Much has been said about the need for a moral crusade and the revival of ethical systems in society. However, far less has been written about the problems that arise in associating right and wrong behavior with the moral imperatives that underwrite ethical systems. Yet, disregarding religion, as most of the educators and politicians seems prone to do now days, the history of social relationships, the statements of great humanitarian leaders, and the annals of moral principles all throw light on the issue. The problems of moral principles, ethical systems, and the erosion of social values are especially illuminating in pointing out the tragic and difficult choices, which confront local churches, and the uncertain course we must follow simply because the immoral has been mandated. This is particularly true in these opening years of the twenty-first century where the tasks of teaching young people that which they were not taught by home, school, and the society at large, seems almost insurmountable.

Definitions

Anyone pretentious enough to discuss the relationship of moral principles and ethical systems must first strive to ensure that everyone understands what is meant by the word or words being used. This clarity becomes even more relevant when determining which spirit or attitude one will approach the subject with. There are far too many people today who would argue that you cannot make an absolute statement concerning behavior, which is an absolute statement within itself. They would argue that one must speak in generalities and only the most limited terms when dealing with others. If not clarified at the very outset of the dialogue, then when turning for discussion or counsel with others, the guidance will most often be opposing and mutually contradictory.[82]

- **Absolute:** Not limited by restrictions or exceptions; in Law, complete and unconditional; in Philosophy, considered the ultimate basis of all thought and being.
- **Amoral:** Is outside or beyond the sphere of moral distinctions or judgment, neither moral nor immoral. In the broader sense it means: "lacking the ability to make a moral judgment." In simple terms, an amoral person has no reference point from which to draw the moral distinction of what is right or wrong in behavior toward others.
- **Immoral:** Contrary to accepted moral principles.
- **Imperative:** Having the authority or power to control or command; constituting the mood of a verb that expresses a command or request; in Urgency, obligatory.
- **Moral:** In the broad sense it is: "of, or concerned with, the principles of right and wrong in relation to human action and character; teaching or displaying good or correct behavior; standards of what is right or just in behavior." In the context of being it is: "Arising from conscience or sense of right and wrong; based on conviction rather than evidence; a judgment."

- **Precept:** A principle or rule imposing a standard of action or conduct.

The Educational Debate

Everyone seems to have an answer to why Johnny is carrying guns to school: can't read, has Attention Deficient Disorder, is anti-social, etc. However, nothing seems to be working, and the problem just keeps getting larger. Most states now have mandatory skill level tests. They all seem to proudly point to better scores each year, and yet the number of children killing children and the number of individuals coming into the Armed Services still reading at the eighth to ninth grade level is alarming. The truth is that most schools now take anywhere from three to four weeks out of the school year to prepare for the skill level test. One can but wonder what would happen if the education administrators placed as much emphasis on learning moral values as they do on passing the annual test. "*By wisdom a house is built, and through understanding it is established; through knowledge its room are filled with rare and beautiful treasure*" (Proverbs 24:3,4).

In the last ten to twenty years, there has been a new emphasis on avoiding value judgments. There is also a new resurgence on creating scientific, value-free wisdom in the behavioral sciences and on eradicating any teaching that smacked of the earlier parochialism. The scientific school of thought maintains that the student of such concepts as morality, ethics, or values, should strip oneself of any trace of commitment or personal belief. The best of modern social science is, or at least I have been told, value-free. It would be science if it were lacking, or free from, misleading prejudice or preconception that would lead to a predetermined end. However, in morality, we are dealing with a theory that has its basis in universal societies. It has long been accepted that society has the right to impose certain behavior on the masses for the good of the group, society and not the individual denoting what is "good."

An opposing school of thought, however, enjoins the student to keep aim and purpose ever before him or her and before those who would hear or read his or her words. If I seek to establish moral behavior, then I must allow neither fact nor the ordering of events ultimately to deter me from my stated goal. Were my purpose religious faith, or public law and order, my task would be to arrange what I say primarily to instill convictions and values conducive to these aims. As I understand this concept, the end justifies the means. I sincerely hope that I am not the only person to have trouble with this concept. Both schools would argue that theirs is the only viewpoint in which valid facts are to be found.

I hope to direct this discourse to a point somewhere between the two extremes. I believe that value-free social science, except for the most narrow and frequently insignificant subjects to be an absurdity. One might use it to test limited areas of consumer behavior, political attitudes, or trends. However, goals and purposes permeate the great and timeless literature on humanities and social behavior.

I believe one of our supreme tasks in training young people is to bring moral purpose and ethical realities into proper alignment, and to understand their relationship more deeply and in terms that carry meaning for those whom we teach. I also believe that this overarching goal can be subjected to intellectual discipline, can be safeguarded from cynical nihilism[83] or hypocritical moralism, and can be measured against the living, and oft time changing standards of modern society.

According to the German philosopher Kant, reason approaches nature "not in the character of a pupil, who listens to all that his master chooses to tell him, but in that of a judge who compels the witness to reply to those questions, which he himself thinks fit to propose." I believe that all would agree that this new generation of young people ask questions and seek answers rather than just following an edict they do not understand. They do not seem willing to accept the knowledge and wisdom of the masters but rather seek to emphasize the questions that reality imposed upon them. New realities in the twenty-first century may call for new insights as well.

Imperatives and Absolutes

Until recent times, the bulk of the writing on morality fell to the lawyers. While political theory goes back to the speculations of Plato, philosophies of relationships are largely embedded in law (religious or otherwise). The contemporary development of interpreting the law was affiliated with the breakup of Western Christendom. The task of the writers was either to salvage from the old or to put something in its place. They chose to demonstrate that the legal and moral bonds drawing collective society together still existed. The Papacy with varying effectiveness asserted its authority primarily with respect to things spiritual but beginning in the Middle Ages with an impact on things temporal as well. The church, not the Empire, comprehended the moral universe. Since there was no widely successful political unity, the "Respublica Christianum" possessed both the moral and the political oneness, which was almost alien to the fragmented modern state systems.

The moral problem does not lay in searching out accepted higher standards that somehow will transcend partial or parochial loyalties. Today, moral writers seek some form of higher order, whether in ecumenical movements, in the building of common functional interests, or in the philosophical system. "*Open my eyes that I may see wonderful things in your law... Give me understanding and I will keep your law*" (Psalms 119:34).

What we need to do is return to the moral and ethical conduct that God provided us via the Deuteronomic law.

> God gave Israel a code of laws that offered a guideline to follow in order to accomplish His purpose. The Mosaic code was a civil, political, religious, and domestic code all in one. The legislation of the Hebrews was a definite and absolute. It regulated the whole life of the Jew, his home, dress, employment, food, the distribution of his property, domestic arrangements politics, and civil and religious life.[84]

By the seventeenth century, Grotius[85] was required to substitute universal natural law for the ecclesiastical order. Now it was not the church, but the "law of nature" that bound humanity irrespective of national allegiances to one another. The law of nature was a precept of "right reasoning." This precept pointed out that an act has in it a quality of moral baseness or moral necessity. In consequence, such an act is either forbidden or enjoined by society. Humanity was driven to achieve not exclusively for one's own advantage but the maintenance of the social order. Thus, moral behavior was judged valid, although an individual might be compelled or coerced into obedience.

From Grotius to the present, the stress in a fundamental way has been on positive law. With the notable exception of the somewhat hesitant and uncertain invoking of concepts such as the "principles of law" generally recognized by civilized nations, an identifiable higher natural law has tended to disappear. Karl Marx once noted that where there is no absolute (God), man himself will become the absolute.

Niebuhr starting from the point of philosopher-theologian rather than lawyer asserted that society, as we know it rests fundamentally on man as history reveals him through the ages. The practice of rooting morality and legal theory in modern institutions and processes rather than probing deeper to the level of human nature has been a peculiar affliction of the law and relationship theory. In the search for absolutes, the study begins in trying to understand humanity. "Man has always been his most vexing problem. How shall he think of himself?"[86] Any confirmation humanity makes of itself will involve humanity in contradiction. If we stress humanity's unique and rational qualities, then greed, lust for power, and our own pure brute nature betrays us. If we hold that humanity is the product of nature and is unable to rise above circumstances, we deny the individual free will and the ability to rise above one's station in life. If we assert that humanity is essentially good and attributes all evil to concrete historical and social causes, then we are but creatures of habit and upon scrutiny, to be the consequences of the evil inherent in humanity. "*The Lord saw how great man's wickedness on the earth had become, and that every inclination of the thoughts of his heart was only evil all the time*" (Genesis 6:5). Such baffling paradoxes of human self-knowledge point out the troublesome problem of doing justice to the uniqueness of humanity and to our affinities with nature. The paradox of man's existence arises from the fact that we are suspended perilously between freedom and finiteness, spirit and nature, and to stretch the point between right and wrong (Romans 7:14-20).

I believe that I would be correct in saying that the closer we move toward vital questions such as "how to preserve moral principles and ethical systems," the less influence the larger community has on its members. The morality that people practice in their mutual relations is in large measure the product of their historical partitioning. They are refractory to a higher morality only because their sentiments, like their interests, continue to gravitate exclusively about the culture (which is today the social group). These cultures, though theoretically subordinate to the higher community (state, country, etc.) are in fact real and almost absolute centers of moral cohesion.

No social or legal reform that would succeed can ignore the moral infrastructure, or the lack of it. The failure of ventures like collective morality and sweeping appeals to community wide public opinion are examples of thinking that suffers from the illusion that moral foundations are unimportant. The teaching of moral and ethical education, from a purely academe point of view, can be defined as the pursuit of the common good, understanding that in the majority of societies, the good of each is to be found in the good of the collectivity. I believe that the Army's attempt at teaching core values has been dealt with somewhat naively and impatiently in declarations that we should teach values without first ensuring the young men and women understand the moral principles that under-gird the ethical systems that lead to the internalization of the desired values.

The Target Audience

Into this discussion I have to add the American youth and the interesting concept of growing up American. Who are we trying to reach and why? Have we become so youth oriented that we now disregard the countless millions over thirty in an attempt to win the hearts and minds of the American youth? I do not discount that we should certainly be trying to reach young people, but who and what is our target?

In order to determine the target audience of moral education (the youth of America) we must look to reality, not the publicity of self-interest and societies ethos, which is the need for self-preservation. Our Armed Forces have been targeting frustrated individuals by striving to fulfill them vicariously by projecting their hopes, dreams, fears, and aspirations to the needs of our services. In the military today, collective attainments offer possibilities of self-realization and self-aggrandizement for the individual, which the civilian culture no longer offers.

At the same time, appeals are made to the loyalty, self-sacrifice, and devotion of individuals to the collective values and culture of the military. In this way, military cohesion is built on the virtuous as well as the selfish side of humanity's nature. In this way, the two elements of collective strength become self-sacrificial loyalty and frustrated self-attainment. I have to acknowledge that this conception of the primacy of self-interest broadly conceived has not been popularly acceptable or widely congenial in military circles.

In seeking a target audience, we first have to acknowledge that they do not come from the same generation as we do. Today's audiences are from what has been termed the "X" and "Net" (or dot com) generations. Just as Vietnam, Woodstock, and the Civil Rights movement shaped my generation, the Digital Revolution is shaping them. To complicate the equation, playing catch-up and winning these generations over to a more moral lifestyle will not be that effective, because we have a new generation that comes of age post the year 2000. Somewhere around 2005, we will have a new generation of young people dubbed the "Millennial" generation. Trying to determine which survey[87] to use to catalog these generations is like trying to pick your worst fears, everyone has a different slant on them, and no two look exactly alike.

There are some similarities in the studies in which we can seek to draw some conclusions on these emerging generations. After sorting through the material, I have placed the information in no specific order. Collectively, to these new generations, big is not better. They want intimate, long-term, protective kinds of relationships. Although out for a good time, they are looking for "the long haul." At the same time they have grown up feeling "it is up to me." They are not inclined to look to others for help. With the exception of grandparents, they tend not to trust the over forty crowd (go figure). They are on the move. They feel no loyalty to job or place. They do not expect to live in the place of their birth all their lives. "They do not like generation labels, seemingly to cry in unity: 'I am who I am, why label me?' They resent the effort to tag their collective psyche…,"[88] but marketing experts and sociologists are keenly interested in their values and tastes.

These generations will be cyber-literate. Chat rooms, text messaging, and e-mail will be a common mode of communication. In a chat room, a young person can manifest any kind of personality that they want. They will meet people who may similarly be shielding their true personality, gender, age, and sexual preference. They view these encounters as a form of virtual reality and acknowledge the danger of a personal encounter, even when that knowledge does not stop them from meeting the cyber-individual in person. The remote control symbolizes their reality; change is constant; focus is fragmented; generation pulse runs fast. They are bombarded by frequent images. They process information in narrative images, and consequently, they need continual "hits." They consume media at an accelerated pace. It is not uncommon for them to have the television and radio on while they talk on the telephone and do their homework. There is some evidence that they have, or are, developing the cognitive ability to process multiple streams of information at the same time. Ironically, most agree that today's youth are very perceptive shoppers, making it harder and harder for marketers to "get into a kid's mind." They do not buy into large-scale or slick promotions, preferring instead more individualized micro-marketing campaigns.

They are a jaded group, having a "been there, done that" attitude. Nothing seems to shock them. Drug abuse is down with the exception of heroin. It is called the "end-all" drug. Take it and sooner-or-later everything ends. There is an increase in alcohol consumption. Alcoholism is on the increase as well in the under thirty crowd. They have a pick and mix approach to spirituality, and their heroes include: Puff Daddy, God, Jeff Gordon, their grandfathers and grandmothers, Jesus, Michael Jordan, Madonna, Will Smith, and John Travolta.[89] Most of them state that there is no clear distinction between right and wrong, good and evil, and they have a hard time discerning the differences society places on them.

> For what the law was powerless to do in that it was weakened by the sinful nature, God did by sending his own Son in the likeness of sinful man to be a sin offering, and so he condemned sin in sinful man, in order that the righteous requirements of the law might be fully met in us, who do not live according to the sinful nature but according to the Spirit. (Romans 8:3,4)

The stereotypical image is often that of a self-centered, lazy youth with few goals beyond their plans for the evening. In reality, they have many concerns and interests beyond themselves and appear motivated to realize their hopes and aspirations for a bright future, while at the same time acknowledging that they do not have a clue as to how to get there. There seems to be an evenly split debate as to whether they believe that a lucky break or hard work will get them where they want to go.

There is a decisive split along economic lines as to how they see the future. The upper-middle and affluent class sees more possibilities in life. There is a growing softer edge to their music. They are wearing less name brand clothing, choosing to save their money for college. Working during the school year has become the norm. They take an active interest in politics and what the government is doing. Those who are registering to vote are overwhelmingly independent. They are turning to their families for a stronger support group than past youths, using the family as a sanctuary against the world. They display a greater desire to be with the family and to please them.

Middle class youth seem to associate themselves with the upper middle class rather than the lower-middle class. Despite their worries, they are into having fun, and they are not bored with life. Their top worries include: getting a good job, their parents' health, finishing their education, AIDS, the environment, and finding someone to love. Of this group, a small number who plan on entering the service have set goals and believe hard work is important to success. Eighty-eight percent have established specific goals for the next five years and see the service as a way to complete their education but not necessarily a career option. This statistic is interesting because the last Army survey showed that less then ten percent are taking advantage of the educational opportunities offered by the military. More than three-quarters of them believe that someday they will be where they want to be in life.

For the lower middle class and poor there is not nearly as much expectation for the coming years. Brand names are at an all time high. The cry is: "know these names, wear these names, live these names!" The individual identity is in the brand name. They are more pessimistic or cynical. Many of them feel alienated. Despite the national debates along racial lines, these youth support affirmative action but are skeptically optimistic about the American Dream, believing it to be a myth. Most have never held a "good" job, and an equal number have never had a checking or savings account. They describe their parents as "Latch-Key" children and alcohol or drug impaired. Seventy-three percent do not want to end up like their parents. Over eighty-six percent will earn a high school diploma with a grade point average of between 1.75 and 2.5 (D+/C+). It is estimated that over half will be dysfunctional in one or more areas of the social skills. One of the most disturbing findings is that a great majority of these youth expect to die young, and that their lives will end by violence. It is this latter group, in great numbers, that is seeking a way to improve their station in life and rise above their environment. These then are the ones, who come seeking a new life in the nation's military services.

Before moving on, a word of caution must be given. Most of the social research currently being done is actuarial in its concept. Although such research may provide a somewhat dependable prediction when conducted in the hundreds or thousands, it does not necessarily follow that it will provide the same dependability when applied to a single individual or congregation. Causation will always be personal, never actuarial, and there will always be the exception. "The only way to make a certain prediction of effect from cause is to study the life in which the causes operate and not a thousand other lives."[90]

The Moral Based Model

The basic approach to individual development lies in the identification, articulation, exploration, and internalization, by the individual of the moral imperative, the ethical system that supports that imperative(s), and the value that is associated with it. From the foundation of morals, we as individuals and groups draw the rules, habits, or values of conduct by which we chose to live. These morals range from concisely expressed precepts to general truths. They have through the ages become well defined and are often absolutes to the society at large. It is within the society that morals become imperatives. Society has the authority to command or control individual behavior. Society often sees them as obligatory.

According to philosophers, we differ from animals in that we have an intellect and a will. We have the ability to think and to choose what we think and what we do. Within the concept of intellectual investigation and moral self-discipline, every human act is either right or wrong. Society does not necessary force us to choose; yet, every act is an expression of our choice. Humanism, building on philosophy, tells us that to be free, an act must flow from the unimpeded working of the intellect and will. As noted earlier, the first choice that anyone must make is the spirit or attitude in which he or she will approach the subject or choice.

Within the intellectual pursuit of right reasoning and the larger concept of morality, three and only three choices are available. One may choose to be moral, exhibiting right or correct behavior. One may be immoral, or choosing to act contrary to right or correct behavior, and therefore at odds with the majority of society. Lastly, one may be amoral, and lack the moral judgment to discern right from wrong behavior.

An act can be seen as a unit, of measurement depicting progression toward, or away from the moral norm. It has three elements: 1) the act itself, 2) the purpose for which it was performed, and 3) the circumstances, which accompany it. In practice, these three elements form a single unit. They may be separated in the abstract, but not in concrete practice. Therefore, when reduced to action, an act is either right or wrong. It is never (which is an absolute statement) indifferent.

The laws of morality are laid down to ensure peaceful coexistence within humanity. The basic laws of morality are fixed and stable. They do not change with people, place, or time. The ultimate norm of morality is the eternal law.[91] For the humanist, this eternal law is transmitted to us through "right reasoning" and is then called the natural law. Subsequently, only human acts can then be right or wrong, because they are the only ones that can be controlled or mastered and made to conform to law. Based on our individual moral position we conform, or non-conform, to accepted principles of right or wrong, which governs our culture, group, or profession. "*When tempted, no one should say, 'God is tempting me.' For God cannot be tempted by evil, nor does he tempt anyone; but each one is tempted when by his own evil desire, he is dragged away and enticed*" (James 1:13-15).

Gross immorality can be viewed as "affected" ignorance. The person takes definite steps to avoid learning the precise moral value of an act in order to make it easier to commit the wrong. With few exceptions, every individual knows when something "feels" wrong. They already strongly suspect the moral character of an act and this suspicion steers their course of action. An individual understands that should they acquire the precise knowledge, their conscience might so disturb them that perhaps they will defer from the wrong. "*The Spirit clearly says that in later times some will abandon the faith and follow deceiving spirits and things taught by demons. Such teachings come through hypocritical liars, whose consciences have been seared as with a hot iron*" (I Timothy 4:1,2). This is not a negative attitude. It implies a distinct choice to embrace the wrongness of an act and reject the right course of action.

Lest I face accusations of not allowing for latitude in human thought, there are degrees of ignorance. That one cannot choose what they do not know is a fundamental principle of psychology and religion. "*How, then can they call on the one they have not believed in? And how can they believe in the one of whom they have not heard? And how can they hear without someone preaching to them? And how can they preach unless they are sent*" (Romans 10:14,15).

The next stage in immorality would be "vincible" ignorance. The person is unaware of the precise moral value of an act, but they are keenly aware of their deficiency. In such instances, the element of knowledge is only imperfectly present and the individual wants it to remain so. The individual knows that should they investigate they must acknowledge the wrongness of the act. The lack of effort accounts for the immoral act. Given such individuals, proper training removes this stage of immorality and denies them excuse for their actions (Colossians 3:5-10). Before moving on I need to reiterate my understanding that immoral behavior is chosen behavior, just as sin is a choice.

Amoral behavior is based in "invincible" ignorance and is defined as the state of being blamelessly unaware of the moral wrongness in an act. As an example, a person who knowingly drives a vehicle with defective brakes and has an accident is considered morally responsible for the act and at fault by the courts. A person who borrows a vehicle not knowing that the breaks are defective is not considered morally responsible for the act. This individual acted with invincible ignorance of the defective brakes.

The lack of knowledge might have resulted from one of several factors. Perhaps the person lacked the capacity to learn, or the information was in a remote place and difficult to obtain. Perhaps they were not informed. A more common cause is that there was no one to model the desired behavior, and therefore, the individual is completely unaware of the need to investigate. An amoral act lacks one of the essential elements of a responsible act, namely, sufficient moral awareness. Such absence of knowledge can normally be overcome with proper role modeling and instruction. "*The man who says, 'I know him,' but does not do what he commands is a liar, and the truth is not in him. But if anyone obeys his word God's love is truly made complete in him*" (I John 2:4-6).

There must be three things present before we can incorporate cultural, or social, morals into an ethical system that will ultimately form our value-based norms. First, there must be individual and/or social responsibility. Unless the individual and society take responsibility for their actions, to paraphrase Scripture, the individual and society labors in vain. Second, there must be individual self-discipline. By this, I mean that the individual and the society as well must willingly support and defend the laws of morality in its object, purpose, and circumstances. Last, there must be a willing internalization by the individual. The days of "don't do as I do, do as I tell you to do" are gone. The individual must make the moral position a part of their very being (I Peter 1:13-16).

International law normally allows that a person is responsible only for those actions, which they can control and make their own. In order to meet this requirement of law, the individual must freely choose to perform them. The will cannot be compelled to do (or to consent to do) anything, but there are certain impediments which can hinder the will from functioning correctly.

Impediments to Right Reasoning

The psychological impediments are habit, fear, emotion, and force. A habit simply modifies morality only when the person knows that it is a wrong habit. It is more than possible in today's societies for a young person to form habits which they do not realize are wrong. Because of the oft asked question: "Whose morals, ethics, and values do we teach," I have deliberately stayed away from the concepts of "good and evil," choosing to use the more humanistic terms of "right and wrong."

It is difficult to know that one has a wrong habit without knowing, in a general way, its strength and seriousness. This principle calls attention to the fact that the person performs several complete human acts. Each is deliberate. A habit does not necessarily mean that all acts, which flow from it, are automatic and stereotyped. One can consciously commit the wrong that flows from it automatically.

The second impediment is emotion. Most agree that the emotions are hatred, anger, sorrow, fear, love, and joy. They are part of humanity's psychic being. In themselves, they are morally indifferent and derive their quality from the way they are used. They are said to be good if used according to right reasoning in order to reach a good goal. They are said to be bad if they are used against right reasoning to reach a wrong goal. They should be kept in check by the intellect and will, but experience proves that they do have the power of asserting themselves in the disciplined as well as the undisciplined will. An individual is within intellect and will if one knowingly lets the emotion continue and increase in force. One knows what one is doing and foresees or suspects what will happen if the momentum is not stopped. It is commonly said to be a wrong act if an individual allows this type of emotion to go unchecked. "*Get rid of all bitterness, rage and anger, brawling and slander, along with every form of malice. Be kind and compassionate to one another, forgiving each other, just as in Christ God forgave you*" (Ephesians 4:31,32).

The third impediment is fear. This is perhaps the most important emotion for our discussion. The cause of fear does not have to be rational. Such fear can become irrational as in a wild animal or inanimate as a storm. The type of fear that has bearing on moral responsibility is the fear that causes one to act. The degree of influence on the performance of an act may vary greatly depending on its cause and even on the persons influenced. With the exception of war, it is rare when fear is so great that it completely impedes the intellect and will in their performance of right reasoning.

The last psychological impediment is force. The compulsion spoken of here comes from another person, for only people can compel the performance of an act. In law, it is not enough merely to attend to the degree of force exerted. One must prove the intrinsic moral value of the act resulting from the force. Some acts are forbidden even under compulsion. An act that is intrinsically and formally wrong is an attack on the social order. The disruption of that order is not in the person's intention or in the circumstances. It is rooted in the act itself. Force remains a disruption no matter where, when or by whom it is performed. Nothing external to the act of force can ever render it permissible. Force in social relationships is an extrinsic circumstance, which can never justify the intrinsic nature of an act.

The Educational Impediment

Before moving on I would add to these four, a fifth impediment being seen in society, that of "education." More to the point, the educational system that has the responsibility (to use the Biblical imperative) "*Train up a child in the way he should go and when he is old he will not depart from it*" (Proverbs 22:6). Unless I be accused of being too secular, I believe that the parental unit has the first responsibility to educate children.

Traditionally society held parents responsible to erase the deficiencies of their children in the three major aspects of their development. These aspects being physical, intellectual, and spiritual or attitudinal depending on which school of thought you embrace. All schools of humanity agree that the person suffers if the whole person is not developed. Nature law entrusts this initial unfolding to parents at a time when their young have limited or no means to provide for themselves. Each of these three aspects of a person's formation carries with it specific duties. It is considered wrong by society to neglect one aspect although the others receive proper attention.

Society expects parents to give their children an education in the required areas commensurate with their means to give and the child's ability to receive. This means to give and the ability to receive proper moral upbringing is fixed on two phases of education. The parent has the responsibility to teach, and the child has the responsibility to learn each within his or her own capabilities.

Parenting is interpreted as being a "right" to bear, as well as raise, children. Within this right, so do they have the duty to secure their welfare. One phase of this welfare is an adequate education in the social mores. The State has the right to have responsible citizens. However, it is usurpation for the State to take over the rights of qualified parents simply because they do not agree with the method being used. The State can accomplish this usurpation in two ways. First and the most direct is to take control of all public and private schools and mandate the curriculum. The second is to penalize parents who do not provide the "proper" training. Neither of these is acceptable to the American people.

When parents fail, either through design or deficiency, it falls to the society to take up the responsibility. Current news reports about school violence, teen pregnancy, and drug abuse form the perception that our public schools have failed to educate our youth in social mores. There is a growing outcry for change.

One of the changes that has come about is "Outcome Based Education" (OBE). This program is not about education, at least not in the traditional academically based, teacher-lead instruction. From this grew "Values Clarification" which was publicized as an approach to student decision-making. Values Clarification emphasized feelings and personal growth, but with a non-judgmental attitude toward self or other.[92]

Many of today's youth have a difficult time seeing any moral dimension to their actions. There are numerous reasons why, but none seem more prominent than a failed system of education that abstained from teaching the traditional moral values that have bound Americans together as a society and a culture. This type of system makes the teacher into a "facilitator" or coach in place of conducting a directed learning environment.

The military, as with many large businesses has seen fit to buy into this type of training, especially in "Consideration of Others" and "Values" based training. This decision-making replaced the more traditional "Character Guidance." This old program did not ask the soldier to reinvent the moral wheel; instead, it encouraged them to practice habits of courage, justice, and self-control. Today's young person is told to decide for him or herself what is right and what is wrong. Values education programs that are little more than courses in self-esteem further encourage this kind of moral illiteracy. These programs base themselves on the assumptions that if the individuals feel good about themselves, they will not want to do anything wrong. However, it is just as reasonable to assume that the individual who has uncritical self-regard will conclude that he or she cannot do anything wrong.

Ethical Systems

From morals, we draw the imperatives of what is right or wrong in behavior to others. In ethics, we form those moral imperatives into a system of specific choices. Based on our individual moral position we conform, or non-conform, to accepted principles of right or wrong. An example of an Army ethical system would be the West Point Credo. "I will not lie, I will not cheat, I will not steal, I will not tolerate those who do." Taken individually, they are four separate moral imperatives. However, when combined they form an ethical system that provides an accepted code of behavior, which leads to a value called "Honor."

Any study of ethical systems should incorporate two noteworthy features. First, it should present each ethical system in three ways: 1) by stating the moral principle(s) involved; 2) by discussing the ethical system in an explanatory manner; and 3) by giving an example of how the moral principle(s) should be followed in an actual situation. Second, the instructor's emphasis should be on principles and definitions, which are the very framework of any branch of learning, and are especially important in moral based education.

Society has certain powers, which are properly used only when their use conforms to the laws of morality. If these powers are used in any other way, they are used improperly. Their use can never be indifferent. The conformity or nonconformity with moral laws is rooted in the way the society uses those laws. If, as example, society makes the moral imperative that lying is wrong, then lying is always wrong. It remains wrong even when used for a right reason or to achieve a greater right. Every moral act is performed in a definite set of circumstances. They give the act its individuality and precise ethical character. These circumstances are over and above the basic moral act. There are right acts (lying to save a life) which are wrong if not done. In like manner there are socially perceived right acts (lying to cover your friend's unauthorized absence from work) that are wrong if they are done.

The correct application of an ethical system insures a true appraisal of an act. Difficulty arises because the act has two directly opposite effects, one right and the other wrong. If it is a person's intent to tell a "half" truth in order to protect someone, in effect it becomes a "whole" lie. The lie therefore is wrong, although it was done for a right or wrong reason. An act must be judged in its entirety. Since an ethical system can either preserve or disrupt the moral order, it too must be considered right or wrong. There is normally no difficulty in seeing why one is responsible for an act that's wrong effect is wrong within it. Neither is it difficult to see the responsibility of one who commits an act whose only effect is wrong. However, there are times when it is not so easy to determine the permissibility of committing an act, especially an act, which has two effects, one right and the other wrong.

A Concluding Note on the Problem

It is certainly no secret that many courses offered or required in certain curricula are dangerous to the moral life of the students. These courses are deceptively labeled "objective" or "scientific" but are anything but that. Many courses in comparative religion, history, philosophy, economics, natural and social science are often studied from texts with an amoral coloring or which receive this coloring when they pass through the hands of certain instructors.

The moral education of young people has a positive and negative phase. Positively speaking, an individual's moral education must parallel his or her secular education. On the negative side, one cannot base education on that which does not exist. To call attention to the political corruption of his time, Diogenes lit a lantern and went out to look for an honest man. Someone cynically said that if he were alive today he would re-light his lantern in the search for an educated man.

There are few words in the English language more misunderstood than the word "education." It consists of more than sharp pencils, stacks of books, scores of lectures and slides culminated in a dusty file. True education not only answers the question "what?" but also the question "why?" It not only deals with cold facts but also with fertile ideas. While explaining the meaning of life, it does not neglect to explain the mystery of death. How many times has a young person attended Sunday school, hear that Jesus loves them, and leave having been bored to tears, and has learned nothing of moral or ethical value?

The structure and realities of Christianity must set the framework for any serious discussion of the moral problem. It is not; so much, that absolute moral imperatives are relevant to the teaching of values. Rather, humanity acts in a variety of structures, which in turn evoke an immense variety of codes of behavior and conduct. The central question is what does the education leadership think of the endless variety of human situations? By example, a Superintendent of Education for South Carolina publicly stated that homosexuals not only have a legal right to teach in public schools but also have a moral right to do so. On what morality does she base her opinion? Add to this the self-righteous attitude of the modern homosexual educators, and, what is the youth of America to believe? Most of the time given to moral education is now being spent, not with the family, but with the education system and the social group, both of which society now gives if not verbal, certainly tacit approval.

By example I submit a part of a letter written in *The State*, the local paper in Columbia, SC: "The families of gay and lesbian couples are not the cause of moral decay in our country. Gays and lesbians can be just as moral as straight people. My partner and I both attend Mass every Sunday, tithe 10 percent of our income so our church might do good works, strive within our local community to see that others are clothed and fed and love our enemies as much as we love our neighbors. We try to follow the teachings and example of our Lord and the spirit of the homes in which we were reared... However, as elementary and middle school educators, my partner and I can both attest to the weakening of the family support system, especially in the last 10 years..."[93]

Certainly, from the sound and subject of the letter one is led to believe that this God fearing, Christian couple would be just the type of people who we would want teaching our children. Do they not live by and show the same virtues that the Christian faith demands? Doesn't the church, at least by the letter, accept these two as members in good standing? Or do they? What do they teach the children of these weaken heterosexual families with regard to family morals? The message that both the education and secular systems attest to is that homosexuals are normal people who have as good, if not a better, lifestyle than do "straight" families.

In our drive to honor the Constitution, we have legislated morality, or more to the point, the lack of it. We as a society have given permission for homosexuals, and pedophiles, both male and female, to corrupt our young people (twenty years and under), and have turned America down the path to Sodom and Gomorrah. "*...Get out of our way, they replied. And they said, 'This fellow came here as an alien, and now he wants to play the judge'*" (Genesis 19:9). As if that were not bad enough, the very churches of Christendom which should be protesting the loudest are either strangely silent or on the side of immorality.

Society and not the individual has the right to dictate that certain people will not hold certain jobs for the good of society, even though the individual may be refused certain "rights." Judge Bork once said something to the effect that "when you give one group a right, you inherently take a right away from another group." A thief cannot work in a bank; a sexual predator cannot work in a safe house; a pedophile cannot work in a day care center, why do we open our schools and our churches to such people? And should one think that I go to far astray, the homosexual community began its forward progress toward full acceptance by aligning themselves with the civil rights movement, even though the civil rights people did not want them to. The homosexual is now striving for full recognition as a respectable lifestyle, and the pedophile is doing the same thing with the homosexual movement, even though the homosexuals protest such joining of agendas.

Questions for Consideration and Discussion

The point of our problem is that American society is morally complex, probably far beyond many other countries. In effect, varied social systems appear to create moralities of their own or at least moralities not identical in immediate application with the "pure" truths of social ethics as a whole. All of this points out the profound nature of the moral problem in America. Whose morals, whose ethics, and whose values do we teach?

For the Christian the answer should be the Judaic/Christian values of the Bible. Far too many churches are attempting to reach the new generations by hiring a minister that is closer in age to those they seek to reach, or by offering events that will emotionally lift the youth to a higher plane of morality. As with days of old it is not the messenger that will bring them to a distinctive moral lifestyle it is the message. The only absolute to the questions is that you cannot teach Christian values without first having taught Christian morals and ethic.

1. What are the individual's, the congregation's, and the church leaders' morality based on? How did they arrive at that conclusion?
2. What recent local, government, or world events have stimulated discussion and how have they assaulted the collective senses of moral outrage, or have they?
3. What are the individual's, the congregation's, the church leadership's thoughts on Christians keeping their faith out of the public and political domains? Does the church encourage

involvement in the political arena or shy away from public and political discussions for fear of violating separation of church and state?

4. Does the pastor from the pulpit and the teachers in the Sunday school rooms and leaders of the Bible studies stress the importance of moral-filled education, in the church, in the home, in the school, at work?
5. What basis of knowledge do the individuals draw upon to determine if something is right or wrong? How do the church leaders assist the congregation in making correct Biblically based decisions on such matters?
6. What are the church leaders', the lay leadership's, and the congregation's understanding of value judgments? How do they relate them not only to church business, but in their daily lives as well?
7. What is the church's understanding of the moral and ethical conduct that God provided us via the Deuteronomic laws? Why do they exist and how do we use them in modern times?
8. What studies has the church offered the leadership both pastoral and laity in trying to understand humanities interaction with itself? What does the Bible have to say about our interactions?
9. What does the Bible have to say about how to preserve moral principles and ethical systems? Does the pastor preach on such topics from the pulpit?
10. What types of discussions or classes are available to the youth of the church? How often are such classes repeated? What does the youth of the church think about subjects such as principles, ethics, and morals?
11. Has the church leadership come to a consensus on whom they are trying to reach and why? Have they set goals and objectives in teaching morals to the youth of the church?
12. Does the church affirm the parental unit as having the first responsibility to educate children in the church, in the community and the nation? How does the church define "parental unit?"

13. Does the church offer classes on ethical and moral parenting to married couples, singles with children, and divorced parents?
14. Does the church leadership encouraged parents, singles, and the youth to practice habits of courage, justice, and self-control at home, at school, and in the work place?

RELIGIOUS SYMBOLISM

From Humble Beginnings

Which came first, the chicken or the egg? The reader will almost immediately recognize the question as a philosophical quandary that children used to and still do play with today. However, Paul said: "*When I was a child, I talked like a child, I thought like a child, I reasoned like a child. When I became a man, I put childish ways behind me*" (I Corinthians 13:11). Wouldn't it be wonderful if the citizens of America could make such a saintly statement today? The battle lines are drawn and there seems to be a mutual understanding by all sides that there is to be no quarter given, no reciprocal understanding reached, and no peace accord that would allow all sides to save face and faith.

This declaration of war by all parties involved would be so much easier if we only belonged to one side of the other. I have spent my entire adult life defending this nation and a good part of that time presenting the Christian faith to the men and women of American's Armed Forces. I love my God, my faith, my denomination, and my country. I don't want to see my country torn apart, nor separated from the belief in God that caused people to risk it all to find a new place where they could worship God, each in their own way, nor do I want to see my faith persecuted. Yet, in the emotions of the movement there seems to be no room for negotiations. The scarlet flag has been raised over the bell tower and the "Duegello" has been sounded.[94]

How did we get to this impasse? How did a nation born out of the search for religious freedom reach a point where it is trying to regulate the very freedoms that we were founded upon, and so many have died to defend? Many an early colonist was motivated to leave England, and other parts of Europe, and seek religious freedom elsewhere. At the time of the Constitution's writing, many Americans were acutely aware of the dangers inherent to a state sanctioned church, with its mandated *Book of Common Prayer.*[95] The first amendment was written in such a way that hopefully it would guarantee through the years to come that the government would never be used to support, regulate or control any religion or the practice there of.

Where did those grand ideas of religious freedom go? The U.S. Supreme Court seems to have interpreted the Constitution as requiring a complete separation of church and state. How did we let liberal secular, and in some cases godless lawyers reach the Supreme Court and re-interpret the Constitution as granting freedom "from" religion?

How have we allowed secular historians to destroy the reputations of the founding fathers, misinterpret their ideas, and deny us our heroes? Depending on which source you choose to use, the majority of signers to the Declaration of Independence were deeply loyal Christians. The numbers range from fifty-two Christians and three Deist, to forty-nine Christian, three Deist, and three unknown.[96] Patrick Henry's speech before the Continental Congress seems to have disappeared from the history books, as have many other notable speeches. We still can find the "I know not what course others may take but as for me, give me liberty, or give me death" part of the speech, but now gone are the foregoing words "Forbid it almighty God."

Our founding fathers were not perfect, but they did put together one of the greatest governing documents the world has ever seen. I believe that even an honest but cursory review of history will show that both the Bible and the Christian faith were foundational in our educational, political, judicial, and social institutes. These are certainly a lot of questions to begin a chapter with, but to add one more question: where are the answers?[97]

In our humble beginnings as a nation, history proves out that we were for the most part Christian. There were among those colonists of early America those who practiced the Jewish faith. If there were others who practiced other faiths or did not believe at all, they certainly were of a small number and kept a low profile. In the Revolutionary War there was even a Jewish chaplain among the small band of patriots striving to sever our governmental cords with England. In a process, which violated the very roots of Christianity and the American concept that "all men were created equal," slaves were brought to America. Those slaves brought with them the religions of their counties of origin. We fought a civil war in which brother fought against brother to prove that these truths were now and forever to be held self-evident.

However as the nation grew and as we reached out to the rest of the world calling for them to send us "your huddled masses yearning to be free," more and more non-Christians and non-Jews began to arrive in large numbers; among them were the Chinese who were instrumental in providing the labor that built the railroads that crossed our great divide. With these new arrivals came their faith. With the ending of the First World War, and with it the dream that we were, as a race, becoming more moral and that the inhumanity to mankind would soon be ended, came a new kind of academic theologian who after much study proclaimed that God was, if not dead, certainly precariously terminal.

Prayer in School

These United States became one of the most religiously diverse countries in the world. We were proud of our heritage of religious freedom and we wanted to share our legacy of religious freedom and tolerance with the peoples of the world. The modern struggle for religious identity and symbolism did not begin with the name of Jesus. It did not begin with the battle for the right to post the Hebraic Ten Commandments. It began with the battle for the minds of the children and with the debate over prayer in schools. America's increasingly religious diversity is the obvious explanation given for most of the lawsuits that have been filed. The religious, or lack of religious, incentive was not as obvious to the general public when there weren't as many religious minorities.

Even into the late fifties, public schools were still holding plays in which the children would dress up as Indians and pilgrims and give thanks to God for having provided them with such bountiful blessings. Students would to the joyful laughter of parents and friends re-enact the Christmas story of Mary, Joseph, and the infant Jesus, with the class clown running around in a sheep costume yelling "Baaaaa" at the top of his lungs. Each day would begin with the Pledge of Allegiance offered either by the principle or one of the students. A prayer or moment of silence was often included in the homeroom activities.

Both in the school and on the playground every interaction of students was an opportunity for teaching morals and ethics. There was the occasional fistfight, but both parties were required to shake hands afterwards and put the matter behind them. Some knifes were seen at school carried by the school hoodlums, and some of them were Boy Scout knifes with all the attachments, brought for "show and tell." Guns were never seen, not even in the rough and tough downtown high school. No student in his or her right mind would dare talk back to a teacher. The teacher punished students and the appropriate note was sent home to the parents, and God have mercy on your soul if you had to be sent to the principal's office. Whether the statistics are correct or not, it was just about the time that prayer was removed from school that a moral erosion began to show itself in the schools and in the home. The child in pre-puberty crisis would have to wait until he or she got home to have their faith reinforced that God was still in charge and everything would be all right.

During this time period the New York State Board of Regents published a "Statement on Moral and Spiritual Training in the Schools." The Board of Education of Hyde Park, New York, instructed their school principal to have a small portion of the prayer recited by one of the students in the presence of a teacher at the beginning of each day. That portion of the statement was not particularly Christian in its reading. It acknowledged an "Almighty God," a single, monotheistic God to whom one could pray for "blessings upon us, our parents, our teachers and our country."

Certainly such a prayer would not offend any Christian? Most Deists would not have thought to find the prayer offensive, and although one would have thought the Jewish community would not have minded, there were several Jewish groups that filed "Amicus Curiae"—friend of the court, briefs for the prayer to be ruled unconstitutional.

The main problem with such a prayer is that the Atheists acknowledged no awareness of God; Agnostics were still undecided about what or who God was; Buddhists had no knowledge of a personal God; secular humanists based their beliefs and practices on secular deliberation; and many so called religious liberals opposed any secular show of religion on principle. "*But when you pray, do not be like the hypocrites, for they love to pray standing in the synagogues and on the street corners to be seen of men... When you pray, go into your room, close the door and pray to your Father, who is unseen*" (Matthew 6:5,6). I believe that those who use this verse as reason for no prayers in public schools miss the reason the hypocrites were praying in public.

Of all the families in the Number 9 school district the parents of at least ten students were offended and sought relief by the courts even though the students were to be allowed to either step outside of the classroom or simply remain respectfully quiet with no consequences to be applied to those students who for religious belief or practice did not agree with the prayer. While they failed in both the state court and the court of appeals, the U.S. Supreme Court agreed with the parents and apparently ruled that all state-mandated prayers in public schools were unconstitutional.[98]

The gates were open, and those seeking to end any and all religious symbolism in public were now free to flood the courts with briefs denouncing this display or that resemblance of Godliness in public. They did so because now they believed that they had a good chance of winning, and so far history has proven their view correct. However did the U.S. Supreme Court actually prohibit prayer in school, or even in public, as some people seem to believe? The answer is a resounding no! It has clarified, and in some cases may have even written law rather than just interpreted it, but they did not end prayer either in school or in public.

The cyber-space net is teeming with conservative Christian sites that declare that we must battle to the bitter end to restore prayer in our schools, that the government cannot and should not legislate morality. This seems to be a strange metamorphosis for Christians seeing that just a few years ago, the liberal and immoral groups were bellowing the same battle cry. The thought is just as wrong today as it was then because governments can and do legislate morality. However, the government has seen fit to offer an olive branch to those groups that so desperately want prayer back in school.

Most student-led, special interest, and non-curriculum groups and clubs must be allowed to organize in most public schools. Their right to assemble is "generally" protected under a federal law—The Equal Access Act, (20 U.S.C. Chapter 52, Subchapter VIII >4071-74).[99] I have included the site where those interested can read the act for themselves. It is not a long act as governmental acts go, however I only quote that portion necessary to discuss the subject matter.

> It shall be unlawful for any public secondary school which receives Federal financial assistance and which has a limited open forum… A public secondary school has a limited open forum whenever such school grants an offering to or opportunity... to meet on school premises during non-instructional time.[100]

I use the qualifier "generally" because the school has the right under the act to elect to have no open forum. In other words, they allow no outside school group to use school property, for any reason. Conservative Christian groups seeking to allow students to organize religious clubs in public secondary schools originally were very active in promoting the act, the irony is that this same act now provides the same access for students who wish to organize gay, lesbian, and bisexual support groups.

Although this chapter is titled "Religious Symbolism," I'm going to defer any discussion on the other components of the school prayer debate, i.e. Bible in schools, prayer in hallways, students handing out religious materials, praying in the school cafeteria, religious text on clothing, and religious jewelry. For those who are concerned they can look up "Tinker versus Des Moines." Justice Fortas in delivering the opinion for the Supreme Court stated that neither "the student or the teacher shed their constitutional rights to freedom of speech or expression at the schoolhouse gate."[101]

The battle lines drawn and the sides chosen have resulted in churches finding their congregations split on the issue. It is becoming increasingly complicated to get Christians to present a public front on the more important issues of accepting Jesus as Lord and master, and living a moral life acceptable to God when the public sees us pitting ourselves against one another, even though it may be done in fulfillment of Scripture. "*...a man's enemies will be the members of his own household*" (Matthew 10:36).

Praying at Public Functions

I hope that the reader has noticed that I did not title this subsection "Public Prayer." There is nothing in the law or elsewhere that restricts any person, citizen or otherwise, from praying anywhere, at anytime, in any manner they so choose. There have been rulings and lawsuits and the threat of lawsuits to end Christian prayers in relationship to governmental gatherings. There was even a lawsuit pending seeking to stop the President from having a prayer during his inauguration (it failed).

Most legislative bodies, state and government, open their sessions with prayer. The concern of those who denounce the name of Jesus being used in those prayers state that their intent is not to offend those members of the legislative body that are not Christians. Most legislative bodies have developed guidelines for the guest chaplain of the day who offers prayers for the governing body, the state, or the nation. Most have drawn their guidelines from the National Conference for Community and Justice.

The National Conference for Community and Justice (NCCJ) was founded in 1927 as the National Conference of Christians and Jews. However, in 1990 it evolved into a secular humanist relations' organization whose purposed purpose is to fight bias, bigotry and racism in America. Their expanded mission now includes gender and sexual orientation, and the NCCJ has gone on public record as being against the ruling that barred homosexuals from being Boy Scout Leaders. Based on what I have been able to read on the organization, Christian and Jewish concerns have been replaced by purely secular humanistic endeavors.

These guidelines call for prayer that: 1) seek a higher common denominator without compromise of conscience; 2) call upon God on behalf of the group and avoid individual petitions; 3) uses vocabulary that allows persons of different faiths to give assent to what is prayed for; 4) use inclusive terms for the deity rather than proper names; and 5) opening or closing the prayer with nebulous terms such as "All Mighty God, Creator, In Thy name, or simply Amen.[102] I find it interesting that the guidelines seek to protect the compromise of conscience, yet requires that the name of Jesus, or any other deity, be omitted even when it is a matter of individual conscience requiring that one pray in the name of Jesus, yet at the same time thinks that prayer should "remain faithful to the purposes of acknowledging divine presence."[103] What about the atheist or the agnostic who may be in the gathering; won't they be offended by the prayer, any prayer?

I can find no argument for disallowing Christian prayers in governmental gatherings, and for those dear souls who have no problem watering down their prayers to exclude their god, not I, but the Scriptures say:

> Live such good lives among the pagans that, though they accuse you of doing wrong, they may see your good deed and glorify God on the day he visits us. Submit yourself for the Lord's sake to every authority instituted among men… For it is God's will that by doing good you should silence the ignorant talk of foolish men. (I Peter 2:12-15)

If you can pray in such a manner, then do so, and if not then respectfully decline, and tell the group why. Don't take the invitation with the intent of calling upon the name of Jesus if you have been asked not to.

> Do not lie to each other, since you have taken off your old self with its practices and have put on the new self, which is being renewed in knowledge in the image of its Creator. Here there is no Greek or Jew, circumcised or uncircumcised, barbarian, Scythinan, slave or free, but Christ is all, and is in all. (Colossians 3:9-11)

However, I have been talking about governmental gatherings, not public gatherings. That is a different matter altogether.

> "On the contrary, we speak as men approved by God to be entrusted with the gospel. We are not trying to please men but God, who tests our hearts… God is our witness. We were not looking for praise from men, not from you or anyone else" (I Thessalonians 2:4-6).

Whenever someone asks me to pray at a social gathering, I make the common assumption that they know that I am a Christian and will give a Christian (Christ-like) prayer. "*Salvation is found in no one else, for there is no other name under heaven given to men by which we must be saved*" (Acts 2:12).

Prayer has been defined as the raising of one's heart and mind to God and to ask Him for benefits which God is predisposed to grant. There are undeniable elements that one implies when offering prayers to God. First, an individual who prays to God not only recognizes the existence and attributes of God, but also acknowledges God's presence in his or her life. By the offering of a prayer anywhere, anytime, and under any circumstances an individual confesses his or her dependence on God. Prayer is an acknowledgement that we have nothing that God has not given us. My God is an awesome God, an omnipotent God, a God that has "*made this Jesus, whom you crucified* (in word and deed) *both Lord and Christ*" (Acts 2:36). I do not pray in the name of Jesus to be an offense nor a stumbling stone, but to give glory to my savior. However, "*the message of the cross is foolishness to those who are perishing, but to us who are being saved it is the power of God*" (I Corinthians 1:18).

The most faultless of prayers is the Lord's Prayer, the "Our Father" prayer, and it is essentially a prayer of petition—"*give us this day our daily bread, and forgive*" (Matthew 6:9-13). The general framework of the prayer gives us four elements of a proper prayer. By adoration, we acknowledge God's supreme regime over His creation; by thanksgiving, we express our gratitude to God for all that He has done for us; by petition, we seek to enlist God's help in facilitating our progress as children of God to be more like Him; and by contrition we seek to repair the separation that our sins have caused between God and us.

Contrary to many beliefs God is not a heavenly kite that can be drawn this way or that with just the pull of a stringy prayer. He is not a white bearded grandfather figure who has nothing better to do than wait for his grandchildren to call out "what have you brought me this time." And, in like manner prayer is not just an addition for a social function that really has no more meaning than to help us to recognize the pluralism of our society. The fundamental purpose of prayer is and has remained to obtain grace, which, for the Christian, should be used to provide the means of salvation.

What are we teaching our children and our congregations when we support not praying in the name of Jesus in public, so as not to be intentionally divisive to those faith groups different than our own? How can we stand up in the pulpit on Sunday and proclaim that Jesus is the way the truth and the life just to go out into the world and deny that we know Him? It has reached a point in many congregations where they end their worship services with a universal, all-inclusive term as if they might offend some visitor to the church.

Praying in the Name of Jesus

I made a pledge, a vow if you wish, a long time ago not to be ashamed of the name of Jesus. This was partly done because of my study of Scripture. "*If anyone is ashamed of me and my words in this adulterous and sinful generation, the Son of Man will be ashamed of him when he comes in his Father's glory with the holy angels*" (Mark 8:38). I certainly would not want to spend my life in service to Jesus, to have him ashamed of me at His coming. But more importantly, I do it because I believe that Jesus is the Son of God and the Savior of all those who accept Him as such. If as I believe that Jesus is the Christ, the Messiah, then shouldn't I want to share that great news with others?

> But I have had God's help to this very day, and so I stand here and testify to small and great alike. I am saying nothing beyond what the prophets and Moses said would happen—that the Christ would suffer and, as the first to rise from the dead, would proclaim light to his own people and to the Gentiles. (Acts 26:22,23)

I mentioned earlier that in the twenty-seven plus years that I have served as both a pastor and a chaplain, I have never had a single person outside the Christian faith take me to task for using the name of Jesus to close my prayers at a social or religious gathering, and on one occasion I even had a Jewish Chaplain defend me.[104] Of all the senior chaplains that have admonished me about being insensitive to those of differing faiths, only the "Christian" chaplains have advised that I not use the name of Jesus in my prayers. One senior Christian (?) Chaplain even went so far as to tell new chaplains that if they couldn't pray without using the name of Jesus, then maybe they didn't belong in the chaplaincy. I hope that I do not have to use the name of Jesus to show that I am a Christian. I would hope that my lifestyle proclaims it more loudly than any words could ever do. I certainly understand that it is not the use of the name that brings salvation but belief in the one who carries it.

However, somewhere along the line Christianity has allowed a cheap Gospel to enter into the picture. Preachers and Sunday school teachers have all proclaimed that if you will just accept Jesus, all your troubles will be over, and eternal happiness will be yours in this life and the next. As a result some Christians are so badly informed of what the scriptures say, and their understanding of the nature of God is so distorted, that they believe that God hasn't placed any restrictions or requirements upon them at all.

If this were the case then why did Paul list those deeds committed by humanity that would exclude them from the kingdom (I Corinthians 6:9,10; Galatians 5:19,21)? Why is the Lord Jesus going to tell those who had prophesied in His name and driven out demons in His name and performed many miracles all in His name that they were to leave His sight because He doesn't know them (Matthew 7: 22,23)? Nowhere in this discussion should someone seek to infer that I am casting doubt on the Biblical concept of Justification by faith alone. I am not advocating Jesus plus something, and I am not endorsing works. I simply believe that it is time that we tell people that with salvation come responsibilities. Not because we have to but because we are new creatures and we want to do the will of our Father.

Does any of this sound alien to you? Do you have any problems with what I've been saying? Well, don't feel bad; there are a lot of Christians who don't believe that we should have to share the

Gospel with the outside world. There are others who very piously note that we shouldn't hit people over the head with the Gospel as though it were a ninety-five-pound Gutenberg Bible. I agree that we should not shove the Gospel down people's throats, but simply proclaiming the truth of our beliefs shouldn't be viewed as radical, and it definitely should not be unconstitutional.

The Ten Commandments

As much as some Christians would love to believe, God did not give Moses the Ten Commandments for America. We, as a nation, were not promised anything that God did not promise any other peoples who called on His name. "*If my people who are called by my name will humble themselves and pray and seek my face and turn from their wicked ways, then will I hear from heaven and will forgive their sin and will heal their land*" (II Chronicles 7:14).

The battle for publicly displaying of the Ten Commandments began when Christians opting to support a half-truth in order to facilitate a belief that the Ten Commandments were a righteous set of precepts for all peoples, and that America was to be equated with the righteous peoples of God of the Old Testament, took a stand based more on emotion than fact.

The Ten Commandments were created within an entirely different civilization and mindset, and with very distinctive expectations for the people that God chose to call His own. "*And God spoke all these words: 'I am the Lord your God, who brought you out of Egypt, out of the land of slavery. You shall have no other gods before me*" (Exodus 20:1,2). It was to be a theocracy, and only after the people cried unto the Lord to give them a king to lead them like the other nations was there appointed a secular government (I Samuel 8:6). Even then the king was to rule Israel as God's anointed and the church and the state were to be united with the religious leaders and the king as joint caretakers of God's legacy.

Here for Christians enters the half-truth. There is a disparity between what the Ten Commandments actually say and what the public assumes they say. Ask most people and they will incorrectly state that all of the Commandments have to do with moral behavior in society. In reality, the first four commandments are religious in nature, uniquely related to Judaism, and through Judaism to Christianity. "*You shall no other gods before me... You shall not make for yourself an idol... You shall not misuse the name of the Lord your God... Remember the Sabbath day by keeping it holy*" (Exodus 20:1-8). These commandments are offensive to the followers of many other religions; among these are Buddhist, Hindu, Wicca, and those who profess no religious affiliation whatsoever.

I once had the unfortunate duty to talk to one of my enlisted brothers about allowing a Satanist to have his satanic bible in the van while he pulled duty. I asked the Christian soldier if he studied his Bible while he was on duty, and he replied that he did. I then had to tell him that the other soldier had the same right, and that he must be allowed to bring his "godless" bible into the van or the Christian brother would have to leave off bring his "Holy" Bible into the van. The soldier all but called me a heretic. Do I believe in the satanic bible? No! However, as a former enlisted soldier who has seen combat, as a chaplain ministering to the soldiers, and as a citizen, I am bound to "defend the Constitution of the United States of America against all enemies both foreign and domestic."[105] This includes the right to worship, or not worship, as one sees fit, regardless of my personal beliefs. If we can deny the right to worship to one group today, then we can deny it to Christians tomorrow, and all those other faith groups would do well to realize that if they can deny it to Christians, they are next on the list.

All United States government offices to include public schools, and their governing boards, are required by law to remain neutral on religious matters. What this means to the average citizen is that the government will not promote one religion over another, or promote a religious lifestyle over a secular one. In like manner this also means that the government is not supposed to promote a secular lifestyle either. Posting the first four commandments clearly promotes both Judaism and Christianity. We as Christians need to be up front and acknowledge this truth.

Posting the Ten Commandments and proclaiming that they are intended to promote correct moral behavior in our society is a half-truth, told as a whole truth, and ethically that makes it a whole lie.[106] Were our secular laws based on the Ten Commandments? Yes, so were most of the civil laws of Europe. However, to be constitutional the Ten Commandments cannot be posted in their totality. Whether we should seek to post the other six in public schools and offices, is a debate that is best carried on with a cool head, and a calm heart.

Confronting the Public on Christian Beliefs

For far too many Christians' consensus is next to godliness, and conflict means spiritual confrontation that should be avoided in public. I do not consider myself a rabble rouser; however I have always believed that while agreement is wonderful and certainly to be found within my comfort zone, sometimes conflict is better than consensus. As a pastor I have often had to remind my congregation that my goal, and the goal of church leaders, should not necessarily be getting everyone to agree with all that is said and done. There have been times when the church has agreed, and everyone has been wrong! I have also had occasion to learn that most of the time many of the people are hoping, nay praying, that someone will have the courage to speak up.

Concerning the putting forth of Christian ideals in public forums, I have always strived to make sure that three principles were present in my debate. First, is it Christian? Is what I am about to do or say Biblically based? Is it not only consistent with the Bible, but would it be something that the humanist public would expect from a follower of Christ? Second, is it true? Is it honest? Is what I am seeking to present to America something that will improve our condition, or am I just jousting with windmills? Third, is it significant? Is this something that is truly worth fighting for? Often in the military I have had to caution young chaplains to pick their battleground carefully, and choose which swords are worth falling on. If you fight every fight, or the wrong fight, you soon lose your credibility, and with it the right to be a prophetic voice crying in the wilderness.

We as Christians should never seek to instigate heated confrontation. The public debates over the legal definition of what constitutes a family, abortion, gay rights, governments funding of pornographic art, and the ever-present religion, or the purging of religion and religious symbols, from government buildings and public schools is going to be with us for a long, long time. I am not saying that we should not protest, however I am saying that it should be a legal, non-violent, well planned, and "Universal" Christian protest. I have never been able to get a good grip on just how politically involved a Christian should be when it comes to protest, yet I do believe that our voice should be heard and our vote counted.

Someone called it a war of cultures. I'm not sure if it is a cultural war as much as it is a war against evil. "*For our struggle is not against flesh and blood, but against the rulers, against the authorities, against the powers of this dark world and against the spiritual forces of evil in the heavenly realms*" (Ephesians 6:12). I grew up in the slums of Oklahoma City, and I was a part of a subculture that was at war with everyone. We won neither the battle nor the war, as the homeless, the poor, the disenfranchised are still with us. A lesson that the Army learned, and often has had to relearn is that you cannot fight everyone and on every front. You have to pick what you're willing to fight for, and where you will put your resources in order to bring the most effective fire on the enemy, thereby defeating them.

What should be our goal, and what should our struggle be against? Theologically, Christians are to be a people who are "called out" of humanity to continue the mission and the life's work of Jesus. Although we are called to be the salt of the world and a light shining in darkness, our program for both the church and the world should be the program that Jesus gave us. However, this does not mean that we should forcefully pursue impressing the entire agenda on the public at large. "*Do not give dogs what is sacred; do not throw your pearls to pigs. If you do, they may trample them under their feet and then turn and tear you to pieces*" (Matthew 7:22). We cannot and should not expect the public at large, those dear souls who for whatever reason have elected to remain outside the family of God, to endorse every concept that is securely ingrained in Scriptures and the Judeo-Christian life. By activism that is often inadequately conceived and raucously promoted, we have created an image of Christians as being prejudiced and a hateful people.

I believe with all my heart that both abortion and homosexuality are Biblically, morally, culturally, and inherently wrong. I believe that whenever and wherever possible we should stand shoulder-to-shoulder with other Christians and publicly declare what and for whom we are for. "*But if serving the Lord seems undesirable to you, then choose for yourselves this day whom you will serve, whether the gods your forefathers served... But as for me and my household, we will serve the Lord*" (Joshua 24:15). We cannot be of the world and separated from the world at the same time. Jesus said of such trials and attempts "*No one can serve two masters. Either he will hate the one and love the other, or he will be devoted to the one and despise the other*" (Matthew 6:24). You are either for what is Godly or for what is humanistic. I cannot find anywhere in Scripture where you can be for something that has been declared ungodly by Scripture and at the same time proclaim yourself to be a devoted follower of the Lord Jesus Christ.

I was reminded that such attempts to be of, and at the same time separate from, the world can lead to heart rending pain. I was told the story of an individual who had been a Christian for many years and was in fact considered one of the leaders of his church. In a conversation with a long time friend at his place of work he mentioned that he was a Christian and had just been given additional responsibilities at his church. His friend looked at him and without missing a beat said, "I would have never taken you for a Christian." I was told that the individual while hurt by the remarks vowed to never again live the kind of life that does not identify him as a Christian.

I am not saying that the church or the people should become isolationist in their earthly endeavors. For the Christian a simple reading of Ephesians 6, verse 10 and following, should bring the understanding that in putting on the whole armor of God there is no back armor. We are to be a people who neither retreat nor run from the earthly battles. But if we are to fight the good fight then let's do it within God's redeeming love for all humanity. Rather then alienating people just for the sake of alienation, let's focus on the Gospel message. Let's focus on the transforming truth that Jesus came to give life to sinners regardless of their political affiliation, and yes, even their personal lifestyles. Denounce the sin, but do it in a way that does not denounce the sinner, nor limits the opportunity to share Christ with those whose lifestyle we reject.

Intelligent Design

The first five words of the Bible, "*In the beginning, God created*" (Genesis 1:1), are a statement of faith; all that follows is our attempt to understand the grand design of all creation, and of the God who created it. God not only breathed into man so that he became a living soul, he gave inspiration and credence to the Bible and to the men who wrote it. Do I believe that Creationism should be taught to our children and also offered as an alternative to evolution or possible an elective in public school? YES! However, when all around us are using any and all devices to put their agendas before our young, are we justified in doing the same thing? Can we use the same devices and half-truths that they use, and if we do, what is the difference between them and us? Isn't "Intelligent Design" just another way of saying "In the beginning, God created…?"

I can think of no better words to close this chapter with then those from a C.S. Lewis novel in which a senior demon gives advice to a junior one:

> What we want, if men become Christians at all, is to keep them in the state of mind I call "Christianity and." You know—Christianity and the Crisis, Christianity and the New Psychology, Christianity and the New Order, Christianity and Spelling Reform [Dare I add, Christianity and Intelligent Design]. If they must be Christians, let them at least be Christians with a difference. Substitute for the faith itself some fashion with a Christian coloring...[107]

Questions for Consideration and Discussion

It is not that we do not need to voice our concerns about those issues that are destroying the moral fiber of our nation, but we ought to be able to do it as one voice. The threat from within the church is that we are losing the ability to be of one mind. "*Your attitude should be the same as that of Christ Jesus*" (Philippians 2:5). When the children of God cannot agree, then more and more Americans are going to feel justified in having nothing to do with Christians and their divided Church.

1. What are the historical roots of your church, your denomination? Was your denomination begun here in America or was it transported from another country? How has its tradition, by-laws, or dogma changed from the original church or denomination?
2. Do the church leadership and members understand the difference between what is American, and what is Godly? When was the last time a study of religious freedom was conducted? What were the resources used to guide the discussions?
3. What is the church's understanding of prayer and when was the last time a Bible study on prayer conducted? What are the differences between public, governmental, and social prayers?

4. Has the church given any thought to what guide lines to use when praying in public? Has there been discussion on such guidelines to ensure that they are Biblically based?
5. Using Matthew 6:1-14 as a base of study, what are the elements of pray that your study group found in the Scriptures? What do you think of when the term "model prayer" is used? Based on Jesus' conversation with His disciples, how them should we pray, what should be our intent, and why?
6. Why pray in the name of Jesus? When, if ever, should we forgo praying in the name of Jesus? Does our behavior in the presence of nonbelievers match our behavior when we pray? How are they different?
7. Has your church ever conducted a study on the Ten Commandments? When were the Ten Commandments given to the Israelites, where and under what conditions? What do you think God's intent was in giving them to Moses to give to the people? Why should we follow their teachings, and what is the relationship of the Ten Commandments to the general public?
8. What are the differences between a secular and a religious lifestyle? How do the Ten Commandments relate to both secular and religious behavior?
9. What are your church's concepts on consensus, conflict, and spiritual confrontation with the general public? How do they differ from your own concepts, or do they? What does the Bible have to say about spiritual conflict between Christians and others?
10. Using the military concept that it is not wise to fight multiple enemies on multiple fronts at the same time, what should our struggles be against, and what should our goals be, i.e. to change the mind of mankind or to do the will of the Father?
11. What does it mean to be Christians with a difference? How should unity in diversity bring Christians together in presenting a common front based on Biblical precepts?

THE BIBLE, INERRANT OR IN ERROR

What Is the Bible

Basic Assumptions: A religious leader recently deplored the fact that today church members of all denominations appear to be spiritually illiterate. They seem to have lost their inheritance in the Bible and in church tradition in general. Are they truly illiterate or just lazy? Today's society is accustomed to having everything given to them in the abridged edition. Most seem content to hear what someone else thinks on the matter rather then do a pragmatic study for themselves. Adults use questionable helps rather then struggle through difficult passages, students use CliffsNotes rather than read the classics, and everyone surfs the Internet for dubious sources rather than go to the library to do research. Someone might want to ask if such statements could be said of Southern Baptist congregations. Aren't we "People of the Book?" Isn't the Bible our guide, our irreplaceable, inerrant, infallible treasure of truth and life? Could "we" lose our heritage in the Biblical revelation?

The Baptist Faith and Message states:

> The Holy Bible was written by men divinely inspired and is the record of God's revelation of Himself to man. It is a perfect treasure of divine instruction. It has God for its author, salvation for its end, and truth without any mixture of error, for its matter. It reveals the principles by which God judges us; and therefore is, and will remain to the end of the world, the true center of Christian union, and the supreme standard by which all human conduct, creeds, and religious opinions should be tried...[108]

I'm going to do my best to answer some of these and other questions as I take us through what I believe may well be the greatest threat to, from, and within the church. However, before continuing I need to give the reader certain assumptions that I bring to the discussion. First, the Bible is a book of religion. It is the story of God and His relationship with humanity, and therefore of humanity's relationship with itself. Although there are many who would turn to the Bible for insights into history, psychology, and the sciences, the Bible was not written to answer questions on such lofty human endeavors. It must of necessity dwell into these realms; however, it speaks of God and must be judged for its message about God and His mighty works on behalf of His people.

The central problem of humanity as revealed in the Bible is sin. And sin, as revealed in the Bible is alienation from a Holy God. Sin breaches the covenant between God and humanity. Sin violates in a very personal way the extraordinary nature of God, and sin seeks to supplant God by making humanity supreme. As such the central concern of the Bible deals with saving mankind from itself and from the sin that has separated us from the Creator. Salvation, the restoration of a proper relationship with God and humanity involves a healing of the division within persons, alienating them from themselves, from others, and of more importance from God.

For the Christian the fundamental person in Scripture is God the son, revealed in Christ Jesus. He is the Immanuel, God with us of Isaiah, He is the Messiah, the Anointed One of Daniel, He is the Son, the Lamb of God, and He is the Alpha and Omega, the First and the Last of the New Testament (Isaiah 7:14, Daniel 3:25, Matthew 8:29, Mark 3:11, Luke 8:28, John 1:29, Revelation 1:8). Again for the Christian, all Scripture is to be interpreted in the light of Christ. The Bible is not an end in itself; it is the written witness of God and His dealings with, and on behalf of, humanity and as such is His written channel of communications with humanity. In making such a broad statement it requires that one take the Bible as a unified manuscript; a manuscript that can be understood only in relation to its own entirety.

Distortions and heresies come from individuals, religious or not, attempting to interpret parts of the Scriptures outside the relationship of the total revelation. Portions of humanity have, and still are from time to time attempting to place a heresy along side a Biblical truth and present the two as being whole in their presentation. Once spiritual, and Biblical illiterate people become accustom to the concept, the heretic, or false teacher if you prefer, then sits aside the Biblical truth and teaches the false doctrine. In this way many congregations are lured into accepting secular humanistic concepts as being in agreement with Scripture.

By example, if God is love, and God loves the sinner, and we are to love one another even as God loved us, then from the secular humanistic interpretation of Scripture even the sexually immoral have a right to claim church membership and to even serve as pastor or priest to lead God's people in a more perfect understanding of the Scriptures. Thus God's people are lead astray by the very ones who are charged by God to speak the truth. "*For the lips of a priest ought to preserve knowledge, and from his mouth men should seek instruction—because he is the messenger of the Lord Almighty. But you have turned from the way and by your teaching have caused many to stumble*" (Malachi 2:7,8).

Because of such problems there are certain basic skills that are needed in interpreting many parts of the Bible. This requirement arises because some of the truths presented in Scriptures are self-evident; however there are parts of the Bible where Scripture is shrouded in mystery and must be interpreted with the help of scholarly insight, comparison with other sections of Scriptures that deal with the same theme, and always with reliance on the Holy Spirit to guide the interpreter. Peter told his readers that, "*Above all you must understand that no prophecy of Scripture came about by the prophet's own interpretation. For prophecy never had it origin in the will of men, but men spoke from God as they were carried along by the Holy Spirit*" (II Peter 1:20,21). In a like manner Paul stated, "*All Scripture is God-breathed and is useful for teaching, rebuking, correcting and training in righteousness, so that the man* (and woman) *of God is equipped for every good work*" (II Timothy 3:16).

Definitions

Authoritative Word of God: Authoritative, like absolute is one of those words that people don't like to dwell on. It means that the Bible is binding on all people regardless of whether they acknowledge God or not. Everyone will eventually have to give an account for how they lived in light of its teachings.

> And I saw the dead, great and small, standing before the throne, and books were opened. Another book was opened, which is the book of life. The dead were judged according to what they had done as recorded in the books. The sea gave up the dead that were in it, and death and Hades gave up the dead that were in them, and each person was judged according to what he had done. (Revelation 20:12,13)

This concept has obvious difficulties for the bulk of humanity when it is applied to persons who have never heard of the gospel, the Bible, or even Christianity. To these poor souls Paul said:

> The wrath of God is being revealed from heaven against all the godlessness and wickedness of men who suppress the truth by their wickedness, since what may be known about God is plain to them, because God has made it plain to them. For since the creation of the world God's invisible qualities—his eternal power and divine nature—have been clearly seen, being understood from what has been made, so that men are without excuse. (Romans 1:18,20)

A little later Paul offered this observation:

> Now we know that whatever the law says, it says to those who are under the law, so that every mouth may be silenced and the whole world held accountable to God. Therefore no one will be declared righteous in his sight by observing the law, rather through the law we become conscious of sin. (Romans 3:19,20)

Autographic Text of Scripture: This is also referred to as "Original Manuscripts." Since God has nowhere promised an inerrant transmission of Scripture, some find it necessary to affirm that only the autographic text of the original documents was inspired and therefore the need to maintain textual criticism as a means of detecting any slips that may have crept into the text in the course of its transmission. Serious students of Scripture know that studies have shown the Hebrew and Greek texts to be amazingly well preserved, so that we are amply justified in affirming, with the Baptist Faith and Message, a singular providence of God in this matter and in declaring that the authority of Scripture is in no way jeopardized by the fact that the copies we possess are not entirely error-free. I, as with others, strongly affirm that the substance and the spirit of the Scriptures remain in tact.[109]

Bible: From the Greek "Βψβλοσ" (Byblos) which is the Greek term for the Egyptian papyrus. Most commonly the word Bible refers to the Christian Scriptures containing both the Old and New Testament. Perhaps more acutely the Bible is a library or a collection of books manually written by multiple authors, in a variety of literary styles, using several languages, and spanning several thousands of years. The Bible as we know it has come into existence by a long and involved process. For the Christian, its authority rests neither in the individuals who wrote it, nor in it historical accuracy, but in the God who revealed its truths and is able to keep it from error. "*Your word, O Lord is eternal; it stands firm in the heavens*" (Psalm 119:89).

Canon: The word "canon," signifying a rule of standard, is a pointer to authority, which means the right to rule and control. Authority in Christianity belongs to God in His revelation, which means, on the one hand, Jesus Christ, the living Word, and, on the other hand, the Holy Scriptures, the written Word.

Grammatical-Historical Exegesis: This simply means that history must be treated as history, poetry as poetry, hyperbole and metaphor as what each is, generalization and approximation as what they are, and so forth. Differences between literary conventions in Biblical times and in ours must also be observed. Since, for instance, non-chronological narration and imprecise citation were conventional and acceptable and violated no expectations in those days, we must not necessary, on face value, regard these things as faults when we find them in Scripture.

Inerrant: This word's base meaning is to be free from error. It signifies the quality of being free from all falsehood or mistake and so safeguards the truth that the Holy Scripture is entirely true and trustworthy in all its assertions. Since errors, mistakes and duplicity are never regarded as qualities of God, then inspiration by God would imply inerrancy of the text. "*The law of the Lord is perfect, reviving the soul. The statutes of the Lord are trustworthy, making wise the simple. The precepts of the Lord are right, giving joy to the heart*" (Psalm 19:7,8).

Infallible: This word means that the subject matter is incapable of error in its public declaration of doctrine. It signifies the quality of neither misleading nor being misled and so safeguards in categorical terms the truth that Holy Scripture is a sure, safe and reliable rule and guide in all matters. "*Every word of God is flawless; he is a shield to those who take refuge in him. Do not add to his words, or he will rebuke you and prove you a liar*" (Proverbs 30:5,6).

Inspiration: From the Greek "επιπνοια" (epipnoia), "With regard to the Bible, inspiration denotes the doctrine that the human authors and editors of canonical scripture were led or influenced by God with the result that their writings many be designated in some sense the Word of God."[110] It is the belief that God influenced the authors of the Bible so that their writings would be free of error. Some Christians believe that God, in effect, dictated the words in the Bible to its authors; others believe that God allowed the authors to write in their own style, but prevented them from committing errors. Regardless of which view you choose, it was by God's authority and inspiration that men wrote the Scriptures.

Omnipotent: The word is from the Latin meaning to have unlimited or absolute power. There is in the word the understanding of total authority over all creation from its conception to its end. By virtue of this unlimited power, God is also to be found omniscient, meaning processing all knowledge, and omnipresence, or the Godly ability to be everywhere at the same time. Within God's omnipotence His knowledge of past, present, and future events is perfect. Nothing can be added to the knowledge He processes and nothing can be taken away from it.

Revelation: The dictionary defines revelation as being "a dramatic disclosure of something not formerly known or realized."[111] For the Christian this means that the knowledge was conveyed to us by God, either by direct supernatural instruction by the Holy Spirit, or more immediately through the written word, which we now know as the Bible. There are many today who report to have a new revelation. "The Scripture theory seems to be this, that in any new revelation the prophet of God must present a doctrine perfectly consistent with every past revelation and with the knowledge conveyed by nature and must, at the same time, confirm by miracles his authority as a teacher from God."[112]

Translation: A translation is an act or process of accurately converting a passage or an entire writing from one language to another. Most translations tend to be a new work from the original languages. Such a project normally will involve multiple translators from several denominations or groups, numerous revisions and with each step being constantly referenced to the original languages. For the

Bible this means working directly from the best available Hebrew, Aramaic and Greek texts. Such a process will often take thousands of hours and years to reach final consensus from the various individuals and groups participating in the project.

Transcribe: Transcribe means to write out fully or to transfer from one record to another. Because of human error and religious or political preference of the scribe, or person dictating to a group of scribes, it will often involve an adaptation of the original manuscript. The changing of a letter or of the meaning of a word may be made because of a new or special situation. The Dead Sea Scrolls are one such type of transcribed manuscripts, although in their case among the transcribed manuscripts there were also found examples of extended paraphrases.[113]

Paraphrase: While a true translation will involve multiple revisions intended to limit any sectarian bias, a paraphrase can and often is completed by one individual or group. Many new "translations" are really just paraphrases that seek to remove masculine emphasis from the Bible and make the Scriptures as politically correct as possible. Rather than use the original languages most will use an accepted version of the Bible approved by either themselves or the denomination to which they belong. In such works there is almost always a loose handling of the order of the text, numerous mistranslations, changed meaning of passages, almost always easy to read, and lacks consistency often translating one word in many different ways. Such "bibles" are biased and very poor for study, or for discerning Biblical truths.

How Did the Modern Bible Come About

The Old Testament: There are certain questions that people ask about the Bible that cannot be answered through human endeavors. In the realm of theological studies and archaeological finds neither of these can prove nor disprove inspiration. Along with this is the quest for how the modern Bible came into being. Both the

Jewish Synagogue and the Christian Church have the same canon of the Old Testament. The Catholic Church accepts the thirty-nine books of this canon yet also accept the collection of books which are known as the Apocrypha.

As if it were not hard enough to find some kind of consensus concerning the Old Testament, there is at least some agreement that one would be hard pressed to find a single book in the canon that is free from considerable additions and insertions, all attempting to clarify one matter or another. As nearly as can be estimated the last twenty-six chapters of Isaiah were written some 150 years after the prophet's passing. The Book of Esther was at one point nearly twice its original size due to scripts, translators, and commentators. The redeeming factor in regards to Esther is that the additions never got into the Hebrew text. So as far as is possible no scholar of Old Testament studies can fix with confidence, the points where one writer left off and another began. More to the point, no scholar of the Old or New Testament can point to any part of Scripture and say with any certainty that the section was not included by inspiration of the Holy Spirit, which is, or should be the deciding point for Christians.

I assume that there are among my readers some learned individuals who would point to the discovery of scrolls near the location of the Qumran community, and make the assertion that the Old Testament was canonized more than nineteen centuries ago. However, I do not believe that such a statement could be proven because at the Qumran community each book existed as a single scroll. There has been, to my knowledge, no discovery of a bounded collection of all the books at the Qumran community site. Add to this that even though every book is represented, if not as a whole then as a fragment, with the exception of Esther, one can at least make the assertion that there was a collection of recognized books. I must in all honesty also acknowledge that there was an abundance of apocryphal literature found among the Qumran documents.

The books that we regard today as the Old Testament were read, studied, copied and used as a manual in religious practice giving them creditability as being authoritative, as well as inspired. Although there is some disagreement, the Council of Jewish Rabbis at Jamnia circa A.D. 90 is believed to have officially closed the Old Testament canon producing what is called the "Masoretic Text." They did not determine which books were to be included and which were not; they simply formalized and gave religious standing to what had already been in wide circulation.

The New Testament: As with the Old Testament, the New Testament began with the oral traditions of Jesus handed down by apostles and the disciples who were with Jesus during His earthly ministry. Paul did his writings between 45 and 68 A.D.; the latter date being the date of his death. Although there seems to be room for discussion, most scholars agree that the bulk of the Gospel, Matthew, Mark, and Luke were completed somewhere between 50 and 68 A.D. The writings of John, a "Son of Thunder," and the beloved of Christ wrote his Gospel, the three letters, and the Revelation between 68 and 96 A.D. Even after these men of God wrote the New Testament books, they were not distributed equally throughout the early Christian church. Somewhere in the fourth century there came about a canonized list that we now recognize as the New Testament. Athanasius in A.D. 367 used the term in the sense of an accepted list. "His list is the oldest known to correspond exactly to the twenty-seven writings of our New Testament."[114]

As a Christian one is called upon to believe that God providentially guided the early church in its evaluation and acceptance of various books. To believe otherwise is to reject the total concept that the New Testament is the authoritative record and interpretation of God's revelation of Himself through Jesus Christ the Son. This concept being accepted as true, then one must also accept the same concept with regard to the Old Testament as Jesus Himself affirmed the Old Testament.

> Do not think that I have come to abolish the Law or the Prophets; I have not come to abolish them but to fulfill them. I tell you the truth, until heaven and earth disappear, not the smallest letter,

> not the least stroke of a pen, will by any means disappear from the Law until everything is accomplished. (Matthew 5:17,18)

The English Bible: Christianity came to the British Isles with the arrival of the Roman soldiers. However, Christianity did not begin to show any real growth potential until the seventh century when Augustine a Roman monk gave both leadership and direction to the struggling religion in what is now known as England. Prior to the mid-thirteen hundreds Bibles were handwritten copies of the Latin Vulgate, were in manuscript form, and were reserved for only the most prestigious of individuals and churches. In many of the large Cathedrals of England one can still see the beautifully bound copies of the Bible chained to the Pulpit. The Bible was not to be read by the lower and middle classes of English society.

When one takes into consideration the political favor of the times, the fear of heresy and of unofficial sectarian religions which the Holy Scriptures once written in English might cause among the common people who could both read and write, then it becomes apparent why there were no official versions of the Bible in English. When viewed from such concepts, one sees the production of an English Bible as being more a matter of politics than of religious orthodoxy or a crusade to keep the Scriptures pure and untouched by common hands.

During the Anglo-Saxon period some parts of the Bible, most notably Psalms and the Gospels were translated from the Latin into English. It was John Wycliffe in association with others between the years 1380 and 1382 who produced the first English Bible.[115] However it should be remembered that this translation was taken from Jerome's Vulgate, and not from the original languages. It would be some two hundred years, 1525, before William Tyndale would translate the New Testament from the Greek. He also translated portions of the Old Testament from the Hebrew of the Masoretic Text. Tyndale was martyred for the heresy of translating the Bible into the colloquial language.

In 1534-35 Myles Coverdale using most of the text from Tyndale's translation printed the first complete English Bible. The next important printing of the Bible was published in Geneva in 1560 by Protestants who were exiled from England during the reign of Queen Mary, Henry the VIII's Catholic daughter. The Geneva Bible proved to be one of the most popular translations with some two hundred copies being made between 1560 and 1630 and was also referred to as the Great Bible because of the large size of its pages. Before moving on, one other Protestant translation before the King James Version should be mentioned. This was the Bishops' Bible, circa 1568. It was published to counteract the Geneva Bible, which was considered by the English Church to be unsuitable for use in their services.

The "official" Bible of the Church of England, called the King James Bible has perhaps had the most influential effect, and can, rightly so, be considered to be the most widely read Bible of the present age. The 1611 translation was made by a number of scholars, most notably English, using the Hebrew and Greek languages. It is noteworthy to be aware of the fact that the King James Bible went thought several revisions before reaching its present form. Translations continued because where the King James Bible uses language that is both stately and beautiful, it is also archaic, hard to understand, and many of the words used have evolved into different meanings.

I am acutely aware that I have just spanned some three hundred plus years, and no less than eight notable translations of the Bible for the sake of brevity. I would hope that the reader would not take away from this compressed analysis the concept that I do not understand or am somehow disrespectful of the cost in human life that was required to bring us the English Bible. Most of the individuals started with no ambition to translate the Bible, save the love of study. Because of the persecution that followed most became convinced that it was vital to produce an English Bible as quickly as possible.

None of the early Bible translators ended their lives in a peaceful manner. Wycliffe was condemned for heresy at Oxford in 1382. He died in retirement some eighteen months later, however his heirs were persecuted and burnt alive for the perceived heresy of translating the Bible into English. Tyndale was strangled and his body burned; Coverdale unnaturally died in bed. Yet the work once begun would continue on to completion and those who so staunchly condemned the work would now be anxious for a National English Bible. What was begun in secrecy would be completed in enthusiasm and read aloud even while service was going on at the altar.

Inerrancy and Other Related Matters

As with other sections of this book I must offer clarification. This chapter is not intended to be an apology or defense of Scripture. God has and will continue to defend His Word until He comes again to receive His own. However secular humanists continue to try and chip away at the precepts and truths that the Bible contains. One such attempt has been the History Channel's presentation of the concept that Jesus married Mary Marlene; they had a child who was in fact the Holy Grail, and she with the child escaped to France; that once in France the child, a girl, grew up and married into French nobility, of whom many of their descendants were purposed to have had miraculous powers of healing, and that many famous and historical personalities have conspired to hide this truth from the general public. Aside from the "Holy Grail" being nothing more than an old English myth, the program's speculative presentation only lightly touches on there being no basic of reality, secular or Biblical, to the presentation, but leaves the viewer with the thought that all of this might be true and Jesus was therefore nothing more than another frail creature of dust (Genesis 3:19), purposing to be the Son of God.

This misleading presentation, presented as near fact was based on the novel *The Da Vinci Code*. This and other such programs of presence origin are intended to strip Christ of His Divine nature and thereby water down the Scriptural presentation of Christ as the Son of God and the Redeemer of the world and present the Bible as being imperfect in its presentation. They stop just short of denouncing the Bible's claim to inerrancy. *The Da Vinci Code*, Dan Brown's masterfully concocted, and by his own admission fictitious and imaginary, lucid murder mystery marries the enthusiasm of an international murder mystery with a collection of fascinating esoteric myths culled from 2,000 years of Western history. It was intended as a murder mystery and nothing else. However it leads us to the first of several questions that I hope will give the reader the incentive to further investigate their Scriptures in search of God's truth.

Does Inerrancy Really Matter: The authority of Scripture is not just a key issue for the Christian Church in this day and age; it is the main issue. For those of us who profess faith in Jesus Christ as our Lord and Savior, we are called to show the authenticity of our discipleship by respectfully and faithfully obeying God's written Word. To stray from Scripture in faith is to, at a minimum, be hypocritical in our presentation and disloyal in our conduct to our Lord and Master. Recognition of the total truth and trustworthiness of Holy Scripture is essential to an adequate confession of its authority.

The Bible's perpetual interest comes from the fact that it deals with the lesser, but always important and emotional, questions which cluster around its great and ever contemporary themes; humanity's relationship to the God who created it, humanity's relationship to itself, and humanity's relationship to eternity. However is that sufficient to produce a book that has a universal and ubiquitous appeal? Timeless literature, all literature that seems to span the imagination, leap national boundaries, and endures through the chronicles of time, do so because of something magnificent in its thought, or its universal appeal, or its mastery of its construction, or even its charm or beauty of form and line. Many people prefer the King James Version because of its lyrical, oft times poetic, and lamenting flow even though they acknowledge that it is often hard to read and difficult to understand with any certainty.

One cannot reason that this timelessness is the product of a wonderful period of humanity, marked by magnificent experiences, of a great and powerful people, a people who were undoubtedly the religious geniuses of all the humanity that God created. There have been other great people of antiquity who have put forth vibrant and powerful religious literatures, but oblivion has claimed their once proud writings. They were great, but they are gone, gone forever or are only occasionally viewed or studied in the museums of history.

The Hebrew nation as a people, in any living sense of the thought, has also passed. In so much as they retain the body of writings and miss the soul of its intent, they are deferred Pharisees. Where they have missed both the outward form and the inner soul, they are belated Sadducees—one division retaining no power, the other division having no approach. They can but watch and wait for an impending disclosure of God's working to bring them back to the glory that once was theirs, but now is gone.

The Bible's preeminent approach and appeal endures because it possesses certain qualities of eternalness in greater degree than any other literature, it endures because it claims for itself both God's authority and inspiration. It endures because it claims for itself inerrancy.

What the Bible Says about Its Own Inerrancy: Lest I open myself to a charge of dishonesty in my presentation, I must openly acknowledge that the word "inerrant" does not appear in any form in the pages of Scripture, however in my defense neither do the words: Trinity, rapture, millennium, etc. In those early days when Godly men, pioneers of the Hebrew and Christian faith, martyrs one and all, sought to translate the Bible into written form there was no need for such a word. The consensus, even of those who later fought not to have the Bible translated into English, was that the Bible was completely trustworthy and without error. It was only during the age of enlightenment when some European theologians began to approach the Bible from a historical view that doubt arose as to the authenticity of the writings and the truthfulness of Scripture came into question. In response to such heretical thoughts, fundamental theologians instituted the concept of faith in the inerrancy of Scripture.

In beginning this discussion, I am obliged to point out that there are far too many Scriptures to list here that either state without reservation, or imply by association that God's infallible character does not permit Him to do evil, be deceitful with His creation or make mistakes. "*God saw all that He had made, and it was very good*" (Genesis 1:31).

> "Then the Lord said to Abraham, 'shall I hide from Abraham what I am about to do'" (18:17)? "You are not a God that takes pleasure in evil; with you the wicked cannot dwell. The arrogant cannot stand in your presence; you hate all who do wrong. You destroy those who tell lies; bloodthirsty and deceitful men the Lord abhors" (Psalm 5:4-6).

Since the Bible states that it was inspired by God, and since God does not make mistakes, then would it not stand to reason that inspiration by God would by its very relationship imply inerrancy of the content?

Although logical in its arrangement, I doubt that the above would sway the masses away from the present battle over inerrancy, and that certainly is not my intent in this chapter. And so, for the reader's edification, or simply to stimulate the reader's quest for truth, I present the following as a sample of what the Bible has to say about the inerrant Word of God.

- "And God spoke these words: 'I am the Lord your God, who brought you out of Egypt out of the land of slavery. You shall have no other gods before me'" (Exodus 20:1,2).
- "Who has a claim against me that I must pay? Everything under heaven belongs to me" (Job 41:11).
- "The law of the Lord is perfect, reviving the soul. The statutes of the Lord are trustworthy, making wise the simple. The precepts of the Lord are right, giving joy to the heart. The commands of the Lord are radiant, giving light to the eyes. The fear of the Lord is pure, enduring forever. The ordinances of the Lord are sure and altogether righteous" (Psalm 19:7-9).
- "Your word, O Lord, is eternal; it stands firm in the heavens. Your faithfulness continues through all generations; you

established the earth, and it endures. Your laws endure to this day, for all things serve you" (Psalm 119:89-91).

- "Every word of God is flawless; He is a shield to those who take refuge in Him. Do not add to His words, or he will rebuke you and prove you a liar" (Proverbs 30:5,6).
- "The grass withers and the flowers fall, but the word of our God stands forever… Do you not know, have you not heard? The Lord is the everlasting God, the Creator of the ends of the earth. He will not grow tire or weary, and His understanding no one can fathom" (Isaiah 40:8,28).

Lest I be charged with only providing Old Testament Scriptures I offer these from the New Testament:

- "Do not think that I have come to abolish the Law or the Prophets; I have not come to abolish them but to fulfill them. I tell you the truth, until heaven and earth disappear, not the smallest letter, not the least stroke of a pen, will by any means disappear from the Law until everything is accomplished" (Matthew 5:17-19).
- "Jesus answered them, 'Is it not written in your Law, 'I have said you are gods?' If he called them gods, to whom the word of God came—and the Scripture cannot be broken—what about the one whom the Father set apart as his very own and sent into the world" (John 10:34,35).

I have quoted II Timothy 3:16, 17 several times, and yet I need to place it here because it is perhaps the primary Scripture giving reference to being inerrant,

- "All Scripture is God-breathed and is useful for teaching, rebuking, correcting and training in righteousness, so that the man of God may be thoroughly equipped for every good work."

Lest I bore some with my endless quotations, I leave this part of the discussion with the last book in the Bible:

- "I warn everyone who hears the words of the prophecy of this book: If anyone adds anything to them, God will add to him the plagues described in this book. And if anyone takes words away from this book of prophecy, God will take away from him his share in the tree of life and in the holy city, which are described in this book" (Revelations 22: 18,19).

Purposed Errors in the Bible: In my definition of the "Autographic Text of Scripture," I said:

> Since God has nowhere promised an inerrant transmission of Scripture, some find it necessary to affirm that only the autographic text of the original documents were inspired and therefore the need to maintain textual criticism as a means of detecting any slips that may have crept into the text in the course of its transmission. Serious students of Scripture know that studies have shown the Hebrew and Greek texts to be amazingly well preserved, so that we are amply justified in affirming, with the Baptist Faith and Message, a singular providence of God in this matter and in declaring that the authority of Scripture is in no way jeopardized by the fact that the copies we possess are not entirely error-free.[116]

One could add to this that many of the copies that individuals possess are not real translations but are paraphrased copies. Of those translated from earlier texts, the documents in question could have been translated from a copy of a copy, and due to having been improperly translated by the reader or incorrectly copied by the scribe error is now present in one or more contemporary translations. However this would not take into account those portions of Scripture, most notable in the Gospel presentations that disagree in their description of the same event. Having worked my way through college as a law-enforcement officer I was taught at the police academy that when two or more individuals describe the crime in the same identical way, using the same words, then more than likely their stories have been rehearsed and both testimonies are suspect.

I could muddy the waters even more by noting that no one has come forth professing to have an "original" manuscript. The oral tradition of the Jewish faith has been said to have begun some four centuries ago in Ur of the Chaldees, not far from the Gulf of Persia, where Abram an Arabian Emir went in search of a land that God had promised to him and his decedents, and in the process became Abraham a wandering Armenian (Genesis 17:4,5). "The earliest literature of the Israelites, dating from the time of Moses or earlier, would give the first writings a date of approximately 1300-1275 B.C."[117] What could be called the first continuing narrative comes from around 850 B.C., often called the "J" source, followed by "E" 750 B.C., "JE" 650 B.C., "D" 621 B.C., "JED" 550 B.C., and lastly "P" 500-450 B.C. "The earliest attestation for the threefold division of the Hebrew bible (Law, Prophets, and Writings) is in the Prologue to the Greek translation of Ecclesiasticus (132 B.C.)."[118]

The earliest manuscripts available concerning New Testament writings date from the second century.[119] Jesus Christ our Lord and founder of the Christian faith left the fledging church with but the most diminutive of organization and so far as theologians can tell no written documentation at all. Most of the Gospel message was centered in the oral tradition being passed by word of mouth. It is to this murky transition time between occurrences to written records that many have turned their attention in the drive to find and if possible harmonize the Scriptures.

As the disciples spread throughout the known world, churches began to spring up in diverse places, and with them came perplexing heresies to disrupt the fellowship. To meet these threats letters were written, discussing the problems of the time. This gave rise to epistolary literature that encompasses a large portion of the New Testament. Although there is continuing debate as to the dating of the earliest of manuscripts[120] most will accept the dates as being between A.D. 50 for Mark and the late A.D. 80s or early 90s for John, which would allow approximately fifty years for the originals to have been copied several times and spread throughout the known world.

With the death of John the Age of Apostles ends, the time of miracles pass, and Christianity is left to win its own way by means of the efforts and prayers of the faithful. Thus ends the writings, the canon of Scriptures are closed with a completed divine, inerrant, revelation.

The "I" Passages of Paul: In an endnote in Chapter 7, I said that I would attempt to address the "I" passages of Paul. I begin by noting that Paul did not set out to write a portion of the New Testament. I doubt that the thought of a New Testament hardly crossed his mind as he struggled with the problems of the then present age. Many of his and other apostles' and disciples' writings were being produced because questions were being asked of them, questions about behavior that was most notably disrupting the congregations.

I have already stated the verse that gives rise to the most contention, that of I Timothy 2:12. Perhaps a rendering of the entire "I Paul" passage may help the reader to better visualize the setting.

> A woman should learn in quietness and full submission. I do not permit a woman to teach or to have authority over a man; she must be silent. For Adam was formed first, then Eve. And Adam was not the one deceived; it was the woman who was deceived and became a sinner. But women will be kept safe through childbirth, if they continue in faith, love and holiness with propriety. (2:1-15)

Most students of the Bible will readily note that Paul is alluding to that portion of Scripture in Genesis concerning the fall of humanity. However, the most cursory look would lead the reader to agree that at its face value it certainly sounds bigoted. However a search of Scripture will find that Paul was not too much kinder with men who wore long hair,

> Does not the very nature of things teach you that if a man has long hair, it is a disgrace to him, but that if a woman has long hair, it is her glory? For long hair is given to her as a covering. If anyone wants to be contentious about this, we have no other practice—nor do the churches of God. (I Corinthians 11:14-16)

Hopefully someone will note that to use only these to show that Paul was not being lead by the Holy Spirit would be to take these verses out of context. The context of these last verses was concerning propriety in worship.

> Now I want you to realize that the head of every man is Christ, and the head of the woman is man, and the head of Christ is God... Every man who prays or prophesies with his head covered dishonors his head. And every woman who prays or prophesies with her head uncovered dishonors her head... In the Lord however, woman is not independent of man, nor is man independent of woman. For as woman came from man, so also man is born of woman. But everything comes from God. (I Corinthians 11:3-16)

It should be interesting to note that Paul affirmed that women as well as men could both pray and prophesy. Prophecy and very possibly prayer would of necessity denote verbal utterances from women as well as men.

Within the context of the I Timothy passage you will find these words, "*I want men everywhere to lift up holy hands in prayer, without anger or disputing. I also want women to dress modestly with decency and propriety... but with good deeds, appropriate for women who profess to worship God*" (2:8-10). When taken within the content that Paul intended, He comes across more a religious zealot then a bigot. I would encourage the readers to seek out the more positive passages of Paul, "*There is neither Jew nor Greek, slave nor free, male nor female, for you are all one in Christ Jesus*" (Galatians 3:28).

Paul's intent was not to put down women or men, but to call men and women to proper behavior before society and before their God. However, is that the main issue for those who would so readily discount Paul because he stated what for him was appropriate behavior? If all Scripture is God-breathed and profitable, if the Holy Spirit moved individuals to write Scripture, if the Bible is the inerrant, infallible revelation of God's dealings with humanity, then are not the writings of Paul, even those he considered his own, not inspired? Isn't this just another attempt to discredit Scripture in its entirety?

Inerrancy, a Statement of Fact or Faith: James made a declaration of what constitutes real faith when he penned the words,

> Do not merely listen to the word, and so deceive yourself. Do what it says. Anyone who listens to the word but does not do what it says is like a man who looks at his face in a mirror and, after looking at himself, goes away and immediately forgets what he looks like… Show me your faith without deeds, and I will show you my faith by what I do. You believe that there is one God. Good! Even the demons believe that—and shudder. (James 1:22-24; 2:18,19)

"*Now faith is being sure of what we hope for and certain of what we do not see*" (Hebrews 11:1). Faith, like inspiration cannot be seen, it cannot be held, but that fact does not prove either the existence or non-existence of faith.

In like manner inerrancy cannot be proven nor disproved by any one, or even a combination of facts. It must be taken in faith. If you do not believe that all Scripture is God-breathed, if you cannot accept certain Scriptures because they violate your sensibilities or social understanding, or is not politically correct enough for this modern age, then to you I must say that all Scripture is in doubt, and you cannot really believe any part of the Bible with any certainty.

Each individual must choose for themselves whom they will follow, God or humanity, and what they will or will not believe. However, I believe! I believe that the Bible is up-to-date, down-to-earth, and right on the mark. Not only does it struggle with modern day issues, it also gives confidence that we can have an accurate knowledge of God and His created beings. I believe that God has placed within the heart of each and every member of humanity a spark that calls us to seek His face. Some will come to Christ seeking salvation, others will come to the church seeking social standing, and others will come to the fellowship seeking only the liberty to do what they wish without condemnation from the faithful. The Bible is the eternal and inerrant Word of God because the truths it articulates are timeless spanning all generations, always true, always faithful, and always verifying themselves in the minds of men and women who seek the God of Scripture.

It does not answer every inquiry of humanity, nor should it, but it does bring peace to the troubled soul in trying times. It brought peace to the mind and heart of Job as he struggled with the tribulations of human virtue and suffering. It brought peace to Solomon, the preacher who sought some nourishing clue amid the distracting questions of life, liberty and the pursuit of happiness. It brought peace to the great questioning soul of Habakkuk in the fog of teasing doubt. It brought peace to one Saul of Tarsus in the written word of the Old Testament, and to Paul in the earliest stages of the development of truth found in the New Testament.

For the faithful throughout the ages the Bible has solved every problem of reason and conscience and spirit. It has done so for giants of the faith such as Augustine, Luther, Calvin, Jonathan Edwards, Spurgeon, Graham, and all such kindred souls like theirs in each and every decade. It has not solved these problems through intellect alone; it has solved them morally, spiritually, vitally, and it solves them with power! It did this yesterday, it will do it tomorrow. Jeremiah saw a vision of an almond tree, and the message of the vision was, "*I am watching to see that my word is fulfilled*" (1:12). Isaiah looked into the unending circulation of rain and snow and understood "*So is the word that goes out from my mouth: It will not return to me empty, but will accomplish what I desire and achieve the purpose for which I send it*" (55:11). However a greater than all of these said, "*I am the way the truth and the life and no man comes to the Father except through me*" (John 14:6).

Discredit the Bible, disregard the Scriptures, deny the inerrancy, and the witness of the ages would be silenced. However before that day comes the words of John will echo across all Christendom, "He who testifies to these things says, 'Yes I am coming soon.' Amen. Come" (Revelation 22:20).

Questions for Consideration and Discussion

I must admit in all honesty that I accept without question the inspiration and the authority of the Bible as the Word of God. I believe that it contains the Will of God concerning all humanity, not just those of us who hold it sacred, but also those who ridicule its precepts. Within its pages we find the knowledge of the redemption, which God has provided for those who seek such Salvation. The Bible also contains information that can and does furnish the basis of both wise and worthy conduct for individuals, for governments, and for nations. I would to God that all humanity would avail itself of every opportunity to acquaint themselves with its teachings, and that all Christianity should be faithful and even aggressive in their efforts to teach its truths, not only to themselves and to their children but to the world around them.

However the pure truth is that one cannot teach that which they do not know. Before we Christians take one more step outside the church to evangelize the rest of humanity we must first insure that we understand what the Bible is and is not, where it came from and how it arrived in its present form, and most importantly what it is that the Bible teaches as well as what it does not teach.

In my discussion on the Bible I have tried very hard not to furnish an apologetic discussion, which consisted in the assertion that the Bible contains such monumental truths that it should be above all reasoning and which, therefore does not have to enter into competition with other worldly religions and philosophy. Rather, I believe that we should boldly enter into the contest for the souls of humanity and should not ask for exceptional treatment, but should be in the thick of the battle of ideologies, relying solely on the power of the Bible's own inherent truths. Some would call it a fantasy; I call it faith.

1. Using the Baptist Faith and Message passage on the Holy Scriptures (or the creed or declaration of your own denomination), what is your church's understanding on what the Bible is and how it came to be written?
2. Does your church see the Bible as a unified manuscript, or do some in your congregation hold that the Old Testament has been totally replaced by the New Testament?
3. How did the canonized Bible that we have today come into being? Who really decided which books would and would not be in the Bible? Are all Bibles, i.e. Jewish, Christian, Catholic, the same? What are the differences, and why?
4. What version of the Bible does your pastor preach from? Is it the same one he uses for his sermon preparation? Are there Bibles in the pews, and if so what version are they? Which version does the congregation prefer, and why?
5. What version do you use, and do you know who produced it? How many people, denominations, faith groups were involved in its publication? How long did it take, and what process did they use to arrive at consensus?
6. What does the preface of your Bible have to say about its production? Is the Bible you use a translation or a paraphrase? Do you understand the difference between the two?
7. Has your church ever undertaken a study of how the Bible came to be in its present form? Does the congregation understand the great sacrifice that was made in the producing of an English Bible?
8. What is your church's understanding of the inerrancy of the Scriptures? How important is the inerrancy of the Bible to your church, the church leaders, and the congregants? How important is it to you? Does it really matter in the total scheme of worldly pursuits?

9. If someone were to attempt to add to the Scriptures a heresy, or change, or even take away a precept would you know the difference? How would you determine if something were true or not true in its presentation? If you became aware of a heresy that was being taught in your church, how would you address the problem?
10. What makes for perpetual interest and "timeless" literature? What is its attraction? Why do people continue to read it through the ages?
11. What would you say is the reason for the Bible's wide acceptance worldwide? What is its "Universal" attraction? Why is this attraction seen as a threat to those who are not believers in its teachings?
12. What does the Bible have to say about its own inerrancy? If the word is not to be found in the Bible why is there such a debate about the concept?
13. Can one part of Scripture be inerrant and another part be in error? Can we disregard the miracles of the Old Testament and yet still embrace the miracles of the New Testament? Does it really matter that Jesus was born of a virgin, that He lived and died, and that He was resurrected on the third day? Why or why not?
14. Do you think that the writers of the Bible were aware that they were writing Scripture? Did Paul see himself as being outside the realm of Godly inspiration?
15. How did the inspiration of the Holy Spirit take part in the writings found within the books of the Bible?
16. If inspiration and inerrancy cannot be proven by human efforts then how are we to accept the concepts as being true? Are there parts of the Bible that you just can't seem to believe? Why, what stops you from accepting the Bible as the inerrant, infallible Word of God?

WHAT THEN SHOULD WE DO?

It would be so much easier to discuss this transformation had it been done with evil intent from the very beginning. However it began with a misunderstanding of what a church is and who can rightfully be called a member. It continued by a separation of God's children into splintered denominations where one zealous group or another sought to exert control over the other groups rather than being a servant to all.

It began its transformation of conforming to this world with an assault on marriage and the family; it spread through one secular liberating movement after another, until at last the very underpinning of the faith, the Bible, is now questioned as to its authenticity, its accuracy, and its dependability.

In dealing with the threat from within the church I have hopefully led the reader through a maze of human development. By now, some of you may be saying, "OK, you've convinced me that there is a threat coming from inside the church. Who are they, how do we spot them, and what do we do about it?" I will try to answer these questions in this last chapter. Unlike the other chapters, this last chapter will not end with questions to ponder. By now the readers have probably begun to have questions of their own to contemplate.

We did not arrive at our present dilemma by suddenly waking up one morning and saying to ourselves, "Today I think I will destroy the very fiber of Christianity. Today I think that I will violate every moral and ethical principle I have ever received in my life." It began, as all evolutionary thought begins; what was once only a distant, and oft times forbidden, thought slowly transformed into a present day reality.

See Things the Way They Really Are

A professor of preaching once told me to never end a message without having told the people what they should do with what I had given them. I turn back to my foundational text once more to aid in focusing the reader on these last pages, "*This matter arose, because some false brothers had infiltrated our ranks to spy on the freedom we have in Christ Jesus and to make us slaves*" (Galatians 2:4). If we are to make a difference in this world, if we are to turn our congregations, our cities, our nation, and as much of the world as the Lord will allow away from sin and back to the Lord then we must approach the problem with eyes wide open. We must remove the rose colored glasses so many of us have been viewing our part of the world with.

There are of course those among us that would readily tell us that according to the Book of the Revelation we don't stand a prayer of a chance of changing the world before Christ returns, and they would be right. I, like many other Christians have read Revelation, and I know what is coming; however, we must try if the Great Commission is to be realized. In the words of an old hymn, "we'll work till Jesus comes, and then be carried home."[121] The Lord said, "*Open your eyes and look at the fields, they are ripe for harvest*" (John 4:35).

I am not saying that one must become a pessimist, a cynical worrywart, or even a naysayer. But if we are to address the problems, if we are to make straight that which was twisted (Ecclesiastes 1:5), then we must honestly look at the problems as they are, not as we wish they were. Solomon noted that such could not be done, but the Christian heart knows that "*what is impossible with men is possible with God*" (Luke 18:27).

I recently attended a South Carolina Southern Baptist Conference. I listened with joy at the great things we are doing. I also heard with sorrow the failures we have endured. The Southern Baptists of South Carolina were going to start 500 new churches. To date we have started twenty-two new churches. We were going to have 1,000 baptisms. There are to date some 500 churches in the state that have not baptized even one person in the last two years. I listened as convention leaders—leaders with a zeal for missions—spoke as if they had let us down. They had dared to dream dreams, and to have visions of what South Carolina could look like if we were only willing to share their dreams. They did not let us down, we let ourselves down, and more importantly, we let God down. Do not take satisfaction from these numbers just because you may not be from South Carolina; the rest of the nation is not fairing much better and in some cases are even worse.

There are great accomplishments taking place in South Carolina, as well as all across the United States. There are churches that are lead by God-fearing pastors who dare to preach the truth, and are filled with God-fearing Christians who are willing to do the work. Yet for every one of these there are scores of other churches that don't come close to what God wants them to be. They have no dreams, they have no visions, they have no workers, and they perish (Proverbs 29:18). And the question begs to be asked—*Why*?

Obstacles: Well, it did not happen in a day, and it will not be corrected in a day. Although there were outside influences, we did this to ourselves. We turned from the Word of God; we sought to join forces with the world's religions, thinking that through our willingness to compromise our faith we would win millions to Christ. Oh, we didn't call it compromising; we are much too politically correct to use such an archaic word. We were seeking "common ground" from which to better our communities and our world. We lowered our standards on who could and could not be leaders in the church, we were willing to let others have the privilege of determining what we should and should not be doing. We listened to the world rather than the Holy Spirit on how we should live our lives, and we let society dictate what was and was not sin based on the changing times.

And when the faithful of the convention dared to raise questions as to our remaining faithful to the Bible and its precepts, those who sought less restriction on their social lives went off to start a new convention. They have not as yet found the courage to call it a new convention, but when a group has their own places of worship, their own annual convention, their own president, their own seminaries, their own missionaries, and their own endorsing agency, they are a convention unto themselves.[122]

We were seeking to be a Spirit filled Acts 1:8 body of believers "*But you will receive power when the Holy Spirit comes on you; and will be my witnesses in Jerusalem, and in all Judea and Samaria, and to the ends of the earth*" without first understanding that we and we alone hold the keys to the Kingdom. We foolishly believed that we could do better than the Lord Jesus Christ when it came to building churches. What Jesus told us was, "*And I tell you that you are Peter and upon this rock, I will build my church and the gates of hell will not prevail against it*" (Matthew 16:18).

I'm not going to go off the point by discussing whether Christ meant upon Peter or upon the statement Peter made with reference to Christ being the Son of God. You should make that decision based upon your own study of the Scripture being guided by the Holy Spirit and not someone else's thoughts. It is enough that Jesus said, "*I will build my church.*" To his disciple, and therefore to us, Jesus said, "*I will give you the keys to the kingdom of heaven*" (Matthew 16:19). If you are honest with yourself you will have to acknowledge that Christ did not send us into the world to build churches, he sent us to make disciples, to enlarge the flock, to build the Kingdom of Heaven. We are supposed to be Kingdom builders! The Church Universal, the "εκκλεσιαυ̦" the "κοινονια" is the Bride of Christ (Revelations 21:2,9). She does not belong to any one person or group; she belongs to Christ and through Him to His followers, and to them alone. If we are building the kingdom, then one of those things that will be given to us is a larger assemblage of believers.

Hedgerows: Jesus, in the parable of the Great Banquet (Luke

14:15-24), told of a master who had planned a great dinner. He sent out invitations, and at the appointed time sent his servants to tell the people to come. With one accord they all began to make asinine excuses. The master then sent his servants into the cities and towns, to bring in the poor, the blind, the cripple and the lame, which they did. And yet, the banquet hall still was not filled so he sent them out into the highways and the hedgerows to bring others in so that his house might be filled.

We as disciples of the Lord Jesus are those servants. We have, through the Great Commission, been instructed to go out into the cities, the town, the highways and the hedgerows of the world to bring others into the Lord's mansion that His house might be filled. We have been told to build the Kingdom of Heaven "*and all these things will be given to you as well*" (Matthew 6:33). We were told to go out into the hedgerows, yet what we have actually done is build hedgerows around the churches.

I had the pleasure, and sorrow, of preaching to a small church in a town not far from Columbia, South Carolina. They were without a pastor and had called to see if I might be available for supply preaching. I was able to work them into my Sunday worship schedule, and as such preached for them several times. When I talked to the Pulpit Committee in an attempt to understand their goals and objectives for the church, as I sought to grasp what they would both want and need from the next pastor, the committee led me to understand that while they would not turn anyone away, they would not actively seek to bring the community into their services. One person described the church as a "white castle surrounded by a black moat."

Rather than reach out to the community that surrounds the church, or join a church that is within the community in which they live, there are those who will drive miles to worship at the church of their parents. They don't do this to keep the church going, and for most individuals so inclined, church growth certainly is not in their plans unless it is to be accomplished by procreation. They do it to keep the community at bay. They do it so another group—social, economic, or racial—does not assume the leadership of "our" church.

For those who are old enough you may have followed the "Watergate" break-in and the following investigations and hearings. For a while it was better than any daytime "soap" could have ever dared to be. There was shock, disgust, and even humor in reaction to the ensuing cover-up. In seeking to find out who was responsible for the break-in, several things came to light. Among these was an official list of enemies of the White House. As I remember there were over two hundred names on the list. There were of course high-level Democrats to be found on the list. Surprisingly there were also some Republicans. There were movie stars, television and newspaper writers and commentators; there were present and former government officials, and of course there were the major opponents of President Nixon, antagonists one and all!

But were these people really enemies of the White House, the president, or the nation? Were these people really enemies of anyone? None of the post resignation studies of the Watergate incident were able to find any evidence suggesting that the "enemies" were a major factor in the final outcome. Oh, they may have been overjoyed to see the president fall, but they were not the cause. The major contributing factor in the downfall of the president and all the president's men was, in the final analyses, an unprecedented level of paranoia toward their opposition.

In their unfounded fear they had built an invisible hedgerow around themselves. Rather than seeking to be inclusive they had become reclusive. All governments have enemies; all strong leaders whether political or religious attract opponents as well as supporters. However, most of them survive in the gladiatorial arena of their calling. They survive because they do not allow fear and prejudices to distract them from their responsibilities, their objectives and their goals.

They do not withdraw from public view, but rather seek to include the public in their pursuit of wisdom, righteousness, truth, justice, and the American way. To use an old cliché, President Nixon "was his own worst enemy." A cartoon character named "Pogo" put it this way, "we have found the enemy and he is us!" Micah perhaps brought it closer to home when he said, "*...a man's enemy are the members of his own household*" (Micah 7:6).

But we as Christians while being shrewd as the serpent must at the same time be innocent as the dove (Matthew 10:16). Jesus in this same set of Scriptures told us that there would be enemies, that some of them will be within the ranks of our own families. Is it little wonder that they are to be found in the ranks of the churches? They will hate us just as they hated Jesus. He told us be on guard, but elsewhere He also said, "*...love your enemies, and pray for those who persecute you*" (Matthew 5:44). We must be on guard, but we must not become paranoid. We must choose wisely whom we will allow to be members of the Body, but we must not become selective in who can attend the worship service. We must test the spirit, but we must not become prejudiced. We will never become an Acts 1:8 church by building hedgerows to hide behind.

Barriers and Bridges: In a book I read years ago by Margaret Craven, called *I Heard the Owl Call My Name*, a young vicar named Mark, not knowing that he had less than three years to live, was sent to minister to a remote Eskimo village in Alaska. As I remember the story, when he first arrived he was searching for a way to reach the villagers, not unlike most pastors today in a new congregation. Most were fishermen like their fathers before them, so he used the analogy of building boats to join the outside world. He wasn't very successful, but toward the end of his life he came to realize that what he had been saying was that the villagers should leave their homes, their way of life and sail to a far and distant land. He had been dealing with his dilemma and one night told the old Eskimo woman who had been keeping house for him that he had heard the owl call his name. They both knew that it meant he was dying. Toward the end he told the villagers that he had been wrong. They didn't need to build boats; they needed to build a bridge so that the world could join them.[123]

There was a Southern Baptist evangelistic program some twenty years ago called "Bold Mission Thrust." The challenge was that every person in the world would have the opportunity to hear the Gospel of Christ by the year 2000. Its premise was based on short time service to the local church and to the mission fields both here and abroad. God led young and old to make commitments to reaching others for Christ. It was a program that gathered momentum as more and more individuals answered God's call to "go and tell." The way the program was conducted there were none who could plead off. All were called to answer. There were none too old, none too poor, none too busy, none without gifts that God could not use to build His Church human brick by human brick.

While the program had great results in some areas, in other areas there was little or no appraisable growth. It is not enough to hold a great citywide revival if when finished the people you have helped find Christ haven't found a church body in which to grown. It is not enough to get out and do the leg work if you are not prepared to do the soul work. It is not enough to bid others to come and follow Christ if you are not going to welcome them with open arms and Christian love into your own fellowship of believers.

Communities grow and change; yet for some remote reason many of the churches within the communities don't. Churches that have been in existence before the community was formed have built barriers around them to keep the "undesirables" out, and communities that have existed before the church was build have also built those same barriers to keep the church members out. These barriers were built one brick at a time, and they must be disassembled in the same manner. But, who is going to make the first move?

By way of seeking the answer let's look toward the holy lands as an example. Can Arabs and Jews ever live in peace? There are not a few that say no, and there may be some Old Testament justification for such a stance. Others say that there can be harmony among the two, that they are after all of the same ancestry, and again there is Old Testament justification for this stance. There is always the third view, the "let's straddle the fence" view that says both yes and no. Even as I write these words, leaders of both peoples are scurrying about the region in an attempt to find out. While one may doubt the other's good faith, the leaders of both nations have seized, yet again, the initiative and are trying to reconcile their differences. Complete reconciliation will, most likely, not have come by the time the reader may read these words, but the reader should be able to evaluate the attempts toward this end.

Are the local church and the surrounding community any different? Certainly there are differences that separate the two, but in the same breath there are similarities that can draw us closer together if we are willing to seize the opportunity. However for this to begin, the leaders of both the local church and the community must be willing to dare to try. If someone must take the first step toward reconciliation, shouldn't it be the church?

The Greek word "κατνλλαγημεν" were reconciled (Romans 5:10) means to bring together or to restore a relationship between two parties who have been kept apart by hostilities or differences. Now days in America, we are more apt to use the word with regard to a divorce than to a spiritual condition. Even my concordance tells me that the word reconcile appears only five times in the New Testament. Add the related words, "-ed, -ion, -ing," and I only find twelve references. However, in spite of the obscurity of the term, the idea is a gigantic one and stands at the heart of what God did in Christ.

Perhaps Paul used this word more than other New Testament writers because his entire ministry was spent in bringing the Gentile population to Christ and then in bringing the Gentiles into fellowship with Jews and vise-versa. It was not enough to have everyone believing in Christ, yet standing alone, Paul understood that in order to live the life of a Christian it meant being inclusive of all other believers. Someone once said that the most segregated time in American is 11:00 AM on Sunday morning. Why is that?

From his writings there were very few days when Paul was not keenly aware of the need to bring the two peoples together in Christ. Indeed, one of the purposes of gathering a collection from the Corinthians was to demonstrate the unity of the two Christian groups. In fact Paul's second letter to the Corinthians was written to the very church which had caused Paul deep pain and with whom he had just been reconciled (2:4). So, it should be no surprise that Paul thought of Christ's redemptive act as a reconciling one (Romans 5:10; Ephesians 2:12-17).

Within II Corinthians there were apparently some who charged that Paul's behavior was unchristian (10:8), and others who may have suspected his motives because he did not accept pay (11:7). No one can be sure of all the charges brought against Paul. He spent most of four chapters (10-13) defending himself.[124] In answer to the charge that his behavior was somehow unchristian, Paul testified that it was the love of Christ that controlled him (5:14), and therefore whatever he did, it was because of the moving power of the love of Christ. Christ's love "συνεχει" constrained Paul. This word normally means "to force" someone to do something, but the word that Paul used didn't have quite that meaning in his own language. Certainly he didn't mean that God forces anyone to minister for Him. Paul used the same word in Philippians 1:23 to describe how two desires pulled at him in different directions. The pull that determined the shape of ministry for Paul was neither self-interest nor self-gain; the love of Christ moved Paul to act in the way he did.

What shapes the lives of people today in America, in South Carolina, in Columbia, in your home town, in your own community? Has life become so routine that the question of why it is lived as it is, never gets asked, or worse yet answered? Do you know people who could honestly say, if asked, that they live as they do because of the love of Christ? If so, what is there about their lives that comes directly from the influences of the love of Christ? Being influenced by the love of Christ is a marvelous experience. When one thinks of all the ominous and threatening forces within the community today, surrendering to the love of Christ can hardly be thought of as surrender. It is much more like a rescue from fear, fright and panic.

The mystery of how Christ's death and resurrection actually accomplished the transformation remains cloaked in the very words intended to reveal it. Clearly, for Paul the thought of Jesus was as a substitute for all humanity, all have died in the one who died (II Corinthians 5:14). In the mystery of divine grace it is enough to say that the death of Christ involves a kind of death to self on the part of the Christian. Life can now be dedicated to the one who made life possible.

How strange are God's ways! He took a brash, conceited, blowhard (Peter), who on the same night both proclaimed that he would never forsake Christ (Mark 14:29) and before dawn denied Him three times and made him the spokesman for the early Jewish church and the preacher for the Pentecost sermon that started the Christian movement (Acts 2:14). Then He took a zealous fanatical persecutor (Saul of Tarsus) of the young Christian church and made him (Paul) the foremost interpreter of Christ for his time and for all the ages that would follow. In Paul was to be found a great mind, trained in Jewish theology and capable of organizing Christian truths into a coherent doctrine. Paul knew both the Old Testament and the Greek mind, and was able to build bridges that would be needed for the Gospel to cross over from the Jews to the Gentiles.

Ties That Bind

In Chapter 2, I asked the question, "What are the minimum requirements for 'being' a Christian?" I think that I want to attempt to answer that question now. In considering my answer I want to draw attention to three ties that bind the wandering hearts of Christians to God, and therefore to one another: 1) Christ is Lord and Savior, 2) Love for one another, and 3) A heart for missions. I am sure that there are those who could and would find many more than three ties to Christian unity, however, for my discussion these three certainly should suffice.

I have also pointed out that Christ did not leave His fledgling church with any real design for growth. The first Christians did not have a very well thought-out theology. Certainly, they had known the awesome experience of meeting God in Jesus. His Great Commission had laid on their young shoulders the task of winning the entire world to Him. The coming of the Holy Spirit on the day of Pentecost filled them with joy, power, and compassion. But they had not yet tried to explain to themselves and to others in any logical way what had happened to them. They had had a tremendous experience, but no one had yet hammered out a Christian theology.

Like all that would follow him, Paul did not come into the Christian movement as a full-grown interpreter of the Gospel. When God called him to be an apostle he withdrew for a year in what must have been a time of intense thought as he struggled to understand how his new life in Christ was related to God's covenant with Israel (Galatians 1:17). Only afterwards did he meet with Peter and James the half brother of Christ. Then came the year of teaching at Antioch, followed by his three missionary journeys, and lastly his ministry and death in Rome. As Paul met the Jews in their synagogues, he was forced to clarify his concepts of how Christ fit into God's plan as revealed in the Old Testament Scriptures and the history of Israel. Later Judaizing controversy and Pre-Gnostic thinkers forced Paul to hammer out his interpretation of the Gospel as it spoke to the ideas and philosophies of both the Jewish and the Gentile world.

Christ as Lord and Savior: The first tie that binds Christians is that for the Christian, Christ is Lord and Savior. Having followed their public profession of faith with baptism, the new Christian then begins a process that will ultimately make Christ their Lord as well as their Savior. During the study and preparation for this book I became convinced that there are two courses of instruction that each Christian church should have: a New Christians Class and a New Comers Class.

It is not hard to identify the new Christian. Most often they have been in the church for some time. They may have grown up in the church, or they may have come to the church sometime ago in search of answers to their questions. The fact is that we know them; we know their commitment and their desire to be yoked with other Christians in service and worship to God. We have watched their growth toward salvation in Christ, and we have had a part in their conversion experience. A New Christians Class would then be the starting place for their pilgrimage toward servitude to Christ as Lord. Here they would at the hands of the pastor, or one of the deacons, or even a well established and well studied lay leader, learn what it means to be a servant to all and would receive those helps necessary for good study habits into the depths and the wonders of the Bible.

However, what about a new comer? Where did they grow up? Did they come to the church with knowledge of what it is that we believe and practice? Or, as is most often today, did they come from an understanding of church polity that is different than our own? If the church has a New Comers Class then they would have been invited to attend the class before being granted membership into this part of the body of Christ. This is not to question their salvation experience but to ensure that there is understanding and agreement. If in such a class it came to light that they did not believe as we do, then there could be instruction on how we differ from their own belief system. Perhaps ours is not the right part of the body for them. Perhaps they would be more comfortable in another Christian church of like or even different worship style.

If the individual comes on profession of like faith and baptism or on promise of a letter from a sister church, a New Comers Class will aid them in assimilating into the worship style and belief of the new church. Perhaps they have been a Christian for a number of years and have transferred here from another city or state. They may even have been a Sunday school teacher or deacon at their last church. Perhaps as often happens the church they were attending changed directions and they don't feel comfortable, aren't being spiritually fed, or there may even be a doctrinal disagreement between them and the present leadership of their last church.

These things happen; however, we need test both the knowledge and spirit of the new member before allowing them to teach or serve in the Deacon Body. This is not a pleasant thought for some people. They have been Christians for many years and are not in need of additional training to serve the church. A New Comers Class doesn't seek to train them to be servants; its only intent should be to ensure that they understand how and why this church worships and serves as it does.

There may be those who are thinking, "No one has a right to judge my Christianity!" To those well meaning dear souls I say, yes they do. Christ said, "*Do not judge, or you too will be judged. For in the same way you judge others, you will be judged, and with the measure you use, it will be measured to you*" (Matthew 7:1). Christ did not make a blanket statement that said, "don't ever judge." He said judge by the same standard you judge yourself. If you do not measure up to the standards your churches set then don't try to place those standards on others. John told the faithful "*Dear friends, do not believe every spirit, but test the spirits to see whether they are from God, because may false prophets have gone out into the world*" (John 4:1). And, I might add: and into the church.

Paul went so far as advocating that the church should judge between fellow Christians on even small matters:

> If any of you has a dispute with another, dare he take it before the ungodly for judgment instead of before the saints? Do you not know that the saints will judge the world? And if you are to judge the world, are you not competent to judge trivial cases? Do you not know that you will judge angles? How much more the things of this world. (I Corinthians 6:1-3)

And with regards to deacons He said, "*They must first be tested; and then if there is nothing against them, let them serve as deacons*" (I Timothy 3:10). This would also be sound counsel for the church body in this day and age concerning any who would seek to be leaders including pastor, teachers, and church staffs.

Love for One Another: One of the facts of human existence is that people within any given social grouping or assemblage tend to behave alike. I think that I can safely say that everyone knows what it is like to stand out in a crowd; it is uncomfortable to be different. When a person is not like others, or feels in some way left out of the loop, the experience, or the fellowship, alienation can result. The inevitable clash of human needs and human situations provides the backdrop for such encounters.

Yet, it ought not be that way for Christians. Aren't we all of one Spirit? The unity of Christians into one body is accomplished by the act of conversion when like Cornelius, and other early converts, all received the Spirit. "*For by one Spirit are we all baptized into one body, whether we be Jews or Gentiles, whether we be bond or free*" (I Corinthians 12:13). Paul's point is that everyone received the same Spirit. Neither previous religious ties nor social status altered that fact. Which is exactly the line of reasoning Peter offered before a meeting in Jerusalem when the Jewish Christians were skeptical of accepting Gentiles as true converts (Acts 15: 6-9). The unity of the conversion experience makes all Christians one in the Spirit.

A Christian who has been possessed by the love of God and who possesses the love of God can be depended on to express that love by loving the other members of the body even as Christ loves them. Jesus said, "*A new commandment I give you: Love one another. As I have loved you, so you must love one another. All men will know that you are my disciples if you love one another*" (John 13:35). There are some who take this to mean that we must have love for the whole world and everyone in it. There is some validity to the notion that we should love the unlovable and the lost of the world, but that concept is not to be found in this verse. This verse deals with the love that Christians are to show other Christians. And it isn't an option. It is a commandment, it is authoritative, and it is an essential sign to all others that we truly belong to Jesus.

John said, "*If anyone says, 'I love God,' yet hates his brother, he is a liar. For anyone who does not love his brother, whom he has seen, cannot love God, whom he has not seen. And he has given us this command: Whoever loves God must also love his brother*" (I John 4:19-21). Once again we are dealing with other Christians. Without minimizing the dangers of the sins of the flesh, the Bible emphasizes more strongly the sins of the spirit, which include attitudes toward other people and the behavior that grows out of these attitudes. Paul's list of sins in Romans 1:29-32 and II Timothy 3:2-7 names more sins of the spirit (i.e. covetousness, pride, ingratitude, without natural affection, covenant breakers) than sins of the flesh.

The sins of "good" people may be the worst sins of all. Sin is sin no matter who commits it, but the sins of those who profess to practice high moral standards, who profess to love one another, and who profess to be in Christ are worse in quality and degree than those of other sinners. Why? Because they are sins of attitude and spirit and they are committed against those whom Christ commanded us to love.

Many people who have been believers for a long time lose the wonder and freshness of their faith. Of course, it doesn't happen to everyone, and never automatically. However, it almost certainly happens to those who forget what God did for them when they were first saved, and what He continues to do for believers every day of our lives. When such a thing happens individuals begin to cut themselves off from the rest of the body.

They pull back into small groups and practice selective inclusion as to who may or may not be in the group. They begin to limit "sin" to those that are not particularly tempting to them but others in the church have problems with. Such individuals develop a righteous and judgmental spirit that says, "You may be of the body, but you are not one of us." Such attitudes begin to affect the Spirit ministering to the church. Some begin to feel unwelcome in the choir, in the Sunday school for their age group, or in the Bible studies being conducted. The fellowship and the worship experience begin to falter, and finally one can barely hear the calling of the Spirit in the sermon.

What has happened in such cases is that the Love of God is not being practiced with regard to those in the body that may be different in social, economical, or educational status. Loving others is not always easy. Sometimes there are problems in relating to other people. There may be disagreements. Those disagreements may occur in your Sunday school class, Bible study, or worship service. When this happens, what can the class or congregation do to preserve or to regain the close fellowship desired? Learning to deal with such matters is part of developing a close Christian fellowship, and more importantly it is part of developing Christian love for one another.

A Heart for Missions: What a particular group of believers do about missions is mostly determined by what the members believe the Bible teaches about missions. Although the word "missions" is moderately new when compared with the Christian faith, the idea of missions is one of the major themes of the Bible. From Genesis to the Revelation, the Bible teaches of God's wish that all should know Him. Jesus saw His responsibility in the Father's plan. He explained that His coming into the world was because of God's love, "*For God so loved the world that he gave his one and only Son, that whoever believes in him shall not perish but have eternal life*" (John 3:16). And when at the end of His earthly life, His mission completed, Jesus commissioned His followers to continue His work.

To discover God's missionary plan, the Christian must go back to the beginning of Godly history. Genesis is the book, and along with the story of creation is also to be found the story of missions. God gave humanity the ability to think and to make choices. Because humanity could think, they could choose between keeping their fellowship with God or going their own way, to find their own destiny, to create a world of their own making. Because they could choose, they could be tempted.

The choice was there; which would it be: God or man? Humanity chose, and in the choosing all the good things that life in fellowship with God had brought were lost. Sin had entered the world.

The Old Testament tells the story of the way back, God working with sinful man to restore the broken communion of God with humanity. It is interesting that many Christians don't see the Old Testament as a missionary book. The Old Testament paved the way for Jesus' coming. Jesus told His followers that the Scriptures told of His coming, and "*beginning with Moses and all the Prophets, he explained to them what was said in all the Scriptures concerning himself*" (Luke 24:27).

The basis for Christian missions is that God was in Christ, living on earth in the form of humanity. By His coming, Jesus showed the depths of God's love for His creation. By His death, Jesus showed how far God was willing to go in order to save humanity from their sins. Jesus was willing to die so that humanity could again enjoy fellowship with God the Father.

When Jesus began His ministry, He called upon humanity to follow Him. He selected a small group of twelve to be His inner circle, to be His close friends and helpers. Jesus taught them about who He was, and about God's plan for the world. They watched Him day after day as He put His teachings into practice. In wonderment they watched as He healed the sick, preached the Good News, and met human needs wherever He found them. For more than three years they had followed and watched and learned until at last it was their turn.

Jesus told them what they were to do and He sent them out. He reminded the disciples of the attitude with which they should go and minister. He said, "*Freely you have received, freely give*" (Matthew 10:8b). There was no choice in the commission. Jesus did not say, "If you go;" He said, "You are going, and as long as you're going, make disciples." This is an important truth about missions. All people have the right to the Gospel, whether they are around the world or around the block! Those of us who have received the Good News of Salvation as a free gift from God have the responsibility for passing it on to those who have not.

Now it is our turn. God still uses people to get His message out to the masses. Not all of those people are pastors, deacons, and Sunday school teachers. Jesus took a group of fishermen, a hated tax collector, and a Jewish zealot, and sent them off to do missions. These were ordinary people with ordinary skills, and yet they began building a kingdom that is still growing today. A secretary can be a missionary at his or her desk, an employee at Wal-Mart can be a missionary at his or her work, a teacher can be a missionary at his or her school, a nurse or doctor can be a missionary at his or her chosen profession, and a homemaker can be a missionary to the friend or salesperson that may come to the door.

> Then the righteous will answer him Lord, when did we see you hungry and feed you, or thirsty and give you something to drink? When did we see you a stranger and invite you in, or needing clothes and clothe you? When did we see you sick or in prison and go to visit you? The king will reply, "I tell you the truth, whatever you did for one of the least of these brothers of mine, you did for me." (Matthew 25:37-40)

God's perfect will for all humanity is that they know Him. He has done all that is necessary for sinful humanity to be saved.

Jesus praying to the Father said, "*Sanctify them by the truth; your word is truth. As you sent me into the world, I have sent them into the world. For them I sanctify myself, that they too may be truly sanctified*" (John 17:16-19). We are a called people who have been chosen to preach the Good News to the nations. Jesus' Great Commission is as binding upon Christians today as it was upon the first-century believers. If the church is to assume its mission responsibility, the members must do the same. With faith in God's love, and in response to the commands of Jesus, Christians today can become fishers of men. Christians today can and must be on missions.

Every individual Christian can do the same things that Jesus sent the seventy to do. These same needs exist in every community. Through the mission action and outreach programs of a church, Christians can find ways to be involved in missions right where they live. How encouraged Christians everywhere should be to know that God is for us and available to us because of what Christ has done for us. Every Christian is to be a priest, and a prophet proclaiming that the day of the Lord is at hand. Christians serve God, not in order to be saved, but because they are saved. They serve God out of loving gratitude for what God has done and continues to do for them. That is what Christians do, however the more important question is, "What are you doing?"

Share the Vision

Well, I have, to the best of my ability shown the reader what some of the threats are and how they came to be in the church. However, what is done about them must be determined by each part of the body individually. The Southern Baptist Convention as with most Protestant denominations does not tell the individual congregations what they must do about any one specific problem. They do, of necessity, set standards by which a congregation can rightfully call itself Southern Baptist, or by which non-conformity will result in a break in the fellowship of the offending congregation. I would assume that other denominations do the same with respect to their parts of the Body of Christ.

Yet, as with Southern Baptist, all Christian denominations should share in the same vision. "We want to win souls for Christ!" This may not be a great objective statement for a church to hang a program on, but it's a great starting point. There are three very important questions that each Christian must ask themselves: 1) "Why was I born?" 2) "What is God's purpose for my life?" and 3) "Where am I going?"

Moses came to understand that beginning with his deliverance from the river he was under the direction of God. It has to be noted that he resisted God's direction at the burning bush. However

Moses' awareness of God's will in his life was realized only after he had surrendered to God's will. God used Mordecai to influence Esther to save her people from destruction. Mordecai even went so far as to tell Esther that God would find another way to save the people if she didn't seek their deliverance. However, it was his words, "*And, who knows but that you have come to royal position for such a time as this?*" (Esther 4:14b) that moved Esther to place her very life in the hands of God, to act and to accomplish God's purpose for her life.

Throughout the Bible there is evidence that God has a purpose for every Christian. Paul referring to his own calling said, "*...called to be an apostle of Christ Jesus by the will of God*" (I Corinthians 1:1). Paul felt that he had been set apart at birth for the purpose of God, even though he did not surrender to the will of God until he was saved on the road to Damascus. Paul was told, "*Get up... and go into Damascus. There you will be told all that you have been assigned to do*" (Acts 22:10). What Paul discovered was that he was to be the Apostle to the Gentiles.

Most in America look to the days of their retirement with anticipation. Most of us will reach that day somewhere between sixty-two and sixty-seven years of age. However, for the Christian there is no retirement from the will of God. God's plan for one's life here on earth continues as long as he or she lives. There are really only two choices for the Christian, "Do I live my life to suit my own purpose?" or "Do I live my life in God's will seeking to serve His purpose?" Joshua called upon the people to make a decision, "*...choose for yourselves this day whom you will serve... But as for me and my household, we will serve the Lord*" (24:15).

There is a story told of a lump of clay that was taken by the master potter and placed on a wheel. The clay was pounded and beaten until the pain was almost unbearable. It was then spun and molded until it didn't know which end was up. Finally having been molded into a cup, it thought its ordeal over, only to be put into an oven and heated to such a high temperature that it thought surely it would perish. The agony finally over, it was covered with a smelly substance and placed in an even hotter oven. Now, finally set to cool upon a shelf it caught a glimpse of itself in the window. "Is that beautiful thing me?" it asked. "Yes," said the master potter, "you are not only beautiful, but now you are also useful."

God is not wasteful. In nature one can see that God does not make anything without a purpose for it. God does not create robots or duplicates. Therefore, each of us is unique, with a unique purpose in life. I can look back to when I committed myself to God's purpose, and I can see the various experiences God has given to me. There have been instances of God's protection and guidance even before I had asked for it. There were times when having been faithful to His purpose I asked for promotion, and He said, "No, you have accomplished what I asked; it is time to move on." There havc been times when I activity sought to find a church that I could pastor after having retired from the chaplaincy, and God said, "Wait upon me; I will show you where you are to serve." Through all of this my skills have been sharpened, and my desire to be where and to do what God wants me to do has been strengthened. Almost every experience of life, for the one seeking God's will, will point toward God's effort to reach us and use us for His purpose.

> For everything that was written in the past was written to teach us, so that through endurance and the encouragement of the Scriptures we might have hope. May the God who gives endurance and encouragement give you a spirit of unity among yourselves as you follow Christ Jesus, so that with one heart and mouth you may glorify the God and Father of our Lord Jesus Christ. (Romans 15:4-6)

What is your purpose in life? Have you taken time to ask God what it is that He wants you to do? Human nature is so easy to read. One can say to oneself, "I am not a Moses, I certainly am not an Esther, and I will never be a Paul, therefore I do not have anything to do!" And, although most of that may be true, and we may never be asked to serve in such a capacity, there are areas in our lives where we can serve. The real question is, "What are you going to do?" For God's sake, do something. God Bless, and May God's grace be with you today, tomorrow, and truly for the rest of your life.

ENDNOTES

1 Sun Tzus wrote a Chinese Military Treatise in the 6th Century B.C. titled *The Art of War*. It contains 13 chapters and was translated by Samuel B. Griffith. It is required reading at the military academies, and the Army War College.

2 The New Hampshire Confession of Faith defines a church as a visible and local institution.

3 The Baptist Faith and Message, Revised Edition, Herschel H. Hobbs, Convention Press, Page 64.

4 One is tempted to view the Church Universal as being the same as the Kingdom of God. This unscriptural concept would swallow up the individual churches, and destroy the very identity of the New Testament churches.

5 John Burnaby, "Augustine: Later Works," *The Library of Christian Classics*, Vol. 8, SCM Press, Page 321-22.

6 P.L. 84-140Law 36 U.S.C. 186

7 This passage of Scripture may best be understood as having lost or forsaken their first encounter with Godly love.

8 Baptist Faith and Message, Revised Edition, Page 94

9 The Christian Persuader, Harper and Row, Page 47

10 See also chapters 2 and 3

11 Paul's warning from past history, quotes Exodus 32:6

12 I fully acknowledge that there are female pastors. However, sometimes he, she, him and/or her becomes distracting to the thought that is trying to be presented.

13 DocDevos, Christian Publications, Inc., Camp Hill, Pennsylvania, 2002, Section Two: The Absolute Need for an Absolute Authority, Day Two.

14 Fleming H. Revell Company, Old Tappan, New Jersey, 1976, pg. 246

15 While I do not wish to enter into a theological debate here as I will discuss this more in Chapter 7, I cannot deny that which the Scriptures affirm. See Romans 16:1. Here Phoebe is described as a deaconess.

While I Timothy 3:11 most likely refers to the wives of deacons rather than deaconesses, I Timothy 5:3-16 and I Corinthians 7:8 are accepted by most as pointing to the earliest origins of the development of the later office of deaconess.

16 Not unlike my pastorate in Texas. There was a one square block area downtown that had four or five churches that competed for parking spaces and members every Sunday. None of them could afford a full time pastor.

17 In a distinctively Christian sense of the activity, it referred to a church official who oversaw those belonging to Jesus, and was likewise overseen by Christ. In 3:8 Paul applies the same concept to the deacons.

18 "God helps those who help themselves."

19 John Morton was my pastor at Springdale Baptist Church in Oklahoma City and has been instrumental in helping many a struggling Christian see their calling to preach the word.

20 It is my intent to cover the issue of sexual misconduct in a later chapter.

21 Zero based budgeting simply means that if we get the money we spend it, and if we don't then the program will not be completed.

22 I understand that there are those who will feel that this is overkill. However, at the yearly denominational meetings, if you don't have a ballot, you don't vote. This is to ensure that the desires of only those who are about our Father's business are heard.

23 *Looking in the Mirror*, Abingdon Press, Page 15

24 When dealing with staff, one must include both the paid and unpaid personnel. Besides the pastor, in a small church this could also include the music leader, the piano player, and the part-time secretary, all of whom more than likely will be related to one or more leaders in the church.

25 When I was in Texas I was considered by many to be conservative, when I moved to North Carolina, I was considered by many to be fundamental. The only change I could determine was that I had crossed the Mississippi River.

26 "Letters and Papers from Prison," Dietrich Bonhoeffer, Macmillan Company, New York, Copyright 1967

27 Also known as Herod Antipas; was one of several sons of Herod the Great. When Herod the Great died, his kingdom was divided among four of his sons. Herod Antipas ruled over Galilee and Perea (4 B.C.-A.D. 39) and was the one who killed John the Baptist. See Matthew 14:1-12

28 It is interesting to note that Paul put a qualifier on the remarriage—"But he must belong to the Lord."

29 There are no secrets in government quarters. You have an argument, and everyone knows about it.

30 I offer a sidebar here for the reader's consideration. Just as the Scriptures admonish parents to cherish children, there is also to be adoration for the elderly. Abortion is not that far removed from euthanasia. If one can kill the unwanted, society will eventually find a way to kill the aged and the unproductive.

31 The Baptist Faith and Message, Revised Edition, pg. 121

32 Ibid, pg. 121

33 Ibid pg. 112

34 This is the concept that one can reach a higher spiritual state of being by rigorous self-discipline and self-denial.

35 Andrew Sandlin, *The Christian Statesman*, Volume 139, Number 5, 1996, "The Christian Libertarian Idea"

36 I have for many years tried to understand at what junction in history the word "fundamentalist" became a bad word.

37 William Williams, *Charles Haddon Spurgeon: Personal Reminiscences*, London: The Religious Tract Society, No Date, Page 104

38 The Tower of Babel, Genesis 11; the destruction of Sodom and Gomorrah, Genesis 19.

39 Gorgias, born in Sicily, 483-375 BC, introduced Solipsism philosophy in Athens around 427 B.C. The theory was believed to have died out due to Plato and Aristotle being two of its most pessimistic critics.

40 *Webster's New World Dictionary*, Second College Edition, Simon and Schuster, New York

41 1596 -1650, French philosopher, scientist and mathematician, educated

at the Jesuit College of La Fleche, in Anjou. The quote comes from his discourse on method, Willis Doney, "Descartes: A collection of Critical Essays," Doubleday, New York, 1967.

42 Here the word is intended to mean the worldly in general or universal rather than the more accepted concept of the Christian Church as a whole.

43 "The principle that women should have political, economic, and social rights equal to those of men," *Webster's New World Dictionary*, Second College Edition, Simon and Schuster.

44 Keil-Delitzsch, "Commentary on the Old Testament, vol. 1, The Pentateuch," p.103

45 Perhaps I will find opportunity later on in the book to discuss this concept of authority and Christian marriage more fully. It certainly is deserving of more comprehensive discussion than I can allot here.

46 Phyllis Trible, "God and the Rhetoric of Sexuality," Philadelphia, Fortress Press, 1978

47 It would be a poor student of Scripture that did not admit that by the time of Christ the role of Hebrew women had for all but a few been lowered to a status of just above a bond slave.

48 "Biblical Affirmations of Woman," Philadelphia: The Westminister Press, 1979, p. 309

49 A hatred of women, especially by a man.

50 There are numerous books on religion in America, woman in religion, and denominational growth and schisms. I do not seek to create another one but rather to simply give an overview for the discussion that follows.

51 "Women in American Religion," University of Pennsylvania Press, 1980

52 Janet Wilson James editor, "Women in American Religion", p. 3-20

53 Russell C. Prohl, "Women in the Church," Grand Rapids, Mich., Eerdmans Press, 1957

54 "Women in American Religion," p. 171

55 "Women in the Church," p. 16-17

56 "Women in Church and Society," Nashville, Abingdon Press, 1972, p. 206

57 I make no secret that I believe the ACLU to be the most godless, secular humanistic, and immoral organization in America today.

58 For brevity's sake I will mention only I Corinthians 6:9 and 7:1-4. There are varying levels of concordances and topical Bibles for the student who wishes to note all the passages, however, I counsel them that the list is extensive.

59 Linda K. Kerber, "No Constitutional Right to be Ladies," *Women and the Obligations of Citizenship*, New York: Hill and Wang, 1998, p. 185-199

60 New York, W.W. Northon & Company, 1963

61 This loss of membership was in part due to such actions as the women of NOW's Ecumenical Task Force in Detroit burning part of the newly released *Roman Missal*, which restricted the right of women to be lectors at Catholic Mass, enraging Christian women's groups.

62 An interesting note here is that most homosexual groups are moving away from trying to convince the public that they were born that way and therefore have no control over their desires or even their own bodies. These groups are now focusing on having it proclaimed an alterative and healthy lifestyle.

63 Adoption is not considered a form of propagation. There is in the case of lesbians the option of artificial insemination, however even this is outside of the normal concept of propagation.

64 Most psychologists agree that the so called "free" marriage where wife swapping and "dating" outside of the marriage are accepted is very detrimental to a marriage, to the individual's self image, and is no better than just living together outside of the limitations of the marriage vows.

65 AIDS can be transferred by body fluids during oral sex, birthing by a contaminated mother, and as some claim there is the remote possibility of transference by kissing, or that the condom leaked, however, I believe that I have, for the most part, correctly stated the main reasons for contacting AIDS by heterosexuals.

66 The term "closet" when used in conjunction with homosexual simply means that the individual homosexual has not openly announced their sexual preference. Within the homosexual community it means that they have not had their homosexual behavior made public. This making public has also been called "outing."

67 Men and women seem to act the same, the men flattering and complimentary, the women flattering and flirtatious.

68 Many professional counselors agree that the physical act of fornication without emotional involvement is nothing more than the use of another person's body for self-masturbation.

69 This discussion on Electronic Affairs and Emotional Adultery was taken from a discussion paper I did while a chaplain in the U.S. Army.

70 The proper term is "infanticide."

71 In all the years that I have been counseling, I have never met a woman who has had an abortion that did not admit to having some form of self-guilt over the loss of the child.

72 If the person actually committed such sins in a sacred place or desired to commit any external sins in such places, they would be considered to be guilty of additional malice.

73 Before the secular humanists or the radical feminists draw on this as proof of why women should be pastors, they should consider the number of homosexuals who have also pointed to such a meeting as their first homosexual encounter and the reason leading to their sexual persuasion.

74 See Romans 1:22-27. Paul draws his entire discussion from creation in Genesis 1 and 2. For a more detailed discussion of "General Abuse" see Ralph Blair, "An Evangelical Look at Homosexuality," revised edition, New York, Evangelicals Concerned, 1977. Also, Robin Scroggs, "The New Testament and Homosexuality," Philadelphia, Fortress, 1983

75 For those who may be interested the concept of adultery being an offense punishable by the UCMJ, comes from an old European military concept that goes: "If I can't trust you with my wife, I can't trust you with my life."

76 I refer the reader back to Chapter 1 where I noted that membership in the Christian Church is reserved for the repentant sinner who accepts Christ as their savior. Anyone who chooses may attend any Christian church they wish, however, they may not become a member unless they are willing to renounce their sins and accept Jesus Christ as their savior.

77 C.E.B Cranfield "A Critical and Exegetical Commentary on the Epistle to Romans," 2 Vols. International Critical Commentary, Edinburgh, T&T Clark, 1975, vol. 1, p. 125

78 Both the NIV and The Interlinear Bible, J.P. Green, Sr. General Editor and Translator, Grand Rapids, Michigan, Baker Book House, 1981 translate the word as "homosexuals," while Liddell and Scott, A Greek-English Lexicon, 9th ed. Oxford, Clarendon, 1968 provides the definition of "sodomite."

79 This chapter incorporates two papers, one on Moral Based Training, and the other my thesis for the U.S. Army War College

80 Sunday School Board, The Southern Baptist Convention, 2004

81 Father Anthony F. Alexander, Formally of the Department of Religion, John Carroll University

82 Unless noted otherwise, all definitions are taken from the Webster's II, New Riverside University Dictionary, Riverside Publishing Company.

83 In modern society, this is a doctrine that states all values are worthless and that nothing is knowable or can be communicated. Such individuals reject all distinctions in moral value.

84 Clarence H. Benson, "A Popular History of Christian Education," Chicago, Moody Press 1943, p. 15

85 Hugo Grotius, 1583-1645 considered to be the "Father of the Science of International Law." He defined natural law as a perceptive judgment in which things are good or bad by their own nature.

86 Reinhod Niebuhr, "The Children of Light and the Children of Darkness," p.20.

87 For the purpose of this study I concerned myself with the under-thirty age group. "The Next Generation," *Youthwork Magazine*, May 97. "The Youth Market," Woods & Poole. "Generation and Race," Mitchel, American Generations, 1998. "Generation Y," and "The Teen Planet Survey," The Coca-Cola company, 2000. "Generation 2001 Survey," Louis Harris and Associates, Inc., Jan. 1998. "Facts and Figures," Northwestern Mutual Life, Annually.

88 "The Millennials," an article by Sandra Frederick, March 1998.

89 I placed the names alphabetical and as such the listing does not imply placement in ranking of favorite.

90 This quote was taken from some old college notes from a psychology class. It was attributed to Cordon W. Allport, "The Use of Personal Document in Psychological Science," 1942, p.157

91 These laws are found throughout the major faiths and populations of the world. The Hebraic "Ten Commandments," Exodus 20; the Islamic "Al-Qalam," the Quran, chapter 68; the Christian "Sermon on the Mound," the New Testament book of Matthew; the Buddhism "Four Noble Truths," the Vinaya; and the Confucianism "Jen/Yi," found in the Analect.

92 William K. Kilpatrick wrote in his book, *Why Johnny Can't Tell Right from Wrong*: "With our children having been taught psychiatric and psychological methods of 'Values Clarification' in their schools' programs, it becomes clear why their scores are low and why morals are on a steep decline," p. 47.

93 *The State*, Columbia, SC, Opinion page, December 27, 2004

94 Santa Anna had ordered a scarlet flag raised over the bell tower of the San Fernando Church and the "Duegello" sounded announcing that there was to be "no quarter" given to the defenders of the Alamo.

95 *The Book of Common Prayer* belongs to the Church of England, a state sponsored church, with the Queen of England as its sponsor.

96 "The Founding Fathers," National Archives and Research Administration, www.archives.gov, "A Table of the Religious Affiliations of American Founders, compiled by Ian Doran, copy righted 1997,Religion and the New Republic: Faith in the Founding of America, Edited by James H. Hutson, Library of Congress, 1998

97 A good starting place would be to view "Religion and the Founding of America," at www.lcweb.loc.gov, Library of Congress, made possible by grants from the Pew Charitable Trusts, Mr. and Mrs. Henry J. Smith, and the Lilly Endowment Inc.

98 U.S. Supreme Court, "Engel et al. v. Vitale et al.," 1962

99 http://www4.law.cornell.edu/uscode/20/

100 Ibid sections (a), (b)

101 393 U.S. 503, section 1, paragraph 2.

102 Taken from the NCCJ publication on "Public Prayer In A Diverse Society"

103 Ibid

104 Chapter 6

105 This is part of the oath an office or enlisted soldier takes when entering the United States Armed Forces.

106 See discussion in Chapter 9 on the same subject.

107 C.S. Lewis, *The Screwtape Letters*, Harper Publishers, San Francisco, Parentheses mine

108 Herschel Hobbs, Revised Edition, pg 19

109 I will discuss errors in Scriptures more fully later on in the chapter.

110 B.M. Metzger & M.D. Coogan, "The Oxford Companion to the Bible," Oxford University Press, New York, NY, (1993), Pages 302 to 304

111 *Webster's New World Dictionary*, Second College Edition, Simon and Schuster, New York

112 James P. Boyce, "Abstract of Systematic Theology," pg 50, Copyright 1887, reproduced by Southern Baptist Theological Seminary

113 Charles F. Pfeiffer, "The Dead Sea Scrolls and the Bible," Baker Book House, Grand Rapids, Michigan, pg. 121

114 Frank Stagg, "New Testament Theology," Broadman Press, Nashville, Tennessee, 1962, pg. 2

115 The Interpreter's Dictionary of the Bible, Abingdon Press, Nashville, pg. 921

116 Ibid, page 276

117 "The Interpreter's Dictionary of the Bible," Vol. 1, Abingdom Press, New York, pg. 500

118 Ibid, pg. 511

119 The earliest known fragment of Gospel literature is the Rylands Fragment of John dating from about A.D. 135.

120 There is some uncertainty as to whether Mark wrote his Gospel before or after the martyrdom of Peter somewhere in the year A.D. 64

121 *We'll Work Till Jesus Comes*, Elizabeth Mills, 1805 – 1829,Baptist Hymnal, Edited by Walter Hines Sims, Convention Press Nashville, Tennessee, pg 284

122 For those dear Southern Baptist souls who may not know to whom I am speaking of, check out the Cooperative Baptist Fellowship (CBF).

123 I hope my remembrances have done justice to the book. It was a beautifully told story, and I highly recommend it to young readers.

124 The charges for the most part lurk in the background of the printed verse, and the reader must read Paul's responses to find them.